INSTRUCTOR'S MANUAL

LITERATURE
of the
WESTERN WORLD
Neoclassicism
Through the Modern Period

fourth edition

Brian Wilkie James Hurt
University of Arkansas *University of Illinois*

PRENTICE HALL, *Upper Saddle River, NJ 07458*

© 1997 by PRENTICE-HALL, INC.
Simon & Schuster / A Viacom Company
Upper Saddle River, New Jersey 07458

All rights reserved

10 9 8 7 6 5 4 3 2 1

ISBN 0-13-267410-6
Printed in the United States of America

CONTENTS

PREFACE vii
SOME THEMATIC THREADS 1
FORMAL GENRES, MODES, AND STRATEGIES 8
LITERATURE AND SOCIETY 20

VOLUME I

Gilgamesh 25
The Old Testament (Hebrew Bible) 27
Homer 30
Sappho 36
Greek Drama 38
Aeschylus 40
Sophocles 43
Euripides 45
Aristophanes 47
Plato 48
Aristotle 50
Catullus 52
Virgil 53
Ovid 56
The New Testament 58
The Koran (Qur'an) 59
Beowulf 60
The Song of Roland 61
Andreas Capellanus 62
Marie de France 64
Saints Anselm and Thomas Aquinas 66
Dante Alighieri 68
Sir Gawain and the Green Knight 72
Geoffrey Chaucer 74
Christine de Pizan 77
Everyman 78
Francis Petrarch 80
Giovanni Boccaccio 82
Niccoló Machiavelli 84
Marguerite de Navarre 85

iii

Michel de Montaigne   87
Miguel de Cervantes Saavedra   89
William Shakespeare   91
John Donne   94
John Milton   96

VOLUME II

Molière   103
Marie de La Vergne de La Fayette   106
Jean Racine   109
Jonathan Swift   111
Alexander Pope   114
Voltaire   115
Jean-Jacques Rousseau   117
Johann Wolfgang von Goethe   118
William Blake   121
William Wordsworth   124
Samuel Taylor Coleridge   127
John Keats   128
Mary Shelley   130
Alexander Pushkin   133
Alfred, Lord Tennyson   135
Robert Browning   136
Frederick Douglass   138
Walt Whitman   140
Herman Melville   142
Emily Dickinson   143
Gustave Flaubert   145
Fyodor Dostoevsky   147
Leo Tolstoy   149
Henrik Ibsen   151
Kate Chopin   153
Anton Chekhov   156
French Symbolist and Modernist Poetry   158
Sigmund Freud   160
Joseph Conrad   162
William Butler Yeats   165
Luigi Pirandello   167
Thomas Mann   168
James Joyce   170

Virginia Woolf 172
Franz Kafka 174
D. H. Lawrence 175
Isak Dinesen 176
T. S. Eliot 177
William Faulkner 178
Bertolt Brecht 179
Jean-Paul Sartre 181
Albert Camus 182
Jorge Luis Borges 184
Samuel Beckett 186
Richard Wright 187
Italo Calvino 188
James Baldwin 189
Cynthia Ozick 191
Athol Fugard 193
Jamaica Kincaid 195

SELECTIVE MEDIA GUIDE 197

PREFACE

To the extent that it is a road map designed to help teachers find their way around the fourth edition of Literature of the Western World, this instructor's manual is addressed to both veteran and less experienced teachers. As a guide to classroom teaching of the works included, the manual is addressed more particularly to the latter group and therefore includes some information and tips that veterans will not need.

Even the veterans, however, may find the manual of some interest as shop talk. The editors like to talk about literature and have viewed this manual as a chance to converse with fellow teachers about the writers and works included in the anthology. The conversation, admittedly, is one-sided, but we hope that in some sense it is a genuine one, that those who dip into this fourth edition of the manual will continue to respond to our notes and questions, whether with agreement and development, with reservations and revision, or with downright rejection. In the teaching profession, argument is the spice of life.

Literature of the Western World is a big book, a fact that reflects its fundamental aim: to serve the needs of as wide a variety of teachers as possible. A similar rationale informs the manual, which contains a variety of material that different teachers will use in different ways. We begin with a section, "Some Thematic Threads," in which we identify a dozen recurring thematic concerns in the works anthologized. This section, needless to say, is highly tentative; a dozen other editors would have produced a dozen different lists. But it may jog the imaginations both of teachers who wish to organize their courses thematically rather than chronologically and of teachers who, although they use another scheme of organization, nevertheless want to draw thematic comparisons between works as their course progresses.

Much the same might be said of the following section: "Formal Genres, Modes, and Strategies." This is an index to the anthology arranged by genres such as the drama or novel, modes such as comedy or fantasy, and strategies such as journeys or problematical narratives. In compiling this index, both editors did some squirming; we could not always agree, even with each other, on the precise definition of certain categories, we were far from confident that our audience of teachers would see why we classified certain of the works as we did, and the whole notion of classifying world literature seemed a little presumptuous, if not megalomaniac. Be it understood, then, that this index, even more than the thematic one, is meant to be suggestive rather than definitive, to prompt an awareness of connections rather than to define; like Polonius, we are more than willing to see a cloud as either camel, weasel, or whale. Again, teachers may find suggestions here for organizing their entire course or units within it, or else for drawing comparisons between works on their syllabus, however organized.

The section "Literature and Society," concluding the introductory portion of the manual, makes some suggestions for helping students to see the connection between literary works and the cultures from which they emerged and to compare with one another these cultures and their literary embodiments.

The main body of the manual is made up of author-by-author study guides. Each begins with a few general comments on the work: possible strategies for teaching it, potential problems, tendencies in student response, or the like. We then offer a number of questions that the class might consider. In these questions as in the introductory remarks, we have been more interested in provoking thought and discussion than in attempting to anticipate everything that might come up in a class, where, as every teacher knows, anything can happen. Occasionally, we have commented on or tried to answer our own questions, especially when the line of thought underlying the questions seemed to need clarifying. But we have left most of them unanswered; some of them, indeed, we would have trouble answering.

Although the lengthier selections in the anthology usually get more space in the Manual than shorter ones, the space devoted to each author bears no consistent relationship to our judgment of the importance or even the complexity of the work. Some very complex works yield up their secrets in response to a very few simple questions, while other more accessible works call for examination from a number of critical angles.

We have tried to keep ax-grinding to a minimum, presenting for the most part what we perceive to be consensus readings of the texts and proposing questions open enough to be answered from a number of critical perspectives. But no doubt close readers of the manual (if there are any) will be able to identify recurring concerns that reflect our own biases about literature and perhaps about life. To edit out all such biases would perhaps have been impossible, and we have not aimed at total impersonality. But we hope our personal approaches, where they are detectable, will not obscure our attempt to encourage a wide variety of other approaches.

The manual ends with a "Selective Media Guide" that tabulates films, videotapes, sound tapes, and similar materials currently available in connection with the works in the anthology. New materials of this kind will become available (quite a few, it will be noted, have appeared since our earlier editions were published), and old ones will disappear, but the list of distributors and their addresses will help the teacher set up his or her own continuing guide to such materials.

One of the most exciting (and long overdue) projects in literary studies in recent years has been the Modern Language Association series on teaching the masterpieces of world literature. Almost every author in the anthology is or soon will be represented by a volume in this candid, nuts-and-bolts series. Except for a few, we do not specifically mention these volumes, but all of them are valuable and some are inestimably so.

Our thanks go to Paula Brickey and Rhonda Benish Adams, whose help with earlier editions of the Manual has left its print on this fourth one as well.

SOME THEMATIC THREADS

To identify the themes of world literature is to identify the themes of life itself, and not even anthology editors are rash enough to attempt that. But here is a list of a round dozen themes that we were especially conscious of as we worked on the book and that may serve as a starting point for developing thematic links in a world-literature course. The concept of a literary theme, we realize, is somewhat problematical. If literature is a rendering of life, the rendering is at least as important as the life, and exclusive attention to thematic content can distort somewhat students' understanding of how literature works. The problem is aggravated in that many students--most of them, probably--find it easier to concentrate on the "content" of a work than on its artistry. Nevertheless, most of us were probably first drawn to literature, and continue to be drawn to it, by its power to help us understand the world and our lives. However great or little the attention given to formal matters, the class will probably come back finally to the question of how these works render human experience--what they "mean." Here, then, not necessarily in order of importance, are twelve areas of human experience that the works in the anthology explore again and again.

Codes and Value Systems

Perhaps the most general of the thematic threads are codes of behavior and belief. Often the values of an entire culture and of the literary works that express that culture boil down to a simple question: "What are the rules and values by which one should lead one's life?" At the dawn of Western culture stand two contrasting, or complementary, value systems: the Hebrew and the Greek. The successive patriarchs in Genesis embody stages in the development of a distinctive ethical and moral code. It is a code very different from the code embodied in Homer's Akhilleus and Odysseus, which itself was transformed in later works of Greek literature such as the Oresteia and Oedipus the King. The Christian gospels and the Koran attempt something supremely difficult: to maintain the lifeline with Old Testament codes while radically superseding them. The Roman code, epitomized in Virgil and actually thrown into higher relief by raffish challenges to it on the part of Catullus and Ovid, might be seen as a precarious balance between Hellenism and Hebraic moral earnestness. Beowulf and Roland on one hand, and on the other hand the lais of Marie de France, The Art of Courtly Love, and Sir Gawain introduce two related but sharply different medieval codes: the masculine heroic code and the relatively feminized courtly code. Shakespeare's Henry IV provides a telling evaluation of such codes, in Renaissance retrospect, as does the profound and complex irony of Don Quixote. In their diverse ways, Petrarch, Machiavelli, Marguerite de Navarre, Montaigne, and Milton are all Renaissance modernists who, paradoxically, assert their modernity by reviving various aspects of antiquity. The code of refined honor governing the world of Mme de La Fayette and Racine is one of the most intricately articulated of all societal codes. "An Essay on Man" advances, among other things, a rationalistic Enlightenment ethic, which in turn is illuminated by the challenges to it from Romantics as different as Mary Shelley and Walt Whitman. As we approach the present, we encounter a proliferation of codes, societal and personal. Ibsen, Dostoevsky, Conrad, and Freud are all voices of the future who anticipate it with vastly different mixtures of hope and apprehensiveness. As for our own time, what seems from close range like fragmentation will probably come to be seen, in the future, as a set of distinct and definable codes, and students can be challenged to discern--from within, as it were--the codes they themselves are living by.

Growing Up

Someone once wrote that life consists of twenty years of growing up and another fifty of trying to understand what happened during the first twenty. Certainly growing up, if measured by the temporal duration of childhood and adolescence, receives a disproportionate amount of attention in literature, and the anthology is full of stories of development and initiation. The accounts of Jacob, Telemakhos, Electra, Orestes, Antigone, the Princesse de Clèves, Candide, Rousseau, Blake's Thel and Oothoon, Victor Frankenstein, Frederick Douglass, Freud's Dora, and the youngsters in Blake's Songs, Wright's "Big Boy Leaves Home," Fugard's "Master Harold" . . . and the boys, and Kincaid's Annie John--the list, though long, is not exhaustive--are all focused on the phenomenon of growing up. The crucial experience in maturation narratives is probably initiation, the movement from innocence to experience through a shattering encounter with some aspect of adult reality, such as Telemakhos' forced confrontation with his mother's murderous and rapacious suitors or the Princesse de Clèves's introduction to the storms of sexual passion. Nor is initiation confined to the young. Nora Helmer is a married woman with children before the affair of the forged note shatters her still-girlish fantasies, and the crucial spiritual rebirth in Camus' "The Adulterous Woman" occurs in middle age. The challenge of maturely facing reality comes even later in life in Ozick's "The Shawl." The theme of growing up not only spirals out to engage a number of other themes but also speaks with a special urgency to students who are experiencing their own particular initiations.

The Family

The structure of the nuclear family is related to the theme of growing up, but the family is a crucial subject of literature in its own right. Adam, Eve, Cain, and Abel provide a paradigm for literary families whose dynamics often reflect basic tensions in a literary work or in an entire culture. The roles of Father, Mother, Daughter, Son, Brother, and Sister are endlessly explored in the literature of the anthology, from Genesis, The Odyssey, and Greek tragedy, through Henry IV and Paradise Lost, to Frankenstein, Douglass's Narrative, Freud's Dora, Six Characters in Search of an Author, and Fugard's "Master Harold" (to give only a scattered sampling). It is worth noting that, in several of these works, existent familial tensions are posed against an ideal of the family that exists only in theory or vision. As with all the themes of literature, students are likely to be struck (if they are good readers) not so much by the similarities of literary families (their "universality") as by their differences. The patriarchal Hebrew family becomes the model for social and cosmic organization in the Old Testament, as the Greek family is a model for the relations of both human beings and gods in the Oresteia, but family structure is conceived very differently in the two works. And, to leap over two and a half millennia of literary families, the psychologically wholesome (or is it?) family of Victor Frankenstein, devastated by the consequences of his actions, provides an interesting comparison with the equally wholesome, almost somnolent family atmosphere startled into new awareness by the French chef in "Babette's Feast" and the psychologically distorted family situations in Kafka's Metamorphosis, Ozick's "The Shawl," and Kincaid's Annie John. Like growing up, family structure is a topic that often leads straight to the heart of a work's system of values.

Love and Marriage

Wooing is another human activity that is likely to engage issues far beyond its own literal scope. For a story about a mature married couple, The Odyssey contains a remarkable amount of courtship, and an examination of the relationships of Penelopé and her suitors, Odysseus and Kirkê, Odysseus and Kalypso, Odysseus and Nausikaa, and even Odysseus and a flirtatious Athena--especially in light of the epic's ending in that bed with a tree for a bedpost--can uncover some basic Homeric values, as a study of the Dido and Aeneas story can reveal some fundamental things about Roman culture. A very special instance of wooing occurs in Gilgamesh, when Enkidu is converted from the life of nature to societal life through being seduced by a temple prostitute. Sappho's and Catullus's poems of yearning, the sexual campaigning in Ovid, Marie de France's lais, the nearly contemporary Art of Courtly Love, the temptation of Sir Gawain by Morgan, the relationships of Dante and Petrarch to their idealized ladies, the tales told by Chaucer's Miller, Wife of Bath, and Nun's Priest, The Decameron and The Heptameron, Don Quixote, The Princesse de Clèves, Phaedra, Faust's pursuit of Gretchen, the poems of Baudelaire and the French symbolist poets, Chopin's The Awakening, Freud's Dora, Joyce's "The Dead," the complex relationship in "Under the Jaguar Sun"--all these involve romantic love stories that imply a wide range of views not only about love but also--in many cases--about even vaster subjects. In connection with all these works one can ask whether love is the ultimate subject or a vehicle for exploring, say, the possibilities of human nature, or its limitations, or the condition of society, or even the nature of divinity.

Conceptions of Gender

Conceptions of masculinity and femininity have been another fundamental concern of Western literature. The male domination of literature as of culture has usually placed man at the center, woman at the margins, of what matters. What it is to be a man has, frequently, been generalized into what it is to be human, while woman has frequently been regarded as the Other, a supplement to the male, an object seen in male perspective. To what extent this perspective represents a diminishment of woman, to what extent the opposite, is a matter that needs discriminating from one work to another. The very centering of the Odyssey in its male protagonist, for example, prompts an identification of the feminine with experience itself, with a large and varied world to be encountered and explored. However one reads the story of the Fall in Genesis (and it can be read several ways), it has formed a central myth of our sexual natures through Western history. One illuminating view of Greek drama is that it consists of a continuing debate on the role of the feminine in human values. Aeschylus casts his culture-history of Greece, the Oresteia, in the form of a struggle between female and male gods and between their female and male human counterparts; Sophocles in Antigone pits Creon's male values against Antigone's female ones in what amounts to a radical critique of Aeschylus' rather optimistic rationalism; the great "she-dramatist" Euripides, in such plays as Medea, ironically demythologizes the views on femininity of both his predecessors. The Greek opposition of "male" rationalism and "female" vitality in the tragedies illuminates the joke in Lysistrata, a work with unexpected thematic complications. The quasi-divinization of woman in Andreas Capellanus, in Dante, and (ambivalently) in Petrarch, is put into a radically different perspective by the Wife of Bath in her Prologue and Tale in The Canterbury Tales, and significantly modified by Christine de Pizan in The Book of the City of Ladies, by Marguerite de Navarre in the "problem" tales of The Heptameron, and by Goethe in Faust. Milton's revisionist view of Genesis in Paradise Lost is implicitly answered by Mary Shelley's revisionism in Frankenstein, where the Monster's Eve remains uncreated. Racine's reworks his spiritual forebear Euripides in Phaedra; Blake reworks Mary Wollstonecraft in Visions of the Daughters of Albion. The assumptions about women that underlie Freud's treatment of Dora have in recent years become a genuine cause célèbre. The resurgence of feminism in the late nineteenth century brought new questionings of the ways we divide up "male" and "female" in our culture. Ibsen's A Doll House and Chopin's The Awakening represent early stages in the debate, which is consolidated forcefully in Woolf's A Room of One's Own. Brecht's Good Woman of Setzuan recalls Sophocles' Antigone in finding a link between sexual division and a fundamental flaw in society.

The Hero

It is sometimes useful, early in a world-literature course, to arrive at a fairly explicit definition of hero, not as just a larger-than-life person but as one who exemplifies an entire society's values or an important part of them. The crucial point is not that Gilgamesh and Akhilleus are both heroes but the different value-systems their kinds of heroism imply. Job, Antigone, Medea, Lysistrata, Plato's Socrates, Aeneas, Jesus, Beowulf, Roland, Dante the pilgrim, Sir Gawain, and Milton's Adam and Son of God (possibly also his Satan) lend themselves well to such a view, as do such later heroes as the Princesse de Clèves, Faust, the protagonist of Douglass's Narrative, and Nora Helmer. The term heroine does not seem very functional from this point of view; gender is less important than the courage to act upon strong beliefs. The distinction between hero and anti-hero, too, is worth making, but it is far from clear-cut. The Kurtz of Heart of Darkness and Prufrock in Eliot's poem may embody a society's negative qualities, but so, to some extent, does Oedipus the King. And where do Victor Frankenstein and his Creature fit on the spectrum of hero / antihero? Or Virgil's Dido?

The Good Society

The creation stories in Genesis (and in Ovid's Metamorphoses) and the culture myth developed in the Oresteia announce another prominent theme in the anthology: the attempt to envision or create a good society. Students frequently find it easier to deal with personal issues than with social and political ones and sometimes have difficulty in even conceiving of a society organized differently from their own. To trace, say, the conception of kingship through Gilgamesh, Oedipus the King, Beowulf, and Henry IV, or--from another viewpoint--to examine the patterns of rights and obligations that tie societies together in the Old Testament, Greek literature, Roman literature, and medieval literature is to define important issues in the works and the societies they mirror. The utopia anticipated in a slant way by Christine de Pizan in her City of Ladies (is it a model for male society as well?) is one key point of departure for the many hypothetical societies later literature offers. Candide, like Gulliver's Travels, is organized around a series of real and imaginary societies, analyzed satirically--a telltale of the future development of literature, wherein panoramic or symbolic views of society tend to become progressively more baleful. The sardonic speaker in Notes from Underground presents a soured view of rationalistic utopias, and Heart of Darkness is a powerful exploration of the dark underside of "enlightened" Western society. Wright's picture of racial hatred and violence in "Big Boy Leaves Home" takes increased resonance from Douglass's picture, in his Narrative, of the slave society of a century earlier. Brecht's Setzuan is really an imaginary dystopia that mirrors the injustice of our own society; Fugard's

St. George's Park Tea Room anatomizes the racist society of South Africa; Kincaid's <u>Annie John</u> reveals not just a person but an environment. Some of these works are notable in that, paradoxically, they use intensely private or eccentric experience to suggest the entire surrounding culture.

God and Religion

It is sometimes as hard for us to imagine a God not our own as it is to understand an alien society, and we are all tempted sometimes to read our own ideas of God back into places where they do not belong. "Who is God?" is a question that runs throughout Old and New Testaments and the Koran, as "Who are the gods?" runs though all Greek tragedy (becoming startlingly literal and immediate in such works as Aeschylus's <u>Eumenides</u>). Tracing the successive answers to these questions is a good exercise in understanding and sympathetic imagination. Just as illuminating as the question of the nature of Abraham's God or of Sophocles' gods are the questions of what God means for Dante, the anonymous playwright of <u>Everyman</u>, Milton, Goethe, Blake, Dickinson, and Tolstoy. The proofs advanced for God's existence by Saints Anselm and Thomas Aquinas imply notions of God that differ, at least in emphasis, not only from those of other religions but even from each other. In certain works, the emphasis shifts from God to religion as an institution, as in <u>The Canterbury Tales</u>, <u>Tartuffe</u>, <u>Candide</u>, <u>Faust</u>, the "Grand Inquisitor" section of <u>The Brothers Karamazov</u>, and <u>The Good Woman of Setzuan</u>. And what, in this whole context, are we to make of Montaigne?

Illusion and Reality

All imaginative literature inevitably raises the question of the relation of fiction to truth, and so all such literature in a sense is "about" illusion and reality. But a substantial body of literature, since its beginning, has dealt specifically and directly with the problems of reality and of imperfect humanity's difficulties in perceiving it. Plato's Parable of the Cave can stand as the most haunting early expression of this theme in the anthology, introducing a series of works in which protagonists struggle through veils of illusion to arrive at what (in various senses of the word) is real. <u>Don Quixote</u> is the most searching of these works, which also include among many others Ovid's <u>Metamorphoses</u> and <u>Heroides</u> (the Paris-Helen letters can be read as a dance of deception and possibly self-deception), Montaigne's <u>Raymond Sebond</u>, <u>Phaedra</u>, <u>Candide</u>, "The Queen of Spades," "The Death of Ivan Ilyitch," Freud's <u>Dora</u>, <u>Heart of Darkness</u>, <u>Six Characters in Search of an Author</u>, "The Mark on the Wall," the Borges pieces, and Ozick's "The Shawl." The roles played by the human imagination and sensory apparatus in the creation or definition of reality also underlie the whole enterprise of the Romantic and symbolist poets. An important sub-theme appears in a number of works wherein illusion is identified with literature itself and the quest is, paradoxically, to catch reality in a net of the illusory. Pirandello's <u>Six Characters</u> and the Borges stories are obvious cases in point, along with Yeats's "The Circus Animals' Desertion," where the poet seeks to move past the circus animals of his art to descend into the "foul rag and bone shop" of the heart's reality.

Nature

It is often useful in reading a literary work to look at how physical nature is represented. At their simplest, natural landscapes are important as the setting of literary works. Marie de France's magic landscapes are as appropriate in her world of romance as, in <u>Don Quixote</u>, are the harsh, dusty Spanish plains traversed by the knight and Sancho Panza. The wintry landscape of <u>Sir Gawain</u> is both grim and, somehow, lyrically haunting. But in a number of key works, physical nature is not merely setting but a central theme. In <u>Gilgamesh</u>, Enkidu's sexual initiation by the temple harlot alienates him from nature while it brings him into the human community. The Eden myth in Genesis presents human beings as cast out into a natural world forever alien to them and, though precariously, subject to their authority. That authority has never been complete, and recurringly in Western literature writers have reminded us of the power and mystery of the non-human world. In <u>Oedipus the King</u>, the opposition of the man-made palace of Thebes and the continual offstage presence of Mount Kithairon, locus of the wild, the mysterious, and the nonhuman, reminds us of what Oedipus has forgotten: the fragility of the means by which humanity holds the forces of nature at bay. The titanic Leviathan and Behemoth have a similar function in the very different world of Job, as reminders of the awesome might of nature. Beowulf's submarine struggle, Wordsworth's rapture at storm or sunset, Thel's obsessively questioning of flower and cloud, the haunting threnody of Whitman's bereaved singing bird, Marlow on the Congo, Gregor Samsa suddenly changed into the non-human natural Other, Camus' Janine imbibing the life of the nocturnal desert--these represent a sampling of responses to the enigma of our place in the natural world.

War and Violence

The horrifying wars of our century have, understandably, given the theme of violence a special urgency. Cain's murder of Abel is a prototype of man's lethal violence in Western literature, and the inner theme of that story--that killing expresses not only alienation between human beings but the individual's alienation from the self--is elaborated throughout literary history. The most explicit, large-scale treatments of the theme are the war stories. Paradoxically, the "holy" wars of the Hebrews later in the Old Testament are sometimes shockingly idealized, but the exemplary war of Greek literature, the Trojan war, is never idealized and is sometimes presented with an abrupt, anti-mythologizing realism. As a description of the war's grisly mechanics and logistics, nothing could be starker than the <u>Iliad</u>; in Aeschylus' <u>Agamemnon</u> it is called a war "fought for a whore." The Peloponnesian War--modern history for the fifth-century Greeks--is treated by Aristophanes as a catastrophe. Virgil's war scenes, Roman though he was, are as unidealized as Homer's, as the killing of Turnus intimates. The meaning of war is also central, in rather different ways, in <u>Beowulf</u> and <u>The Song of Roland</u>. In light of the frank treatment of war in many of these works, one might ask how "satiric" Voltaire is in his accounts of war in <u>Candide</u>. The treatment of armed conflict in Yeats's "Easter 1916" can make an interesting modern comparison with these accounts. In relating the theme of war to the more general theme of violence, teachers may wish to consider the question whether war is simply an extreme case of the kind of violence found in other works: the rape in Blake's <u>Daughters of Albion</u>, the brutal whippings in Douglass's <u>Narrative</u>, the genocide suggested in <u>Heart of Darkness</u>, and the disturbing overtones or explicit depiction of violence in such disparate works as Mann's "Disorder and Early Sorrow," Faulkner's "An Odor of Verbena," Wright's "Big Boy Leaves Home," Sartre's "The Wall," and Ozick's "The Shawl."

Art and the Artist

Inevitably, art itself has engaged the attention of artists as a subject since the beginning of literature: Odysseus is moved to tears by a bard's recounting of his own story, Aeneas by the same story rendered in pictures on a wall. Paradoxically, some of the most interesting studies of the artistic imagination are in works not overtly about art at all, while some of the works which seem to deal with art really use art as a metaphor for other matters. Odysseus, whatever else he may be, is also an artist, and a study of his virtuoso lies leads us into a number of truths about the way art has been used to structure human experience. Pirandello's Six Characters in Search of an Author seems to be directly about the nature of art, but the more we study it, the more art seems to be secondary to the theme of the nature of human personality. It would be interesting to study Aristotle's Poetics not only as an analysis of tragedy but as a statement about life. The theory of catharsis, for example, goes far beyond dramatic technique in the assumptions it makes about the role of such passions as pity and fear in the personality. Something analogous can be said about Plato's Ion, which on one level is about the role of irrational inspiration in poetry and on another level is about the role, in general, of intuition in mental life. Don Quixote, like The Odyssey, takes art as an important indirect theme, and all the Romantic poets--Keats, for example, in the "Grecian Urn" ode, and Coleridge in "Dejection"--explore the creative imagination as the chief instrument for human beings' encounters with the world. Art has been an almost obsessive subject of modern writers, from the experiments of the symbolists, to Yeats's searching explorations of his own art, to the devastating vision of art as compulsive self-delusion in Beckett's Krapp's Last Tape, to Baldwin's moving exploration of the meaning of the blues in "Sonny's Blues." Even the culinary art has been brought under this rubric, as in Dinesen's "Babette's Feast" and Calvino's "Under the Jaguar Sun."

FORMAL GENRES, MODES, AND STRATEGIES

Some teachers may wish to organize their courses neither chronologically nor thematically but by forms, genres, modes, or literary strategies. One time-honored paradigm consists of epic, drama, and lyric; another consists of poetry, drama, fiction, and discourse. But along with these large families and orders of literature there are of course many more particular genera, species, and varieties, some of them definable as groups (love stories), others by the quality of imagination (fantasy), still others by narrative or rhetorical strategies (problematical narratives with, perhaps, unreliable narrators). Sometimes these categories go half-disguised as themes, but the distinction is real and important. It would be tenable, for example, to say that "The Horse Dealer's Daughter" is a love story that is also centered on the theme of love, that Faust and The Awakening are love stories but are not about love, and that Lysistrata is about love but is not a love story. In fact, one of the reasons to organize units of material around, say, journeys is to show the astonishing variety of themes that can be explored through what might seem at first glance to be a common subject but is really a common generic way of ordering experience.

Even teachers who do not want to stress such formal matters to the extent of making them the basic organizational principle of their course may want to draw regular comparisons between works in similar categories: to compare Gilgamesh with the Iliad or Aeneid as epics (or as visionary literature), or Gulliver's Travels with The Good Woman of Setzuan as fantasy (or as satire), or the Odyssey with Don Quixote as self-reflexive literature (or as journeys).

Our categories overlap freely, and we have tried to be as inclusive and suggestive as possible, even at the risk of making some highly debatable classifications. Most of the categories are self-explanatory. We mean nothing pejorative by melodrama but include under this category works that are characterized by supercharged emotional intensity, confrontations between extreme good and evil, and lurid events, or by some combination of these. Problematical narratives we take to be ones which raise basic questions of reliability or verifiability. Theodicies are works that defend God's goodness and power despite the existence of evil in the world; anti-theodicies deny that goodness and power. Surrealistic carries no connotations of the historical movement of the 1920's but merely means "fantastic or dream-like."

ALLEGORY AND SYMBOLIC NARRATIVE

    Gilgamesh
    Iliad: Book XVIII, shield of Akhilleus
    Republic: Parable of the Cave
    Aeneid: Book VIII, shield of Aeneas
    Beowulf: inset stories
    The Art of Courtly Love, inset narratives
    Bisclavret
    Yonec
    Divine Comedy
    Canterbury Tales: The Pardoner's Tale
    Sir Gawain and the Green Knight
    Book of the City of Ladies
    Everyman

Gulliver's Travels
Book of Thel
Visions of the Daughters of Albion
Frankenstein
Bartleby the Scrivener
Because I Could Not Stop for Death
A Voyage to Cythera
Dora
Heart of Darkness
The Metamorphosis
Under the Jaguar Sun
Annie John

AUTOBIOGRAPHY AND BIOGRAPHY

    Apology
    Rousseau's Confessions
    Narrative of the Life of Frederick Douglass, an American Slave
    Dora
    "Master Harold" . . . and the Boys
    Annie John

COMEDY AND HUMOR

    Odyssey
    Lysistrata
    Ion
    Egnatius Has White Teeth
    Amores (Ovid)
    Heroides (Ovid), Paris-Helen letters
    Canterbury Tales: Miller's Tale, Prologue to the Wife of Bath's Tale,
        and Nun's Priest's Tale
    Decameron: Third Day, Tenth Tale; and Fifth Day, Tenth Tale
    Heptameron
    Don Quixote
    Henry IV, Part I
    Love's Diet
    Tartuffe
    Gulliver's Travels
    Candide
    Bartleby the Scrivener
    The Cherry Orchard

COMIC DRAMA

    Lysistrata
    Henry IV, Part I

    Tartuffe
    The Cherry Orchard
    The Good Woman of Setzuan

DRAMA

    Job
    Oresteia
    Oedipus the King
    Antigone
    Medea
    Lysistrata
    Everyman
    Henry IV, Part I
    Tartuffe
    Phaedra
    Faust, Part I
    A Doll House
    The Cherry Orchard
    Six Characters in Search of an Author
    The Good Woman of Setzuan
    Krapp's Last Tape
    "Master Harold" . . . and the Boys

DRAMATIC MONOLOGUE

    Amores (Ovid)
    Heroides, Paris-Helen letters
    The Art of Courtly Love
    Frankenstein: The Monster's Story
    Tithonus
    My Last Duchess
    The Bishop Orders His Tomb
    Andrea del Sarto
    Notes from Underground
    Helen
    Heart of Darkness
    The Love Song of J. Alfred Prufrock

EPIC AND ROMANCE

    Gilgamesh
    Iliad
    Odyssey
    Aeneid
    Metamorphoses
    Beowulf

The Song of Roland
The Art of Courtly Love, inset narratives
Bisclavret
Yonec
Divine Comedy
Sir Gawain and the Green Knight
Don Quixote
Paradise Lost
The Eve of St. Agnes

ESSAY

Ion
Republic
Apology
Poetics
Proslogium (Anselm)
Summa Theologica
Of Cannibals
Apology for Raymond Sebond
The Prince
A Modest Proposal
An Essay on Man
Dora
Shakespeare's Sister

FANTASY

Gilgamesh
Odyssey: Books IX-XII
Metamorphoses
Beowulf
Bisclavret
Yonec
Canterbury Tales: Wife of Bath's Tale, Pardoner's Tale, Nun's Priest's Tale
Sir Gawain and the Green Knight
Gulliver's Travels
Candide
Faust, Part I
The Book of Thel
Visions of the Daughters of Albion
Kubla Khan
Frankenstein
The Queen of Spades
The Lotos-Eaters
Tithonus
The Grand Inquisitor
Because I Could Not Stop for Death

Parisian Dream
The Drunken Boat
Six Characters in Search of an Author
The Metamorphosis
Tlön, Uqbar, Orbis Tertius
The Circular Ruins

FARCE AND BURLESQUE

Lysistrata
Amores (Ovid)
Metamorphoses
Inferno: Cantos XXI-XXII (Grafters)
Canterbury Tales: Miller's Tale, Nun's Priest's Tale
Decameron: Fourth Day, Second Tale, and Fifth Day, Tenth Tale
Heptameron: Story Eight
Don Quixote
Henry IV, Part I, Falstaff scenes
Tartuffe
Candide
Faust, Part I, episodes

INTROSPECTION AND MEDITATION

Psalms
Apology
Catullus, Poems
Sermon on the Mount
Koran
Everyman
Petrarch, Rhymes
Of Cannibals
Apology for Raymond Sebond
Rousseau's Confessions
Faust, Part I, soliloquies
Songs of Innocence and of Experience
Tintern Abbey
Ode: Intimations of Immortality
Keats, Odes
Frankenstein
Andrea del Sarto
Whitman, Poems
Dickinson, Poems
Notes from Underground
The Grand Inquisitor
The Death of Ivan Ilyitch
French Symbolist and Modernist Poetry
Yeats, Poems

The Mark on the Wall
The Love Song of J. Alfred Prufrock

THE JOURNEY

Gilgamesh
Odyssey
Aeneid
Song of Roland
Divine Comedy
Canterbury Tales
Sir Gawain and the Green Knight
Don Quixote
Gulliver's Travels
Candide
Faust, Part I, Walpurgis Night
Ulysses (Tennyson)
A Voyage to Cythera
Heart of Darkness
Sailing to Byzantium

LOVE STORIES: ROMANTIC AND ANTI-ROMANTIC

Genesis: Jacob and Rachel
Odyssey
Sappho, Poems
Agamemnon
Medea
Catullus, Lesbia Poems
Aeneid: Book IV
Amores (Ovid)
Heroides, Paris-Helen letters
The Art of Courtly Love
Bisclavret
Yonec
Inferno: Canto V (Paolo and Francesca)
Divine Comedy (Beatrice episodes)
Canterbury Tales: Miller's Tale, Wife of Bath's Tale
Sir Gawain and the Green Knight
Petrarch, Rhymes
Decameron: Tenth Day, Tenth Tale
Heptameron
Don Quixote
Paradise Lost: Books IV, IX, X
The Princesse de Clèves
Phaedra
Faust, Part I
Visions of the Daughters of Albion

The Eve of St. Agnes
La Belle Dame Sans Merci
Frankenstein
Andrea del Sarto
A Doll House
The Awakening
Dora
The Dead
Odour of Chrysanthemums
The Love Song of J. Alfred Prufrock
An Odor of Verbena
The Adulterous Woman
Under the Jaguar Sun
The Shawl

LYRIC POETRY
　Psalms
　Koran
　Poems of
　　Sappho
　　Catullus
　　Ovid (Amores)
　　Petrarch
　　Boccaccio, conclusions of Days
　　Donne
　　Goethe (Faust, interpolated lyrics)
　　Blake
　　Wordsworth
　　Coleridge
　　Keats
　　Tennyson
　　Browning
　　Whitman
　　Dickinson
　　Baudelaire
　　Corbière
　　Verlaine
　　Rimbaud
　　Mallarmé
　　Laforgue
　　Apollinaire
　　Valéry
　　Yeats

MELODRAMA

　Medea
　Decameron: Tenth Day, Tenth Tale

Canterbury Tales: The Pardoner's Tale
Phaedra
Faust, Part I
Frankenstein
The Queen of Spades
My Last Duchess
Heart of Darkness

NOVEL (see also NOVELLA)

Don Quixote
The Princesse de Clèves
Frankenstein
The Awakening
Annie John

NOVELLA (see also SHORT STORY)

A Simple Heart
Notes from Underground
The Death of Ivan Ilyitch
Heart of Darkness
The Metamorphosis
Sonny's Blues
The Shawl

PHILOSOPHICAL WRITING

Ion
Republic: Parable of the Cave
Apology
Poetics
Proslogium (Anselm)
Summa Theologica
The Prince
Of Cannibals
Apology for Raymond Sebond
Faust, Part I
Frankenstein

PROBLEMATICAL NARRATIVES AND SPEAKERS

Odyssey
Heroides, Paris-Helen letters
Decameron
Canterbury Tales

Gulliver's Travels
Rousseau's Confessions
Songs of Innocence and of Experience
Frankenstein
The Queen of Spades
Browning, dramatic monologues
Notes from Underground
Gooseberries
Dora
The Love Song of J. Alfred Prufrock
The Mark on the Wall
Tlön, Uqbar, Orbis Tertius
The Circular Ruins
Krapp's Last Tape
Under the Jaguar Sun

QUEST NARRATIVE

Gilgamesh
Odyssey
Aeneid
Beowulf
The Art of Courtly Love, inset narratives
Divine Comedy
Canterbury Tales
Sir Gawain and the Green Knight
Don Quixote
Gulliver's Travels
Candide
Book of Thel
The Eve of St. Agnes
Narrative of the Life of Frederick Douglass, an American Slave
The Death of Ivan Ilyitch
The Awakening
The Drunken Boat
Heart of Darkness

SATIRE

Lysistrata
Ion
Amores (Ovid)
Decameron
Heptameron
Canterbury Tales
Gulliver's Travels
A Modest Proposal
Faust, Part I, episodes

Bartleby the Scrivener
The End
The Approach of Winter
The Good Woman of Setzuan

SELF-REFLEXIVE LITERATURE

Odyssey
Eumenides
Amores (Ovid)
Heroides, Paris-Helen letters
Divine Comedy
Canterbury Tales
Book of the City of Ladies
Petrarch, Rhymes
Decameron
Heptameron
Apology for Raymond Sebond
Don Quixote
Gulliver's Travels
Kubla Khan
Frankenstein
Notes from Underground
Heart of Darkness
The Mark on the Wall
Six Characters in Search of an Author
Tlön, Uqbar, Orbis Tertius
Krapp's Last Tape
Under the Jaguar Sun

SHORT STORY (see also NOVELLA)

Metamorphoses
Bisclavret
Yonec
Canterbury Tales
Decameron
Heptameron
The Queen of Spades
Bartleby the Scrivener
Gooseberries
Disorder and Early Sorrow
The Dead
The Mark on the Wall
Odour of Chrysanthemums
The Horse Dealer's Daughter
Babette's Feast
An Odor of Verbena

The Wall
The Adulterous Woman
Tlön, Uqbar, Orbis Tertius
The Circular Ruins
Big Boy Leaves Home
Under the Jaguar Sun

THEODICIES AND ANTI-THEODICIES

Job
Oresteia
Aeneid
Divine Comedy
Paradise Lost
An Essay on Man
Candide
Faust, Part I
Frankenstein
The Grand Inquisitor
The Death of Ivan Ilyitch
The Good Woman of Setzuan

TRAGIC DRAMA

Agamemnon
Libation Bearers
Eumenides
Oedipus the King
Antigone
Medea
Everyman
Henry IV, Part I
Phaedra
Faust, Part I

UTOPIAS AND DYSTOPIAS

Odyssey: Phaiakian episode
Metamorphoses: Book I
Divine Comedy: Paradise
Book of the City of Ladies
Of Cannibals
Don Quixote, Part II, chapters 22-23
Paradise Lost, Book IV
Gulliver's Travels
Candide, chapters 17-18

Songs of Innocence
Ode on a Grecian Urn

VISIONARY OR SURREALISTIC LITERATURE

Gilgamesh
Odyssey: Books IX-XII
Republic: Parable of the Cave
Aeneid: Book VI
The Art of Courtly Love, inset narratives
Bisclavret
Yonec
Divine Comedy
Canterbury Tales: The Pardoner's Tale
Sir Gawain and the Green Knight
Everyman
Paradise Lost
Faust, Part I
Songs of Innocence and of Experience
Book of Thel
Visions of the Daughters of Albion
Ode: Intimations of Immortality
Kubla Khan
La Belle Dame Sans Merci
Frankenstein
The Grand Inquisitor
French Symbolist and Modernist Poetry
Heart of Darkness
The Metamorphosis
Under the Jaguar Sun

LITERATURE AND SOCIETY

In the preceding sections, on themes and forms, we have emphasized dimensions of literature that are more or less independent of history and sociology. In assembling a collection of world literature, as in teaching a course on the subject, there is a natural tendency to emphasize the universal and to look for threads of similarity running through the works, relatively independent of time and change. But the microcosm of literature is not independent of the macrocosm of history; if literature at its best rises to the universal, it does so through the particularities of specific times and places and social organizations, not independently of them. Literature offers us the chance not only to see what all people have had in common but also to observe how, throughout history, different modes of social organization have generated sharply different ways of thinking and feeling. Paradoxically, a sense of the discreteness of the cultures represented in the anthology, and of their distance from our own, can help bridge cultural gaps today. It might well occur, for example, to students of different ethnic or racial or family or economic backgrounds, that the gap between such backgrounds, however wide it may be in many ways, is probably not as wide as the one separating any one group today from the people who lived in, say, Homer's time.

Like themes and forms, societies could form the basic organizational scheme for a world-literature course. The units could be chronological--Old Testament society, the society of the heroic age of Greece, fifth-century Athenian society, and so on. Even a strictly chronological arrangement of this kind would differ from a work-by-work approach, by highlighting, in groups of works, dimensions that grow out of particular cultures and societies. And, as with themes and forms, teachers who do not want to make social organization a curricular obsession can still make a consideration of the social dimensions of the readings a recurring element in their course.

It would seem that a world-literature course taught with a social or historical approach would be constantly in danger of becoming a history course illustrated by literary works. But that need not happen if one approaches a particular society through its literature. Literature is, arguably, the best source of information about previous societies, if one is interested not only in political and military matters but also in "inner" history: what people thought and felt about living in medieval Europe, say, or in eighteenth-century France.

A teacher can often initiate an inductive, exploratory investigation of the social dimensions of a work by simply asking, "What sort of society does this work depict?" And this question can be broken down into more concrete ones: What is the economic system like? Is it based on tending animals? On agriculture? On trading? On manufacture? How are goods distributed? What things are considered necessities, and how do people get them? Who has the power in the society? By what sanction do they hold it? How is it transmitted? Is there a class structure, and, if so, what is it like, how rigid is it, and what are its visible signs? What is the legal system like? How are children reared? What is the position of women? How are boys initiated into manhood and girls into womanhood? What are the public codes of behavior? Are the public codes observed in private? How are the codes related to the structure of the society?

Such questions, and others along the same lines, can lead students into a working understanding of the dynamics of the societies represented in, say, <u>Gilgamesh</u>, the Old Testament, <u>The Odyssey</u>, <u>Sir Gawain and the Green Knight</u>, Douglass's <u>Narrative</u>, <u>Notes from</u>

Underground, The Cherry Orchard, Joyce's "The Dead," The Metamorphosis, and "Master Harold" . . . and the Boys. But the matters implied by the questions are not significant only in such comparatively panoramic representations of societies as we find in these works. Even such seemingly asocial literary forms as lyric poetry are often illuminated if we consider them not just as vehicles for individual expression but as reflections of certain social conditions. The ideal of manhood implied, for example, in Donne's love poetry could hardly exist if it were not for a particular set of social conditions which a glance at Donne's own life will confirm: a system based on position, office, and favor in which wit, education, and an easy, pragmatic cynicism identify one as a member of a privileged (and in this case all-male) elite worthy of "advancement." Baudelaire's poetry and Emily Dickinson's differ radically from Donne's (and from each other's) not only in sensibility but in the social worlds in which they are grounded.

Writers do not always represent their own societies; obviously they often write about other societies, remote in time and place or even imaginary. In such cases, we are challenged not only to understand the society represented but also to work out its relation to the writer's own society. Understanding then becomes a process of triangulation, of accommodating to one another the writer's viewpoint, the modern reader's, and that of the characters portrayed. King Oedipus' society is clearly not that of Sophocles, despite the regularity with which students confuse them. To the sophisticated Greeks of fifth-century Athens, the Oedipus story was just as exotic and barbaric as it is to us; when Sophocles chose it for the basis of his play, he stood in approximately the same relation to his material as Goethe did when, looking back from the post-Enlightenment period, he chose to base a tragedy on a late-medieval magus. The Thebes of Sophocles' play is a primitive tribal society the (literal) health of which is mysteriously bound up with the character of its king; the little circle of light that is the palace barely holds back a dark, inexplicable world full of sphinxes and inscrutable, threatening oracles. But at the center of this primitive world Sophocles set a man who, in his ways of thinking and feeling, is essentially a fifth-century Athenian, as Goethe put into Faust's consciousness the questions being bruited by eighteenth-century philosophes and their Romantic successors. Understanding these plays involves recognizing that imaginary societies can be veiled representations of real ones and thinking through their relationships. A similar multiple vision is required to understand Racine's Troezen, in Phaedra; Madame de Lafayette's sixteenth-century France in The Princesse de Clèves; and Brecht's fairytale China, in The Good Woman of Setzuan--to name only a few examples from many in the anthology.

American students tend to populate literature with young Americans of their own social class. This is not always bad; identification is an important and valuable part of literary response. But to read accurately, we must go beyond identification to an apprehension of the real differentness of others, just as we must in growing up. In the long run, such an apprehension should probably lead students to revise their notions of what "human nature" itself is. Rather than confidently asserting that the way they think and feel, in a modern, democratic, industrial society, is human nature, they can come to understand the meaning of "other days, other ways" and experience one of the most valuable responses to literature, that of seeing the world for a time through the lenses worn in societies organized differently.

The editors have tried to include in the following sections a number of questions that direct attention to the social dimensions of literature.

One final consideration: If society is understood as the aggregate of communal living conditions and arrangements, then society has always existed, or at least as long as human beings have lived together in groups. In the Introduction to Neoclassicism and Romanticism in the anthology, we try to define also a more modern sense of the word society, roughly analogous in ontological status to the medieval quasi-personification called Fortune. In this modern sense, familiar since the time of Rousseau and ubiquitous in literary works from the nineteenth century on, Society becomes a quasi-conscious force, often a repressive one, that works more subtly than the state but, often, at least as coercively. It may prove interesting to teachers to see how strongly their students have imbibed this idea, and how easily they are inclined to detect this modern notion of society even in the literary works of the more distant past.

VOLUME I

THE ANCIENT WORLD THROUGH THE RENAISSANCE

Gilgamesh

For most undergraduate students, everything that happened in ancient times--before the time of Christ especially--tends to blur and blend together, as things unimaginably distant in time and therefore undifferentiated. Such a feeling is understandable, not only because few of us were well acquainted with ancient history when we were undergraduates but also because it is inherently difficult for anyone to grasp imaginatively what it means for, say, a thousand years to elapse. Yet some attempt ought probably to be made to bring this time perspective home to students, to help them appreciate that Gilgamesh was a very ancient poem even at the time of Homer and the authors of the Hebrew Bible. And, although it would probably be a disastrous mistake to attempt a crash mini-course in ancient history, it might be a good idea to spend ten or fifteen minutes outlining the sequence and dates of the most important ancient empires and dynasties, especially those of Asia Minor, somewhat as geological periods are schematized in basic science courses. Teachers whose own acquaintance with ancient history is less than expert can consult any of several overviews of it--to name just one very brief one, the book History's Timeline, edited by Fay Franklin (1981).

Most teachers, however, will find it more useful to concentrate on the literary dimension of Gilgamesh, and to advert to its cultural and historical milieu only to the extent that that emerges explicitly in the poem and helps define the poem's powerful emotional effect. The questions below are, by and large, framed with this latter approach in mind. Certain of the questions in this Manual about other ancient epics, especially Homer's, and about the Bible can also be adapted to Gilgamesh. Teachers must bear in mind, however, that any single version of Gilgamesh is just that--a version--and that we have nothing so nearly approaching a definitive text of the poem as we do with the Bible and Homer.

1. The opening lines of Gilgamesh have some things in common with the opening formulas used in the later epics of Homer, Virgil, and Milton. There are also important differences, in this respect, from those later epics. Compare the various openings with one another.

2. The last lines of the poem nearly repeat lines 11-15 of Tablet I. What is the effect of this repetition and framing?

3. One way of achieving a figurative immortality is through fame. To what extent does this idea emerge in Gilgamesh, and how convincing is it?

4. In some respects, Gilgamesh is portrayed near the beginning of the poem as an oppressor or tyrant. What happens to this view of him as the poem progresses?

5. The immediate effect of Enkidu's sexual initiation through his encounter with the Shamhat, the temper harlot, is to alienate him from the animals with whom he had previously lived unself-consciously, and perhaps, more generally speaking, to alienate him from nature. Does this make sense? Is not the fact of sexual intercourse one of the most obvious ways in which human beings resemble other animals?

6. How do Gilgamesh, Enkidu, and/or other characters in Gilgamesh define the meaning of death? What, for example, do they imagine as happening to persons after they die? What is there about being alive that makes dying so fearsome or hateful?

One might wish to compare the famous statement by Akhilleus in Homer's Odyssey, Book XI, that he would rather be the meanest servant alive than be king over all the dead.

7. Fearlessness in the face of death, or a kind of disregard of it, would seem to be central in many versions of the heroic code. Yet for both Gilgamesh and Enkidu the prospect of death occasions bitterness or panic or revulsion. Does this fact diminish their heroic stature? Does their sharing of the normal human fear of death throw light on what heroism truly is?

8. What is the meaning of the realm over which Siduri, the "tavern keeper," presides?

9. What is the status of Utnapishtim? The poem seems to insist relentlessly that death is the inescapable lot of mortals, however heroic, but that Utnapishtim is indeed a mortal rather than a divinity (see, for example, lines 1-8 of Tablet XI). How can it be, then, that he has been exempted from death?

10. Compare the accounts of the Flood in Gilgamesh and in the Hebrew Bible (Genesis, chapters 6-9).

Students should note especially the differences in the divine motivation for the Flood and in the moral/ethical implications of the two accounts.

11. In Tablet XI, section viii, a serpent steals the magic plant capable of restoring youth. What do you make of this incident? Compare the role and meaning of the serpent in Genesis, chapter 3.

The Old Testament (Hebrew Bible)

The Old Testament presents formidable challenges in an introductory literature course: the difficulty of the language, the complexities of the text and of the narrative movement in many sections, and the remoteness of the culture presented. But there are compensating rewards. The Bible is so central to our culture and yet so unfamiliar to many students that many will welcome a close look at what it actually says. Because of its very complexity and remoteness, it presents a clear challenge to develop the kinds of interpretive tools that the class will need all through the course. And finally, the issues in the Old Testament--the nature of God, the nature of humanity and its place in the universe, the meaning of good and evil--are so basic that the selections can be used to define themes that will run throughout the course.

A good starting point for Genesis might be a consideration of the terms myth, legend, and saga, as biblical scholars use them. If there are any literal interpreters in the class or even if there aren't, it might be well to establish right away that whatever else the first eleven chapters of Genesis are, they are also a myth, in the sense of a traditional story that embodies characteristic world-views of a culture. Chapters 12-50 contain legends of the patriarchs in that, whatever their historicity, they have taken on the shape of folk tales in the process of being handed down orally. And the story of the Israelites' flight from Egypt into the Promised Land--not in the anthology but at least roughly familiar to most students--is a saga, in the sense of a heroic tale of national origins. (The point that, in literature, truth is not necessarily the same as historicity is not a bad one to make early in the course.)

Harold Bloom's The Book of J (1990), with the accompanying translation by David Rosenberg of the J author's contributions to the Pentateuch, throws into extraordinarily high relief the awesome originality and genius of the J portions, whether or not one finds credible Bloom's historical suggestions (e.g., that the J author was a woman) or even takes his argument at face value.

We have been at pains also to present in the anthology a few other facets of the Hebrew Bible and culture, including the strain of skepticism in Job and the many-voiced lyricism of the Psalms. Apart from their inherent interest and value, these works attest something many students need to recognize: that the Bible is both a book and a set of books.

1. How is the great creation account that opens Genesis structured, and what views of the world does it express?

The serial structure and the use of repetitive formulas--"And God said", "And the evening and the morning were the xth day"--both remind us of the roots of the work in oral literature and give the account an exalted, incantatory quality. The sequence of the six days is very carefully structured, both as a pair of triads (large areas, then populations for those areas) and as three pairs (the luminaries of the fourth day, for instance, are linked to the light of the first day). The ancient Hebrew cosmology, with a flat earth resting on great pillars and covered by a solid, dome-shaped sky, is clearly implied, as well as a conception of God as single, supreme, independent of matter, and the source of design and meaning in the world.

2. Compare the tone and content of the first creation narrative (the P account in Genesis 1:1--2:3) with those of the second account (the J account in Genesis 2).

3. What basic assumptions about such matters as the nature of God, humanity's relation to Him, the relation of the sexes, the nature of work, and the nature of good and evil does the story of the Garden of Eden imply?

4. Explore the parallels between Adam and Eve's transgression and Cain's.

5. What does the Flood story add to the conception of God already presented?

    The concept of <u>covenants</u> as defining the relations between God and humanity is important here. The relation between God and Adam and Eve is implicitly a covenant; the covenant of the rainbow is second in a long series of developing covenants in the Old Testament.

6. The story of Noah's drunkenness and his curse on Canaan is apparently an etiological story meant to account for the presumed depravity of the Canaanites. Show how it also develops the theme of human alienation and division after the Fall.

7. The story of the Tower of Babel ends the section of Genesis devoted to primeval history. Note that it lacks the concluding divine forgiveness and redemption of the earlier stories of Adam and Eve, Cain and Abel, and the Flood. Why should this be so?

8. Compare the role of God in the primeval history portion of Genesis (chapters 1-11) with His role in the legends of the patriarchs (chapters 12-50).

9. Look at the patriarchal narratives as an anthropologist might, using them to construct as complete a description of patriarchal culture as you can, considering its pastoral economy, family structure, marriage customs, patterns of inheritance, and religious practices.

10. The patriarchal legends contain a number of crucial <u>theophanies,</u> in which God makes Himself seen or heard. Identify these and consider their significance.

11. Abraham is principally characterized as a man of complete faith in God. What does the episode of the near-sacrifice of Isaac tell us about the kind of faith the Lord requires?

12. Much of the story of Jacob is in the mode of earthy comedy. What relation do the comedy and the characterization of Jacob as a trickster have to the major theme, in the patriarchal saga, of the Hebrews' developing negotiations with God?

    This question could raise the important issue of whether the Hebrews "deserve" the special favor God grants them or whether God is working out His will regardless of the human instruments. The motif of "wrestling" or "struggling" throughout the Jacob story is also relevant.

13. James King West, in comparing the frame tale of Job with the poem, mentions "the patience of the legendary hero as compared with the impatient subject of the poetry." What other differences of content and style are there? Are the differences necessarily defects? Or can they be regarded as complementary views of the same material?

14. Job is best read in the context of the rest of the Old Testament, since the orthodox interpretation of suffering advanced by the comforters represents an illegitimate extension into

individual life of God's covenant with the Hebrews. What other relationships are there with earlier parts of the Bible? Does Job develop an aspect of God slighted earlier? How does the theophany "out of the whirlwind" compare with earlier manifestations of God's presence?

15. Is there any development of Job's character in the book or does he remain essentially the same throughout until God speaks?

16. Are the Comforters differentiated in any way?

17. Much of the poetic power of Job is in its strong images. Identify some of these, especially the ones that link Job's and the Comforters' speeches with those of God at the end.

18. The Psalms fall into several loose categories, including hymns (songs in praise of God), both personal and communal laments (expressions of doubts and fears), psalms of confidence (laments in which expression of confidence in God outweighs the note of lamentation), and wisdom psalms (expressions of proverb-like advice). To which categories do the psalms in the anthology belong?

19. What are the characteristic devices of Hebrew poetry, and what are their strengths and weaknesses, compared with the devices of modern English verse?

Homer

The transition from teaching the Old Testament to teaching Homer is about as radical a shift of gears as one can imagine; to move from the God-saturated "vertical" world of the Bible to the humanist "horizontal" world of Homer (especially of The Odyssey) can be vertiginous. Many teachers, of course, will welcome the challenge of transition, as a vivid object lesson to their students about the enormous differences between the two strands, Hebraic and Hellenic, from which, according to the familiar formula, Western culture derives. The parallel-in-contrast between the Hebrew and Greek worlds can be further heightened for students by impressing on them the fact that the Old Testament and Homer are not merely conveniences for us in understanding the two cultures synoptically; rather, what we are reading are the basic educational instruments of the ancient Jews and Greeks, the books they considered, in different senses of the word, sacred.

Teachers will differ widely in the degree to which they want to emphasize broadly cultural as opposed to more purely literary-critical approaches; both have their risks. An anthropological approach is somewhat complicated by the fact that neither the biblical nor the Homeric world reflects the milieu and values of a single generation or even century. Strictly literary approaches (whatever that means exactly in the present context) must bear in mind the differences between ancient and modern modes of meaning, most obviously the difference between hearing literature and reading it from a page.

Thematic approaches to The Iliad come more readily to hand than with The Odyssey, since the former is so intensely concentrated and the latter so expansive. Teaching characterization in both works is relatively easy. Homer's narrative method presents greater challenges, once one gets past discussing certain superficial aspects of suspense. (Not that Homeric suspense need be treated superficially; students may recognize that Homer enhances suspense in some ways by telling us what is going to happen.) It may be hard to persuade students that a writer at the dawn of literature is a sophisticated virtuoso of narrative, and Homer plays into the hands of such skepticism through his "paratactic" method, leaving implicit the myriad connections between paired themes, images, and episodes, as in the incident with Meneláos' steward mentioned in the Introduction. One of the most satisfying rewards in teaching Homer is to make students aware of these connections, which are sometimes ironic. The many ironic parallels and contrasts between the two homecomings of Odysseus, one aborted and one successful, provide a good case in point.

Both The Iliad and The Odyssey are definable as belonging to various genres. The Iliad is a tragedy, and perhaps the old view of it as allegory merits some respect. The Odyssey can be understood under several rubrics: romance, comedy, drama, sheer yarn. It is not fanciful to see it also from the modern perspective of self-reflecting art; this perspective is suggested by the poem's interest in bards and their function, the accounts of Odysseus as a fiction-maker, and accounts of his listening to his own story and responding to it. But, most obviously, the poems are epics. A backward glance at Gilgamesh, especially in connection with such matters as heroism and death, can be immensely profitable. For the purposes of course organization, the Homeric epics also cast their shadows forward into many works to come--Aristotle's Poetics, Virgil's Aeneid, Ovid's Metamorphoses, Beowulf, The Song of Roland, Dante's Divine Comedy, and Milton's Paradise Lost. Since the recurrence in these works of the epic impulse and its attendant conventions is always a blend of originality with a kind of echolalia, it seems important while examining the wellsprings of epic to consider the inherent value and meaning of the epic devices: the opening invocation, the descent into the underworld, the intervention of deities (what the classical theorists called "machinery"), the medias res chronology, the extended similes, and of course the theme of heroism.

Questions on The Iliad:

1. The opening invocation states that the theme of The Iliad is "Akhilleus' anger." Is this an adequate description of the poem's theme? Might it serve as the title of the work?

2. The quarrel between Agamémnon and Akhilleus centers on captive slave-women. Does this fact reflect the importance of women in the Homeric age or their unimportance? Is it a paradox that the Trojan war, though fought by men, is all about women?

  There is not only Helen but also, behind her, the Judgment of Paris on the three rival goddesses.

3. The plague of Book I is inflicted by Apollo. Does one's inability to believe that an archer-god really causes fatal illness interfere with the interest of the story?

  This question is one of many that can be used to introduce the problem how the Homeric (and, more generally, the Greek) deities are to be understood.

4. How does the view we get in Book VI of the personality and character of Paris affect our response to the poem and to the ideal of heroism? How does Hektor's interview with Paris and Helen give stronger point to Hektor's subsequent scene with his wife and child? How do the scenes between Hektor and the various women in Book VI clarify or confuse the goals of the war?

5. The scene between Hektor and Andrómakhê is one of the most memorable in ancient literature, posing an ultimate kind of question about the relationship of heroism, or public duty, to private obligations and affections. Does Hektor's choice seem the right one? Even in light of his awareness that Troy is fated to fall?

  This last point is pertinent also to Akhilleus' knowledge that he is fated to be killed in the war.

6. What is the role of Diomêdês in Book IX? Of Nestor? Is the demoralized Agamémnon the same man we met in Book I?

7. To what extent, if at all, is Akhilleus justified in rejecting Agamémnon's overtures in Book IX? Akhilleus' removal of himself from the fighting has often been called "sulking"; is this the right word, or the whole story? If Akhilleus is proud, is his pride justifiable? Is he simply personally offended, or is he defending a principle? How does the matter of honor enter into all this? What, exactly, is honor for the Homeric warrior?

  Thematically, and in terms of the poem's tragic pattern, these are central questions, and the answers are not simple. Moreover, the questions are further complicated by the fact that Odysseus has somewhat sweetened Agamémnon's terms.

8. How does Sarpêdôn's speech in Book XII underline the tragic pattern of The Iliad?

A similar question can be asked about Zeus' speech to Akhilleus' immortal horses in Book XVII and about Akhilleus' dialogue with the horses in Book XIX.

9. In allowing Patróklos to enter the battle, is Akhilleus compromising the principles that he claims have actuated him? Does he, in effect, sacrifice his best friend to his own selfish concerns? Akhilleus has, of course, ordered Patróklos to play a merely defensive role, and Patróklos disobeys. Was Akhilleus merely trying to deny Patróklos a truly heroic role?

10. Should the credit of having killed Patróklos go to Apollo or to Hektor? Compare also Athena's assistance to Akhilleus in Book XXII, at the death of Hektor.

In some ways, this is one of those chicken-egg problems of the relationship of Homeric deities to their protégés. Is Odysseus resourceful because Athena helps him, or is her protection a confirmation of his resourcefulness?

11. Akhilleus' shield presents a comprehensive picture of life in the Homeric age. Do the scenes on it throw light on the meaning of war? Do they make the tragic pattern of The Iliad more stark?

12. Is there any pattern (other than Zeus' fiat) to explain why the deities sometimes intervene in the war and sometimes stay out of it?

13. What is the significance of Akhilleus' fasting in Book XIX?

(Aptly, the earthy Odysseus makes the case that an army "travels on its stomach.")

14. Does Hektor's fear in the face of Akhilleus in Book XXII undermine his heroic stature? Is Akhilleus' savagery after his victory dishonorable behavior?

15. Is the encounter between Akhilleus and Hektor a symbolic one? Do they represent different principles?

16. In the meeting of Priam and Akhilleus in Book XXIV, which is the more tragic figure? If they are both tragic, is the source of their tragedy the same?

17. Is The Iliad propaganda for war? Protest against it? Neither? Both?

Questions on The Odyssey–Structure, Form, Narrative Method:

18. Odysseus does not appear until Book V. Does he seem from the beginning to be the protagonist of the poem? Would his story be more effective if he appeared earlier?

19. In the last twelve books, the scope of the poem seems to narrow, from a vast, mysterious world to a small, domestic one. Is this a letdown?

20. Summarize in chronological rather than narrative order the main events of The Odyssey. What would be gained, or lost, if the time-scheme were more straightforward?

Obviously a paper or overnight assignment. It may seem mechanical, but students can learn much about how the poem is put together from doing this exercise.

21. Between the moment when his old nurse recognizes Odysseus' scar (Book XIX) and his silencing of her, Homer suspends the action for seventy-seven lines to tell the story of how Odysseus got the scar. Why this long suspension?

22. All the narrative of Books V through XV (including the return of Odysseus to Ithaka) elapses in the short interval between the suitors' plot to intercept Telémakhos and his evasion of them and safe return. Consider the effect of this dislocation of narrative time.

23. Books I and V open with a council of the gods. What is the main item on their agenda in the two books? What is the significance of the parallelism of the two councils?

24. What purpose is served by the six accounts of Agamémnon's homecoming from the Trojan war (in Books I, II, III, IV, XI, and XXIV)?

Questions on The Odyssey--Themes and Images:

25. "The Odyssey is not just a story, it's a story about telling stories." In what sense is this statement true?

26. What attitude toward bards does the poem reflect? Does this attitude tell us anything about the standing of poetry in Homeric culture? Does the attitude have a thematic importance?

27. Consider how many old men there are in The Odyssey. Why are there so many?

Among other things, this question invites discussion of the counter-theme of youth and initiation.

28. In Book VIII, the bard Demódokos sings of the adultery of Arês and Aphroditê and of Hephaistos' vengeance. Does the story have a meaningful application in The Odyssey or is it just a comic diversion?

Among other things, the story shows what some wives and their suitors do when the husband is away.

29. As he puts to sea after blinding Polyphêmos (Book IX), Odysseus shouts out his real name to him. What importance does this self-revelation have?

The question is designed to open up the theme of recognitions (and the counter-theme of disguise). A similar question could be asked about the many other recognition scenes.

30. In what ways is it appropriate, or ironic, that the returned Odysseus takes the disguise of an old beggar?

31. In Book XIV, Odysseus tells a false story to Eumaios about an Odysseus who, at Troy, used deception to obtain a cloak for one of his comrades. Besides showing Odysseus' cleverness, how does this story function in the poem?

The intention is to get at the theme and technique of fictions within fictions, lies within lies. (One is reminded of the genteel nineteenth-century euphemism for lying: "telling stories.")

32. What is the function of the dog Argos in Book XVII?

33. After Odysseus strings his old bow in Book XXI, he is compared in some detail to a harper. Analyze the passage--its mood, its timing, and its general significance.

34. Penélopê spends a lot of time sleeping. What do you make of this fact?

35. Are there any girls, women, or supernatural females in The Odyssey who are not clever and capable?

The answer, essentially, is no, and the significance of the fact is worth pursuing further. The poem has more than its share of femmes fatales, and on the other hand several major female characters are exceptionally noble in character.

Questions on The Odyssey--Characterization:

36. In one of P. G. Wodehouse's stories, there is a character who always registers at hotels under a false name. When asked why, he answers, "Just an ordinary business precaution." Compare this psychology with that of Odysseus.

37. The first time we actually see Odysseus, in Book V, he is weeping. About what? What do we learn from this first view of him and from his following dialogue with Kalypso?

38. In Book V, before he makes it to shore in the land of the Phaiakians, the nearly drowned Odysseus resists a goddess's offer to help. Why does he hesitate, and what does the incident tell us about him?

39. In Book X, when within sight of Ithaka, Odysseus falls asleep and his men open the bag of winds. Everyone is blown far away from Ithaka, his homecoming is delayed for years, and his men never get home. What does this incident tell us about Odysseus and his relationship to his crew?

40. The interview in Book XIII between Athena, disguised as a shepherd, and the newly returned Odysseus says much about both of them. What?

41. Compare Telémakhos with Nausikaa. In what ways are they similar, in what ways different? What role do they play in defining Odysseus?

Questions on The Odyssey--The Homeric World; Student Response:

42. What are the rules for treating guests in Homer? Look, for example, at the way Telémakhos, as opposed to the suitors, treats the disguised Athena in Book I.

43. What enduring images (or enduring stereotypes, if you prefer) of women emerge from The Odyssey?

44. What do we learn from Odysseus' visit to the underworld in Book XI that we would not have learned from other parts of the poem?

Among other things, this question allows one to introduce Akhilleus' famous statement about being alive versus being dead. One might prefer to start, more concretely, with that statement. While on the subject of Akhilleus, one might also ask whether he seems to be the same person he is in The Iliad.

45. "The Odyssey is a glorification of primitive life, subject to hardship but free from the rules of social organization." Is that statement valid?

This question is a faintly dirty trick. Many teachers will wish to cite Odysseus' scorn of the socially unorganized Kyklopês, expressed in Book IX.

46. According to one old formula, Western civilization is the result of a cross-breeding between the ancient Hebrew and Greek cultures. Focusing on large matters, such as conceptions of deity, or more particular matters, such as the characters of Jacob and Odysseus, comment on the familiar formula.

47. If you had to reduce the differences between the ancient Hebrews and the ancient Greeks to three formulas, each of fewer than a dozen words, what formulas would you propose?

48. Would The Odyssey make a good movie? What things in it are cinematic? What things would be lost?

49. If a modern novelist were re-writing The Odyssey (while keeping the ancient setting), what probable differences in treatment would there be?

Sappho

The first well-defined examples of lyric poetry in the anthology are the biblical Psalms, but these are rather special, not only because of their distinctive Hebraic form but also because they often seem to represent a collective voice--of the Hebrew people rather than of an individual personality. The poems of Sappho are the first examples of lyric poetry in the modern sense of brief, melodic poems centered around the individual, personal emotion of the poet. They can therefore be studied not only for their intrinsic interest but also as keys to lyric poetry in general and how to read it.

Inevitably, the subject of translation will come up, especially in light of the description of the state of Sappho texts in the anthology introduction. Mary Barnard has chosen not to try to reproduce Sappho's characteristic verse form, to which she gave her name. Sapphics are stanzas with three eleven-syllable lines followed by a fourth line of five syllables. The eleven-syllable lines have the following stress pattern (--- is a long syllable; x is a short one; / is a foot-division):

--- x / --- --- / --- x x / --- x / --- x

The fourth, five-syllable, line has this pattern:

--- x x / --- x

A number of poets have attempted to write sapphics in English, but the pattern is difficult because of the demand for three spondees (feet with two accented syllables) in each stanza. The Thrall and Hibbard Handbook to Literature gives the following example from Swinburne as an English sapphic:

--- x / --- --- / --- x x / --- x / --- x
Then to me so lying a wake a vision
--- x / --- --- / --- x x / --- x / --- x
Came with out sleep over the seas and touched me,
--- x / --- --- / --- x x / --- x / --- x
Softly touched mine eyelids and lips; and I too,
--- x x / --- x
Full of the vision . . . .

Mary Barnard has chosen as a modern analogue to Sappho's verse form a loose unrhymed free-verse triplet. This form makes possible a simple, colloquial directness without distortion of sentence structure to fit a rigid pattern not natural to English. At the same time, it allows a light, subtle rhythmic regularity that raises the language above ordinary prose. The students will also notice a distinctive way of handling titles; sometimes they are used traditionally (as in Poem 39) and sometimes as an integral part of the syntax of the poem (as in Poem 34).

1. What is the dramatic situation in each poem?

As with many lyric poems, simply asking, "Who is talking to whom and in what context?" often opens up the poem to the reader and suggests important issues of interpretation. For example, it is obviously vital to note immediately that Poems 37 and

38 are addressed to Aphrodite. More subtly, Poem 30 is addressed by a woman (Sappho?) to a new bridegroom, but is it to be understood as literally addressed to him aloud? This question leads into matters of tone, the subtle jealousy of the speaker, who in effect ignores the bridegroom-addressee in favor of a quite sensuous description of the bride. The famous Poem 39 is also interesting in terms of dramatic situation. Ostensibly addressed to a female friend with a lover who is "more than a god," it is highly unlikely to be literally so addressed. In its confession of physical desire for the friend and jealousy of the man's privileged intimacy, it seems more likely to be an interior monologue by the poet.

2. What images does Sappho employ and what are their effects?

Poem 34 is useful to introduce the concept of imagery, built as it is around two sharply contrasting similes for a maidenhead. The contrast between the unreachable quince-apple and the trampled hyacinth, sharpened by being assigned to two voices, is very suggestive in unexpected ways and expresses a complex attitude toward the subject of loss of virginity. Natural images of this sort are dominant in Sappho (see Poem 37 for another good example) and repay close study for their subjective associations.

3. What conception of love do Sappho's poems present?

A natural comparison with Plato will suggest itself. Sappho, like Plato, sees erotic passion as not confined to the physical but engaging also the soul. But unlike Plato, she does not see physical love as the foot of a "ladder" which a person should ascend toward a disembodied spiritual or religious love. Flesh and soul remain inextricable in Sappho, a view given divine sanction by Aphrodite, as Sappho presents her.

4. How does the Sappho persona compare with Homer's Odysseus in terms of awareness of self?

Bruno Snell, in The Discovery of the Mind (listed in the Further Reading section of the text), draws an interesting comparison between Sappho and Homer in this respect. Odysseus seems "unaware of the fact that he may think or act spontaneously, of his own volition and spirit." Whatever he thinks or feels, he attributes to an outside agency, either an external event or a god. Sappho, in contrast (the argument runs), directs her attention almost exclusively to her inner life; she is aware of her own consciousness in a way that Odysseus is not. (Poem 39 is an obvious example of such self-consciousness, but the other poems also exemplify it in various ways.)

5. How does Sappho present the tension between public behavior and conventions and her own private emotions and values?

Poem 41 offers a good starting point here, in its contrast between the "beauty" of military spectacles and that of "whatever one loves." But the contrast is pervasive through the other poems as well.

Greek Drama

The teaching of Greek drama presents some special problems, regardless of which specific plays are included in a course. A major early goal in a unit on Greek drama should probably be to help the students imagine the plays as drama. The basic facts about the Greek theater are given in the Introduction to the Ancient World in the anthology. The slides in the VRI Slide Library of World Theater will help students visualize the theater, as will also such films as Oedipus the King: The Rise of Greek Tragedy and the Tyrone Guthrie production of Oedipus Rex (both listed in the Selective Media Guide). Fascinating supplemental reading, for either student or teacher, is Mary Renault's novel The Mask of Apollo (1966), which gives an engrossing and persuasive account of how the Greeks produced plays.

When beginning the study of a Greek play, it is usually helpful to talk through the theatrical structure of the play, identifying the prologue (the opening section before the entrance of the Chorus), the parados (the choral song with which the Chorus enters), the alternating episodes and choral songs which make up the body of the play, and the exodos (the choral song with which the Chorus exits). It is also helpful to talk through the staging of the play. The translations used in the anthology are rather more generous in descriptive stage directions than most English versions, but even so students sometimes miss implied stage action which is quite important to the play. Agamemnon's entrance, in most productions, is quite spectacular, with at least one horse-drawn chariot (in which Cassandra remains standing, silently, for a long, significant time) and probably a number of dusty, battleworn soldiers.

Once the students have the theatrical event the play implies firmly in mind, there are a number of general questions which are appropriate for any Greek play.

1. What sort of prologue does the play have, and what is its function?

Aeschylus and Sophocles customarily use a "dramatic" prologue (a representational scene) and Euripides customarily, though not always, uses a "nondramatic" prologue (a direct presentation to the audience, usually by one character). Medea opens with a monologue by the Nurse, directly addressed to the audience. The three varied prologues of the Oresteia are also worth close examination, as is the scene of the suppliants which opens Oedipus the King.

2. Who make up the Chorus, and how do they function in the play?

Generally speaking, the Aeschylean Chorus often provides a sort of timeless, cosmic meditation on the material of the play, the Sophoclean Chorus is more limited in its knowledge and more realistically human in its responses to the action, and the Euripidean Chorus, while realistic, is somewhat removed from the dramatic action, sometimes offering little more than "interlude music" between the episodes. But the variations are almost unlimited. Compare the Choruses of the Oresteia, for example, and consider why the Chorus of Medea is made up of "Corinthian Women."

3. How is dramatic action handled in the play? Which scenes does the playwright choose to present, which to describe? How does he create setting?

Perhaps the central symbol in Greek drama is the skene building itself. Most plays take place "before the palace" (though a number of important ones do not), and it is often illuminating to consider what the palace comes to stand for in the play: established order (Oedipus the King), a prison (Medea), unjust authority (Antigone), or other forces or values. Plays in which the setting changes are especially interesting (The Libation Bearers, The Eumenides). The old critical cliche about the representation of violence being barred from the Greek stage is a half-truth that makes the theater sound more serene and decorous than it actually was. Often violence is withheld only to make its eventual display even more shocking; the exhibition of the bodies of Clytaemnestra or of Medea's babies is even more harrowing for being described in such gory detail earlier.

4. How many masks does the play require and who plays which roles?

All the plays in the anthology can be, and were, performed with three actors (plus Chorus and an unlimited number of silent actors and supernumeraries). Most of the plays offer some possibilities of flexibility in casting, but it is often illuminating to work out a tentative cast. The Greek playwrights may even have intended some mildly ironic effects in their arrangements for doubled roles; when the Protagonist, or First Actor, having been killed as Agamemnon, must return in the mask of Aegisthus, the cyclic nature of blood vengeance is theatrically reinforced. The probable doubling of Electra and Clytaemnestra in The Libation Bearers has the same effect.

5. What was the play's probable source, and what liberties did the playwright take in dramatizing it?

Many Greek plays are based on Homeric materials, and it is instructive to compare the treatment of, say, Agamemnon in the Iliad, the Odyssey, and the Oresteia. Even more illuminating, sometimes, is merely speculating about what the playwright's source must have been like and trying to identify the tension between a stock, received version and the playwright's development of it. Too much is often made of the fact that Greek audiences knew the stories of the plays they were to see--there are few people nowadays who see Hamlet or, for that matter, Death of a Salesman, without knowing how they're going to come out. Despite romantic notions of the Greeks, it seems less likely that they thought of theater-going as a ritual confirmation of traditional themes than that they valued individual and sophisticated rethinkings of those themes, like those of the three great tragedians.

6. What light, if any, does Aristotle's Poetics throw upon the play?

The selection from the Poetics is useful reading in conjunction with the Greek tragedies. Attempting to interpret the plays in Aristotelian terms, though, sometimes ends either in a game of Spot the Tragic Flaw or in a complete rejection of the Poetics. Perhaps Aristotle is most useful as a source of terms--tragic hero, catharsis, tragic flaw, recognition--which must be reconsidered and redefined with each play.

Aeschylus

The Oresteia is one of those works, which the nineteenth century called "world-historical dramas," which attempt a comprehensive and analytical view of great movements in cultural history. Agamemnon is often studied (and is well worth studying) independently, but its meaning is clear only in the context of the rest of the trilogy, which forms one artistic whole, simultaneously simple and clear in outline and rich and complex in detail. In addition to the works in the Further Reading section in the anthology, teachers will find useful a brilliant, hundred-page essay named "The Serpent and the Eagle: A Reading of the Oresteia," by Robert Fagles and W. B. Stanford, which appeared as the introduction to the separate book publication of the Fagles translation of the Oresteia (1975). Also highly recommended is C. J. Herington's essay on the Oresteia in The Reader's Encyclopedia of World Drama, ed. John Gassner and Edward Quinn (1969).

1. The action of Agamemnon takes place in the context of a bloody family history. What are the recurring themes in the curse on the house of Atreus? Note especially sexual competition, vengeance, betrayal by kinsmen, and the slaughter or abuse of children.

2. The parados, or first choral song, of Agamemnon is the longest and most complex in Greek drama. What subjects does the chorus cover and what attitude does it take toward those subjects?

3. C. J. Herington: "Agamemnon has the compulsive, bewildering quality of nightmare, where everything can dissolve into everything else." Trace examples of this perceptual ambiguity and of deception, illusion, and hallucination through the play.

4. H. D. F. Kitto, in discussing the relevance of the Aristotelian "tragic flaw" to Agamemnon, calls Agamemnon a "walking hamartia." What sins is Agamemnon guilty of when he arrives home?

5. The dominant sexual symbolism of the Oresteia is introduced in Agamemnon. Trace sexual conflict on individual, marital, and social levels through the play.

Note the sexual ambiguity of the main characters: Clytaemnestra "maneuvers like a man" while Aegisthus is a "womanly" man. A major motive for the murder is Clytaemnestra's adultery with Aegisthus and Agamemnon's with Cassandra. The Trojan War itself is seen in sexual terms: it was fought "all for another's woman" and the fall of Troy was a "rape."

6. Analyze the scene in which Agamemnon enters the palace on the red tapestries (lines 767ff.). What issues are involved here, and what symbolism is introduced?

The sin of offending the gods by walking on the tapestries seems insignificant compared with Agamemnon's other offenses and should probably be taken as a theatrical "concretization" of Agamemnon's general hubris. The scene also introduces or develops the images of blood and robes or nets: the tapestries should look like a stream of blood flowing out of the palace, and they also anticipate the bloodstained robe which will later be displayed with the bodies of Agamemnon and Cassandra.

7. Troy falls in line 24 of the play, and Agamemnon arrives home, after a presumably long

and eventful journey, at line 767, after what appears to be continuous action. What does this tell us about "unity of time" and the way the Greek dramatists handled dramatic time?

8. Pylades is on stage through much of the Libation Bearers, but he has only one short speech (lines 887ff.). Compare his function as a "silent" character with Cassandra's during the long period when she remains silent in Agamemnon. Can a character's mere physical presence have a dramatic effect?

9. How is Electra characterized in the Libation Bearers, and what are her motives for joining in the murder?

Electra is deemphasized in the play in favor of Orestes, but her story was treated fully by both Sophocles and Euripides. The class may be interested in hearing a summary of the radically different interpretations of the character by the three dramatists.

10. Orestes' killing of Aegisthus and Clytaemnestra is presented as parallel to his mother's killing of Agamemnon and Cassandra, as a perpetuation of the nightmare world of blood vengeance. Are there any differences in the circumstances and the motives for the two killings?

Note that Orestes undertakes his task reluctantly and acts only on the gods' command, unlike his mother. The torments of conscience, personified by the Furies, signal an advance in the moral vision of the culture.

11. In the first episode of the Libation Bearers, Electra identifies Orestes as her brother because her foot fits his footprint and his hair matches hers, by an absurd logic which Euripides parodied mercilessly in his Electra. Can you defend the dramatic logic of this scene?

The scene obeys an emotional logic which is appropriate to the generally symbolic method of the Oresteia but which would be grotesquely out of place in Euripides' earthy, sardonically realistic version.

12. Examine closely the Pythia's speech which forms the prologue of the Eumenides. How does her account of the succession of the gods and the progress of civilization parallel the treatment of the same subjects in the trilogy as a whole?

13. Note that the Furies, who were invisible at the end of the Libation Bearers, are very real at the beginning of the Eumenides. What other indications are there that the mode of the trilogy is modulating from the comparative realism of the Libation Bearers to a kind of dramatic expressionism?

14. What ambivalent "female" qualities do the Furies embody, and what ambivalent "male" ones do the Olympian gods stand for? How are these qualities represented in the earlier, human characters of the Oresteia?

15. Oddly enough, in this play celebrating Athenian justice, Orestes' trial is argued on absurd grounds; it is, in C. J. Herington's words, a piece of "celestial pettifoggery." How do you account for the absurdity? Is it, like the recognition scene in the Libation Bearers, a signal that we are dealing with symbolic rather than literal truth?

16. All the major images and motifs of the trilogy culminate in the final episode and the exodos, including torches, robes, sexual ambiguity and conflict, young children, and blood. Trace these elements backward through the plays.

17. The conclusion of the Oresteia seems to advance the proposition that a just society should acknowledge the claims of both the "female" qualities of irrationality, fertility, and family ties and the "male" ones of reason, order, and objectivity, but that the male ones should be in control. Do you agree with these identifications of female and male qualities and with the conclusion drawn? Do these views appear elsewhere in Greek literature?

Sophocles

A teacher may be pardoned a touch of stage fright as he or she prepares to teach Oedipus the King. It is, after all, the world's most famous play, and it stands there, like its own sphinx, fascinating and enigmatic, at the gates of Western drama, surrounded by brambles of commentary. The first challenge is probably to cut through these brambles, hardly less thick around Antigone, and get a good clear look at the plays themselves. (Sometimes one has to fight through the students' own brambly preconceptions; both plays are increasingly popular high school texts.) A good bramble-clearing essay on Oedipus is E. R. Dodds's "On Misunderstanding the Oedipus Rex" (1966), reprinted in the Norton Critical Edition of the play (1970); one on Antigone is Charles Paul Segal's "Sophocles' Praise of Man and the Conflicts of the Antigone" (1964), reprinted in the Twentieth-Century Views volume on Sophocles (1966).

1. Oedipus the King has a "revelatory" structure; that is, most of the major incidents are revelations of past action. In what order does Sophocles reveal past events, and what is the relation of this order to the actual chronology?

2. Oedipus the King is a masterpiece of dramatic irony, of tension between what the characters know and what the audience knows. Even Oedipus' name, "swollen-foot," is ironic, since we but not the characters know that it is evidence of the truth revealed at the end. Select various points in the play and analyze what we, Oedipus, and various other characters (Tiresias, Jocasta, the Shepherd) know at each point. What is the relation between this dramatic technique and the emphasis in the play upon the existential problems of knowing oneself and knowing what is "true" in the external world?

3. A hero might be defined not just as a good person but as a person who embodies the value system of an entire culture. Could Oedipus be described as a rationalist hero? Describe his personality in these terms, citing specific characteristic speeches and actions. What are the implications, if any, about the value or function of reason?

4. How does the sphinx figure in the play, and how does her riddle echo throughout?

5. Trace the image of blindness through the play.

6. Trace references to Mount Kithairon through the play. Do these references to a dark wilderness, in contrast to the visible, well-lighted palace, come to constitute an important image in the play? What does the opposition mean?

7. Aristotle's analysis of tragedy in the Poetics is largely based on Oedipus the King. Do you agree with his interpretation of the play?

8. Freud thought that the secret of Oedipus' continuing appeal was that it reenacts the universal personal experience of the Oedipal stage of psychological development. Is this an extra-literary observation or can it be used to help understand the play itself?

9. In the prologue of Antigone, Ismene tells Antigone that she is "rash" and implores her to "Remember we are women, / we're not born to contend with men" (lines 96, 74-75). Trace the theme of men's and women's "proper" roles through the play.

10. Analyze the characterization of the Sentry (episodes 1 and 2). Would Aeschylus have included such an earthy, comic character at this point in a tragedy? What perspective does his realistic attitude give us on both Creon and Antigone?

11. Analyze closely the "hymn to man" (chorus 2, lines 376 ff.). Notice, in the light of what precedes and follows it, the irony of its glorification of man's achievements. How are the things cited in the ode--the sea, animals, birds, speech, shelter, and disease--ironically echoed in other parts of the play?

12. Compare the Creon of <u>Antigone</u> with the Creon of <u>Oedipus the King</u>. Are the dogmatism and rigidity he shows in <u>Antigone</u> foreshadowed in the other play? Has Creon in any sense taken Oedipus' place?

13. The third chorus (lines 656 ff.), on fate, seems to refer to Antigone. Can it also be taken as ironically referring, in spite of the Chorus's intentions, to Creon? How?

14. Has Antigone inherited any traits from her father, Oedipus?

15. The German philosopher and critic Friedrich Hegel cited <u>Antigone</u> as an example of a tragedy that consists of a conflict between "partial goods." Do you agree that Creon and Antigone are equally right and equally wrong? Or does Sophocles favor one over the other?

16. Aeschylus' <u>Oresteia</u> may be read as a rather optimistic and patriotic celebration of Athens' achievement of a union of nature and reason, with reason dominant. In this respect, do <u>Oedipus the King</u> and <u>Antigone</u> constitute in any way a reply to the <u>Oresteia</u>?

17. For David Grene, Sophocles' great theme is "the union of the blessed and cursed, of the just and the unjust, and sometimes (not always) of the consciously innocent and the unconsciously guilty." Compare the treatment of these oppositions in <u>Oedipus the King</u> and <u>Antigone</u>.

Euripides

Romantics in your class will like Aeschylus, realists will like Euripides, just as, at the other end of the course, the romantics will like Lawrence and the realists will like Joyce. (Only anthologists can like all four.) Or perhaps Shaw, as has often been suggested, would be a better modern analogue than Joyce. Euripides, like Shaw, is an inveterate demythologizer, a writer of intellectual drama hovering on some indeterminate boundary between tragedy and comedy, turning a blinding spotlight on human pretensions and illusions, and illuminating the real human motivations behind them. Readers coming to Euripides armed only with copies of Oedipus the King and Aristotle's Poetics must abandon their expectations of catharsis and hamartias and attune themselves instead for a dazzling barrage of paradox, irony, shock, and sardonic wit. For an excellent introduction to this dimension of Euripides' art, see the brilliant essay by William Arrowsmith, "Euripides' Theatre of Ideas" (1964), reprinted in the Twentieth Century Views volume on Euripides (1968).

1. Why is the Chorus of Medea made up of Corinthian women? What is their attitude toward Medea?

2. Medea, on her first entrance (lines 199 ff.), laments the woes of both women and aliens; later, she declares that she is distrusted also because of her superior intelligence. In a later episode (lines 474 ff.), Jason tells Medea that she is fortunate that he took her away from a barbarous land and brought her to Hellas, where they live by "justice." How do the words "barbarous" and "barbaric" figure in this play? What ironies are involved in the characters' various views of what is "civilized" and what is "barbaric"? Is Medea in any way a tragedy of the "outsider"?

3. Medea, to the Chorus: "We were born women--useless for honest purposes, / But in all kinds of evil skilled practitioners" (lines 370-371). Does Medea mean this, or is she being ironic? See the following chorus.

4. How is Jason characterized in Medea?

5. In lines 736-739, Medea says:

> Let no one think of me
> As humble or weak or passive; let them understand
> I am of a different kind: dangerous to my enemies,
> Loyal to my friends. To such a life glory belongs.

What would the audience make of this speech if it were spoken by a man, perhaps Jason? Does the play in any way call into question the Greek heroic code by ironically having it followed by a woman?

6. Medea's killing of her children is an example of the major literary motif of kindermord, "the death of children," as are also the attempted killing of the infant Oedipus in Oedipus the King and the sacrifice of Iphigeneia in the Oresteia. The death of children often represents the killing off of some dimension of their parents. Does it in these examples? (See especially, in Medea, lines 929 ff.)

7. The Messenger (lines 1030 ff.) concludes his account of the horrible deaths of Glauce and Creon by saying:

>   those whom most would call
> Intelligent, the propounders of wise theories--
> Their folly is of all men's the most culpable.

Is this a reasonable conclusion? To whom do his words apply?

8. The Messenger (line 1025) asks Medea, "Are you sane, or raving mad?" and Jason (line 1209) says that he is sane now but that he was mad when he married Medea. What ironies are involved in the treatment of sanity and madness in the play?

Aristophanes

With some other ancient works in the anthology, it may be necessary to help students convert themes and artistic methods into meaningful modern analogues. With Lysistrata the problem may be the reverse. The translator renders it with overtones of the American Civil War, and the play has been used for obvious purposes of topical protest in recent times. Moreover, most sexual jokes are timeless. So--what's ancient or Greek about Lysistrata? One answer derives from the context of the preceding tragedies in the book, most of which explore, subtly or more explicitly, the themes of male versus female and of the relationship between sex, war, and heroism. A number of the points and questions about Greek drama earlier in this manual can be recast to examine Lysistrata. And the play is a good example of the tendency in comedy to affirm mythically the life-force while remaining anchored in day-to-day current events.

1. Is it important that the chorus is made up of old men and women? There are many insulting jokes about the old men's decrepitude but none about the old women's. Why should this be so?

2. Does it matter to one's response to the play that all the actors were males? If it were performed by an all-female cast, would the effect be the same?

3. Is Lysistrata about women's power? Do the men give in because they have been converted or because they have been coerced? Would a boycott on something other than sex--on cooking meals, for example--have served the same purpose? Is sex and the withholding of it merely a weapon? Is the moral that hormones take priority over values?

4. In what ways does Lysistrata undermine the notions of masculinity, femininity, and heroism defined by earlier Greek authors in the anthology? Does the play in any significant way accept the traditional identifications and sexual roles?

5. Both the men and the women in the play suffer from being deprived of sex, but the men suffer more. Is this fact consistent with the Greek image of women as earthy and men as more abstractly rational? In Scene II (lines 655-726), Lysistrata gets disgusted with the sex-starved women who are trying to desert. Does this weakness in them underline or undermine the women's role as enlighteners?

6. Are the characters well defined as individuals? For example, could the scene played by Myrrhine with her frustrated husband have been played by Lysistrata with hers?

7. In lines 1022-1066, Lysistrata reminds the Athenians and the Spartans of old days of glory and victory. Is her emphasis the same as in the old men's fond recollections of the good old wars?

8. Examine the end of the play (lines 1097ff). What motifs, in parallel or contrast, does it share with Aeschylus's The Eumenides? What is the importance of Athena in each? What forces in life are evoked in the final chorus of Lysistrata? What is its tone? Is its tone consistent with the appearance of the Drunken Citizen? What's he doing there anyway?

9. How much in Lysistrata needs to be changed to make it effective on the stage today?

Plato

Several ways of approaching Plato are appropriate to undergraduate literature courses. One is to examine him as a narrative and dramatic artist and as a skilled biographer. A second is to examine the ideology of Socrates/Plato, especially the doctrine of Ideas and of the ascent to vision of them (adumbrated in the Parable of the Cave, for example); students who absorb even this much of Plato's thought will have acquired a lastingly valuable key to much great literature. A third way is to use the dialogues as a casebook on ancient Greek culture, including the role it assigned to the exchange of ideas. A fourth strategy is to examine the Socratic method and how Socrates uses it; teachers who themselves attempt this method in class discussions of Plato can gain the heady experience of self-reflexive "meta-teaching."

1. What portrait of Socrates emerges from the selections in the anthology? For example, is his humility genuine or is it a strategic pose?

2. Socrates purports to be a seeker for truth. Is this search for truth consistent with Socrates' resort at times to irony? Is irony consistent with the objectivity often assumed to be a requisite for seeking truth? (For that matter, is objectivity the best road to truth?)

3. Is the Ion a serious work or merely an amusingly comic one? If it attempts a serious statement about the origin and uses of imaginative literature ("poetry" in the extended sense), would not a more solemn approach be more powerful or effective? Shouldn't poetry be represented by someone less dim-witted than Ion?

4. Does Ion have any modern counterparts--people in show business or even, perhaps, television news programs?

5. It sometimes seems that Socrates' interlocutors are straw men, or patsies. If he invariably had to confront intelligent and nimble-witted opponents (someone like you, for example!), would he come off as well? If you were Ion, how would you answer Socrates' questions? More generally, how would you defend yourself and make your case for the value of the rhapsode's profession?

6. Ion is entirely willing to concede that a rhapsode knows less than, say, physicians or horse-trainers about their trades, but he insists that as a good rhapsode he is ipso facto a good general. Why does he make this curious argument? Is there really an affinity between war and minstrelsy?

7. Is the Parable of the Cave an elitist statement? Does it imply that only certain rare and gifted persons can attain the philosopher's vision?

8. In describing the world of shadow images in the Parable of the Cave, Socrates has in mind the world that most of us call reality. (Students, for example, habitually call the world outside the university the "real world.") Should we regard Socrates with awe, as someone who has glimpsed a higher reality than ours? Or is he arrogant in dismissing what most people call real?

9. In defining his own values in The Apology, does Socrates implicitly describe the

generally shared values of the Athenians at their best? If so, is Socrates truly guilty by their standards? In other words, does he die by an abuse of the machinery of justice or because he really is at odds with his people and his time?

10. The "Socratic method," as used by Socrates with Ion and Meletus, is the most time-honored model of teaching by the discussion method. Do you think this method, as Socrates himself uses it, is a) fair to the person questioned, and b) intellectually honest? As most classroom teachers use the method, is it fair and honest?

11. Is the message of <u>The Apology</u> conveyed mainly through the rational and logical use of language or through more "poetic" strategies?

Aristotle

Aristotle can be approached on his own terms, for the inherent value and interest of what he says, or in various comparative contexts. A good many students will have heard of something called the "tragic flaw"; indeed, for certain of them, this seems to be the only thing that really sank in from high-school literature classes. (One wonders why this is so.) After reading the Poetics, and after they have pondered whether or not Aristotle really does talk about a "tragic flaw," they can test the pertinent Aristotelean ideas against ancient plays they have read in the anthology, present-day models of serious and popular entertainment, and modern assumptions about the psychological premises of literature as art. Something analogous can be done with other Aristotelian ideas about drama and epic--the importance of "discoveries," for example.

1. In the Poetics, section I, Aristotle claims that all forms of poetry are based on imitation. What does he mean by this, and is he right? In section IV he states that imitation is a fundamental part of human nature; we first learn, for example, by imitating. Does modern psychology and/or your own experience bear out this statement? Is Aristotle arguing that realism is the only valid form of literary art? Can fantasy not be a valid mode? And does imitation conflict with our usual assumption that great literature is creative?

2. In the Poetics, section II, Aristotle says that tragedy represents human beings as better than they really are, comedy as worse. (Note also his qualification of the statement in section V.) In what sense is this true? Is, say, Clytaemnestra in the Agamemnon a better person than Lysistrata?

3. Tragedy affects the audience by achieving "through pity and fear" the "proper purification of these emotions" (section VI). Some translations use the word catharsis, or purging, instead of purification. Note that pity seems oriented toward other persons, terror toward ourselves. In light of this distinction, what do you think Aristotle means? Perhaps terror needs purification or purging, but why should pity need it?

4. In discussing tragedy in the Poetics, section VI, Aristotle subordinates character to plot, adding that plotting is a harder-acquired skill than characterization. Does this seem convincing to you? In Oedipus the King, for example, or Agamemnon, are character traits less vital than actions?

5. For Aristotle, two crucial plot devices are reversals of situations and recognitions. According to him, the two when combined produce pity and fear (Poetics, section XI). Test this statement against the Greek tragedies you have read. Does Aristotle's statement also hold true for plays (and stories) today? Give an example.

6. Examine Aristotle's remarks in the Poetics, sections XIII and XV, that the tragic hero should be "highly renowned and prosperous" and "above the common level." This would seem to rule out as potential tragedies stories about typical people such as some modern writers have tried to treat tragically. Are Aristotle's ideas on the subject simply irrelevant for such writers?

7. In the Poetics, section XXIV, Aristotle stipulates that poets should "prefer probable impossibilities to improbable possibilities." What does this mean? Give examples of both.

8. In the Poetics, section XXVI, Aristotle argues that tragedy is superior to epic. Is he convincing? For example, he assumes that concentration of effect is preferable to expansion. Is this psychologically valid? Epic, he says, is inferior because it could provide the subjects of several tragedies; couldn't one argue that this fact makes epic superior?

Catullus

Catullus is included in the anthology partly because he represents Roman lyric poetry, as Sappho represents Greek and the psalmist Hebrew lyric poetry. Catullus's debt to Sappho is obvious, and his homage to her is almost overt--by way of imitating certain of her images and twice adopting the stanza named for her, in poems marking the beginning and end of the affair with Lesbia. But Catullus also has ties with two other poets represented by their lyrics in Volume One of the anthology. Petrarch is reported to have owned one of the earliest manuscripts of Catullus, and Donne, who had studied Catullus, sometimes resembles him closely, coming especially near in the love poems that combine passion with zestful hyperbole or audacious playfulness. The Lesbia poems of Catullus capture, with an unguardedness that can seem touching or repellent, the intensity of several variations of happy and unhappy love, while they are also finely crafted works of art.

1. In his poem "Frater Ave Atque Vale" (a title that quotes the last words of Catullus's Poem 101), Tennyson calls Catullus "Tenderest of Roman poets." Is "tenderest" a good adjective to use about Catullus?

2. In certain of the biblical psalms, the poems of Sappho, and those of Catullus, we hear voices that, each in its own way, sound personal. What is the difference in the sounds of these voices?

3. Catullus can be very intense. Does he have a sense of humor too? Where do you find it, and what is its quality?

4. Certain of Catullus's poems sound emotionally boyish. Which ones, and boyish in what sense? Is this quality appealing or not?

5. After the love affair with Lesbia has gone bad, Catullus treats it in several tones and moods. If these poems were mixed with other love poems not by him, do you think you might be able to identify the ones that were his?

6. Does the dedicatory Poem 1 show Catullus as a likable person? What attitude toward his poems emerges from his contrast between them and the writings of the scholarly Cornelius Nepos?

7. Bearing in mind the way he can treat death seriously in Poem 101, identify the devices through which Catullus, in Poem 3, about the dead sparrow, achieves a mock-serious tone.

8. Read aloud Poem 11, the farewell to Lesbia, trying to capture the changes in tone.

9. Poems 109 and 76 invoke the gods in prayer. Is there genuine religious feeling here? In answering this question, does it help to compare Sappho's attitude toward deities such as Aphrodite or the psalmist's toward God?

10. Poem 62, a wedding poem, is meant to be music. If a composer were setting it, what kind of music might be used? What kind of instruments would be appropriate? Which parts should be loud, which soft? Which parts should be in a fast tempo, which in a slow one?

Virgil

Along with the New Testament, Virgil stands at the midpoint of the long line of development from patriarchal times to the Miltonic threshold of the modern world--a fact that, coincidentally, is reflected in the physical makeup of Volume I of the anthology. The Aeneid and the Gospels epitomize the crystallization and refocusing of ancient culture into the forms it thereafter assumed in Western European culture. Homer is doubtless a greater and more vital author than Virgil, but it is Virgil who, at least in the eyes of posterity, created the "literary" epic form through which later authors have attempted to combine high art with a moral or historical vision. That Virgil achieved this transformation so selfconsciously, especially in his adaptation of Homer, makes teaching him the easier; virtually every Homeric motif in Virgil suggests at the same time continuity and radical reshaping, and therefore the tired pedagogical formula "compare and contrast" comes alive with a new freshness when one teaches Virgil on top of Homer. It helps in studying Aeneid III to have read Odyssey IX to XII, in studying Aeneid VI (the Lower World) to have read Odyssey XI, and in studying Aeneid XII (the slaying of Turnus) to have read Iliad XVI and XXII (the slayings of Patroclus and Hector).

The relationship of Virgil to a number of other great works is almost as immediate. As the Introduction to Virgil points out, his view of providence is closer to that of the Exodus saga than to the Homeric world-view, and the model of the fortunate fall adopted in Paradise Lost owes almost as much to Virgil as it does to Christian theology. The Aeneid is the best introduction to Dante, and not only in such obvious things as the correspondences between Virgil's Lower World and Dante's Inferno. Even if we focus more locally than on these vast arches of literary history, Virgil takes on a special role as spokesman for ancient Rome, all the more for being flanked in the anthology by the moody and wicked Catullus and the irreverent Ovid.

Many Virgil scholars and critics insist that Aeneas's encounter with Turnus in the latter books is the true crisis of the poem; our inclusion of the climax of battle in Book XII allows teachers to suggest this view. Book II (the fall of Troy) probably makes the most gripping reading for new readers of the poem. (Many users of the anthology assign it before having their students read The Odyssey.) Book IV is perhaps the most teachable. If the theme of the first six books is the education of Aeneas, the Dido episode would seem to be the turning point within that framework. One may or may not wish to "correct" substantially the tendency of students to side with Dido against Aeneas, but in any event analyzing that episode is a good way to explore the relationship of personal to suprapersonal values in Virgil. The "education of Aeneas" premise is helpful to many teachers because it allows them to regard the Aeneas of Book IV less than favorably without implying that Virgil lost control of his material. Book VI, in the view of many authorities, represents the highest point of ancient Latin literature--a view that has led us to include the whole of the book in the anthology.

1. Compare the epic opening formula in Virgil's Aeneid and in Homer's Iliad and Odyssey. What can we learn immediately about the differences between the two authors?

2. In I.207-19, Aeneas tries to cheer up his men, predicting that some day they will recall in gladness their present distress. What does this speech tell us about the role of Aeneas and about Virgil's world-view? Might Achilles or Odysseus have made this speech?

3. Compare Aeneas's reaction to the scenes in Juno's temple describing the Trojan War (I.470-519) with the still-unrecognized Odysseus' tears at the songs of the minstrel in The Odyssey, Book VIII. Do the two heroes grieve for the same reason?

4. Aeneas's flashback narrative, in Books II and especially III, is obviously modeled on The Odyssey, Books IX to XII. What are the differences in general tone and emphasis? Isolate one or two specific parallels such as the Cyclops episodes (Aeneid III.586-680; Odyssey, Book IX) and show how Virgil has turned them to his own different purpose.

5. In Virgil's view of history, the fall of Troy is ultimately part of a providential plan. Can we appreciate this fact when reading Book II? Does the horror of the story of the sack of Troy enhance Virgil's message of hope or make it seem facile?

6. Pyrrhus, the son of Achilles, plays a prominent role in Book II. How is he characterized? How does his brand of heroism compare with Aeneas's brand of heroism, and with that of Achilles?

7. Aeneas frantically searches for his lost wife Creusa through the ruins of Troy, but the reason she got lost in the first place is that he forgot about her. What are we to make of this incident?

8. Book III of The Aeneid shows the early stages of the Trojans' journey as almost a random wandering in ignorance of their goal. Does this aimlessness have any bearing on the effect of the poem as a whole?

9. As human interest drama, nothing else in ancient Latin literature matches Book IV of The Aeneid. The most compelling question about it has to do with Virgil's sympathies and his management of ours in the affair of Aeneas and Dido. Consider the validity of the following hypotheses (and of any others that occur to you): a) We sympathize with Dido and despise Aeneas, and this is contrary to Virgil's intent; he understands people and love so badly that he defeats his purpose; b) Our sympathies are as just described, but that is what Virgil intended and expected; he believes that mere feelings, however strong, must be subordinated to patriotic and moral duty; c) Our sympathies are, and are meant to be, with both lovers, with Dido for her humanity and the depth of her unhappy passion and with Aeneas because he must reluctantly and tragically stifle his feelings in the name of duty; d) Whatever may be true of Aeneas, Dido is a mad, possessive bitch, as Virgil intended.

10. What is the tone of Mercury's speech warning Aeneas about Dido (IV.595-604)?

This speech includes the famous Latin phrase <u>varium et mutabile semper / femina</u>, rendered by the translator as "A shifty, fickle object / Is woman, always." Since the Latin words are mainly English cognates, the phrase can be used both to clarify Mercury's tone and to illustrate Virgil's linguistic virtuosity, in a way students can readily grasp and appreciate. <u>Mutabile</u> ("fickle") and <u>semper</u> ("always"), placed back-to-back, make a violent and ironic oxymoron, and Mercury's cynicism is rendered even more brutal by his use of the neuter forms of the adjectives instead of the normal feminine forms <u>varia</u> and <u>mutabilis</u>, so that Dido becomes not just shifty and fickle but a shifty and fickle "object." The function and point-of-view of the misogyny in the passage are worth discussing.

11. Compare Dido and Aeneas in terms of their public and private roles.

This makes for an intriguing, and tragic, pattern, since the two lovers are out of phase in the timing of these matters. Both are rulers who have led their peoples from a disastrous past in the eastern Mediterranean. But Dido's city is rising when Aeneas takes time out for personal fulfillment; by the time the gods recall him to his public role, Dido has turned from queen to woman; when Aeneas meets her in the Lower World, he is being prepared for his public ministry while she has become once more the wife of Sychaeus.

12. Compare Aeneas's reception in the Lower World by Dido and by Anchises. Do these meetings help us with the questions raised about Book IV?

13. Compare the treatments of Helen of Troy in The Iliad and The Odyssey with the treatments of her in The Aeneid Books II and VI.

Hardly anything can better illustrate the passionate ambivalence felt by the ancients toward Helen, and perhaps toward woman in general.

14. Compare the versions of the realm of the dead in Odyssey Book XI and Aeneid Book VI. How do these reflect the differences, or similarities, between Homer's and Virgil's world-views? In which version is there more sadness, more hope, more despair? What weight does each poet give to the idea of reward and punishment for one's actions in life?

15. Consider the prospective visions of Roman greatness in The Aeneid Books VI and VIII (the shield of Aeneas). In what tone is this glorious future described? Pride? Humility? Boastfulness? Noblesse oblige?

16. Cleopatra (depicted on Aeneas's shield in Book VIII) and Dido are both African queens. Is this fact significant?

17. Compare the end of The Aeneid, in Book XII, with the ending of The Iliad, Books XXII (the death of Hector) and XXIV (Priam's visit to Achilles). Are the tragic visions similar or different? Compare the father-son motifs in the endings of the poems. What is the effect of the introduction of one of the Furies in Aeneid XII? How does the presence of Juturna contribute to the tragic effect? Can she be compared with Homer's Andromache? Is the rage of Aeneas in character for him, and, if not, is this fact important?

Ovid

The classical principle of decorum itself dictates how one should respond to Ovid: since he is one of the funniest of writers, one's first responsibility in reading him is to have fun. One's second responsibility springs directly from the first: to recognize that certain deep human insights are available only through comedy, which at its best can light up regions of human nature and of reality that heavier or more tragic modes fail to illumine. The upshot of these observations is that to teach Ovid well requires a nice touch. To spoil the fun by approaching Ovid solemnly would be the classroom equivalent of a crime. But it's also desirable, without becoming solemn, to suggest the ways in which Ovid's comic energy, like that of Aristophanes, for all his flippancy and irreverence, leaves a mark on our attitudes toward the things that matter most, in our private lives and even in public affairs.

1. Despite the frequent interactions between deities and human beings in classical literature, one of the most profound realities in such literature was the gulf between the two levels of being. To what extent does Ovid preserve this distinction? To what extent does he modify or subvert it?

2. Some of the poems in Ovid's Amores are close to being dramatic monologues. See, for example, poems I.4 (the address to a wife at a dinner party); I.8 (about the old hag who coaches a woman in how to handle and catch men); and I.14 (about the disastrous experiment with a hair rinse). Take one of these poems and act it out, using appropriate gestures, facial expressions, and tones of voice. How important is it to cast another player in the role of the listening lady?

3. In the Amores, Ovid sometimes personifies abstractions, notably different genres of light or weighty poetry or sources of poetic inspiration. See, for example, poem I.1 or, even better, III.1, which narrates the spat between Tragedy, a puritanical scold, and Elegy (love poetry), a sharp-tongued playgirl. Are these really what we usually consider allegorical figures? Do they not have human personalities that come through independent of their role as personifications?

4. Consider still other poems in the Amores that express Ovid's attitude toward his poetry and the poetic options he must choose from--for example, I.15, II.1, and III.15. How serious is Ovid about his poetry's leading to immortality? How strongly is he tempted to advance beyond elegiac love poetry to "higher" modes?

5. Several poems in the Amores compare or contrast love with war. Poem I.9, for example, draws a long and elaborate analogy between the lover's campaigns and the soldier's. Is there anything more to this than clowning?

6. How does Ovid portray women in the Amores? Do we get a good idea what his girlfriend(s) is (are) like? What is his attitude toward women in general? Is it cruel? Tender? Satiric? Affectionate? Which sex has more power? Which is more selfish? Which is more clever? Which is more easily hurt? Are women mere objects for Ovid?

7. Compare Ovid's notion of sexual love, and his way of expressing it, with those of Sappho and Catullus earlier in the anthology and, in later pages, of Andreas Capellanus, Petrarch, and Donne. Which of these writers is most like Ovid and which most unlike him?

8. Consider the letter of Paris to Helen and her reply to him, in the Heroides, as samples of rhetoric and argument. Could one score their arguments the way a debate competition is scored? Does Paris woo Helen, and does she answer him, more in the vein of passion or in that of debate? How much feeling is evinced on either side?

    The wooing-by-argument in Andreas Capellanus' Art of Courtly Love, later in the anthology, might make a good comparison.

9. "Paris and Helen, in the Heroides, are both self-important, vain, superficial phonies. They deserve each other." Comment on this statement.

10. "Helen, in the Heroides, tries to pull off a neat trick: to convey to Paris that she will indeed run off with him and, at the same time, that she is a virtuous woman shocked at the very idea." Comment on this statement.

11. The elopement of Helen with Paris will ignite the awesome international crisis and bloodbath called the Trojan War. Do we get any hint, from their letters in the Heroides, that the ultimate stakes will be so high?

12. The Metamorphoses is presumably the kind of big, serious poem with which, in the Amores, Ovid contrasts his frivolous elegiac love poetry. Are the two works entirely different in tone?

13. Is there any irony in Ovid's Metamorphoses?

    Consider, for example, the Roman-style class structure among the Olympian deities (I.162-69), the comparison of Jove and Caesar Augustus as avengers (I.196-202), and the grief felt by the gods at the prospect of Jove's destroying humanity, an act that will leave no one to pay the gods homage (I.245-48).

14. Metamorphoses I.1-80 describes the process of the physical creation in detail, in a way that resembles in some respects the opening of Genesis. What are the main differences between the two creation stories? How confident are the respective authors of the truth of what they are relating? What role does a Creator play in each account?

15. The account of the Four Ages in Metamorphoses I.81-154 shows how evil and distress gradually darken a once-idyllic world. Is there anything in Ovid's narrative to explain the emergence of evil as, say, the story of the Fall does in Genesis?

16. The first individual singled out by Ovid as wicked and offensive to Jove is Lycaon (I.204-239), whose name signifies a wolf. How does this story relate to other folk tales about mergers of wolf and man?

    Significantly, Ovid's story is not about a human being whose personality is invaded by an alien animal nature; rather, Ovid suggests that the savage rapaciousness of wolves originated in a human being.

17. Compare the Flood stories in Ovid (I.315-434) and Genesis 6-9. Which has the greater human interest? Which is more stern as a condemnation of human wickedness?

The New Testament

An acquaintance with the Hebrew Bible (Old Testament) is very advantageous in reading the Sermon on the Mount, which so often juxtaposes Jesus' teaching with traditional Jewish teachings. The tense combination of traditionalism with emphatic revision of it, which has often caused Matthew to be considered the most "Jewish" of the four gospels, is worth attention; one notes, for example, that in 5:17-19 Jesus insists that he has come to fulfill the law rather than to destroy it. In this connection, and others, it is helpful to have in the class some religiously well-informed Jews, who are sometimes better able than Christians to assess the degree of Jesus' radicalism, which in fact has some points of contact—despite 5:20—with Pharisaic Judaism.

One general approach to the Sermon on the Mount is to consider whether it is a set of ethical guidelines or a model for a general spiritual transformation in which the notion of guidelines is bypassed. Consider, for example, the passage (5:27-28) in which Jesus equates lustful desire with physical adultery, or the passage (5:21-22) where he implies that anger is a kind of killing.

1. In Plato's Symposium, Alcibiades marvels that Socrates, even when discussing the subtlest and most sublime matters, uses homely images such as pack-asses and tanners. What kind of imagery does Jesus tend to use in his sayings and analogies?

2. The popular image of Jesus is of a gentle person. To what extent is this image borne out in the Gospels?

3. Compare the precepts in the Sermon on the Mount with the Aristotelian ideal of the golden mean between extremes. Is the righteousness that Jesus preaches the same thing that Aristotle calls virtue? What might Jesus have said to Aristotle if he had been among the audience at the Mount?

4. Why does Jesus urge his hearers not to take oaths (5:33-37)? How does this teaching fit into the theme of the Sermon on the Mount?

5. In the Sermon on the Mount, Jesus urges that his hearers allow their goodness to be seen by the world (5:13-16), but later he urges that good deeds be done in secret (6:1-4). Is this a contradiction?

6. In Jesus' well-known analogy with the birds and the lilies (6:24-34), is he telling people that material things are unimportant or that if they ignore such things they will get them anyway?

7. Are the "beatitudes" (5:3-12) a revolutionary program? If so, in what sense? Could they be enlisted in the cause of political revolution?

8. What does it mean to "love your enemies" (5:44)? Jesus goes on to explain that such love shows people to be children of the heavenly Father, who bestows rain and sun on both the good and the evil. Does this mean that God is indifferent to good and evil? How does Jesus' statement fit in with the warnings, elsewhere in the Sermon, about punishment for evil?

The Koran

The brief selection from the Koran, added to the selections from the Old Testament and the New Testament, rounds out the scriptures of the world's three great monotheistic religions: Hebraism, Christianity, and Islam. As sacred texts, all three present pedagogical problems different from purely secular texts. And perhaps all three would benefit from being taught together or at least each in the context of the other two. There are many obvious parallels in subjects: praises of God, accounts of sacred history, moral instruction, and the like. All three must be taught in translation as well, a situation that presents its own difficulties.

1. The winner of the 1995 Pulitzer Prize for biography was Jack Miles's <u>God: A Biography</u>, in which the author reconstructed the "biography" of God by examining how He is presented through the Bible. Can a similar characterization of God be extracted from descriptions of Him in the Koran selections? How would it differ from those in the Old and New Testaments?

2. Point of view and voice are very interesting in the Koran. Much of the text is in the voice of Muhammad, but occasionally it shifts to the voice of God. The translator, A. J. Arberry, has clarified these shifts by capitalizing all nouns and pronouns that refer to God. Trace these shifts through the text. "Ya Sin" is especially interesting in this respect.

3. Verse 177 of "The Cow" is often regarded as an epitome of the core beliefs of Islam. Summarize these beliefs. Notice the respective emphases on belief and on action.

4. Arabic is so different from English that translators have been unable to translate the poetic features of the original into English. Arthur J. Arberry has commented that he has attempted to suggest the effect of sections by finding English equivalents. The class might study how he has done this by analyzing the poetic technique of the selection from "Light." What sort of poetic line does Arberry adopt? (He has said that he uses very short lines to round off each verse.) What sorts of images are used for God, and how are they related? Is the translation reminiscent of any English texts? (Obviously, it has a biblical flavor, but Arberry has commented that he also had in mind medieval Christmas carols!) The class might benefit from comparing the chapter's development of the metaphor of light with the metaphor of God-as-light in the Hebrew and Christian bibles. See, especially, the First Letter of John in the New Testament.

5. "Ya Sin," which is spoken by God to Muhammad, employs narrative, a parable of the dissemination of Islamic teachings. Analyze the narrative structure and the meaning of this parable.

Beowulf

Teachers of Beowulf have an excellent resource available in a Modern Language Association publication, Approaches to Teaching Beowulf, ed. Jess B. Bessinger, Jr., and Robert F. Yeager, 1984. This useful volume is partially based upon a survey of Beowulf teachers and consequently has a refreshingly realistic tone. One section is devoted to teaching Beowulf in translation to undergraduates; it contains four insightful essays in which teachers describe in detail how they go about teaching the poem.

1. In the last lines of Beowulf, four epithets are applied to the hero: "kindest," "most gentle," "most just to his people," and "most eager for fame." Looking backward through the poem, do you find these descriptions justified? (The most surprising may be "most gentle.")

2. The monsters, as post-Tolkien critics have demonstrated, are worth close attention. Look closely at how each is described. Does the poet seem to intend them symbolically to any degree? If so, what are their symbolic associations? How are they differentiated? Does Beowulf approach them differently? Why?

3. Any one of the "digressions" raises basic questions of theme and narrative structure. The opening account of Scyld Scefing is part of a conventional genealogy, but it is developed far beyond what would be required by only that. How? Why? What themes of the poem are announced here? The same sorts of questions might be asked of the other inset narratives: the burning of Heorot, the fight at Finnsburh, etc.

4. Describe the roles of women in the poem, both their realistic depiction and their apparent place in the symbolic structure. If we divide the poem into three, rather than two, parts, part two is especially rich in its treatment of women. Notice that Grendel's mother is introduced just after the scene in Heorot in which Wealhtheow figures prominently and during which we hear the story of another woman grieving for a dead child: Hildeburh. What links, if any, are there among these women, mythic, legendary, and real?

5. One of the peculiarities of the narrative structure of Beowulf is its use of what might be called "flash-forwards," anticipations of future action, some of which is beyond the point at which the poem ends. In describing Heorot, for example, the poet tells us that "The hall towered high, / lofty and wide-gabled--fierce tongues of loathsome fire / had not yet attacked it, nor was the time yet near / when a mortal feud should flare between father- / and son-in-law, sparked off by deeds of deadly enmity" (lines 81-85). Slightly different examples are those in which the poet seemingly destroys suspense by telling us the outcome of an event before it occurs. We are told repeatedly, for example, that Beowulf will not survive his fight with the dragon. Identify as many such passages as you can and comment on their purpose and effect.

6. Does Beowulf have a "tragic flaw"?

7. J. R. R. Tolkien: Beowulf "is a heroic-elegiac poem; and in a sense all its first 3,136 lines are the prelude to a dirge." What is "elegiac" about Beowulf?

The Song of Roland

The details of narrative and of characterization in The Song of Roland are worth close attention, but the value of the poem for students lies even more, perhaps, in its over-all Gestalt, its cleanly delineated picture of the feudal code. To put this another way, Roland would be a good poem for students to read even if one did not have time to discuss it in class. The medieval heroic world, boldly drawn as it is in Roland, provides a neat counterpart with the worlds of Gilgamesh and of the Homeric epics early in the anthology. Roland directs one forward, providing a base on which to understand the more nuanced systems of medieval values in later works such as Sir Gawain and the Green Knight. At the same time, the status of Roland as epic puts the poem in a tradition the narrative conventions of which can be traced back through centrally important classical authors.

1. By the standards of Aristotle's Poetics, is The Song of Roland a tragedy?

2. "Roland's a hero, / and Oliver is wise" (line 1093). Consider the importance in the poem of these words and of the judgments they imply.

3. What kind of person is Ganelon? Is his treachery cowardly? What, exactly, is the nature of the crime for which he is tried near the end? Is he psychologically complex? Do we know how his mind works? In laisses XXIX-XXX, he discusses Roland with the Saracen envoy Blancandrin, paying Roland high tributes; is this in character?

4. In laisse III, Blancandrin suggests that the pagans offer their sons to death as hostages rather than be dishonored by subjugation to the Christians. In light of the poems's system of values, is this offer heroic or is it a sign of pagan evil?

5. Laisses LXXXIII-LXXXV are close to exact repetition. What effect does this repetition have?

6. The nomination of Roland by Ganelon for the post of danger in the rear (LVIII-LXI) closely parallels Roland's earlier nomination of Ganelon for the perilous post of envoy to Marsile (XX-XXVI). What function does the parallelism serve?

7. When Charles offers Roland half of the army to guard the rear, Roland proudly insists that he will accept no more than twenty thousand men (LXIII). Does this gesture enhance Roland's heroism or does it show a flaw in him?

8. What is the relationship between heroism and reputation? See, for example, the crucial laisses LXXXIII-LXXXVI, where Roland refuses to summon help. Later, it is Oliver who objects to sounding the horn (CXXVIII-CXXXI). Why have the two men reversed their views?

9. Ganelon's trial is decided first by the deliberation of the jury, then by combat. What values are reflected by these two kinds of decision?

10. The issues and conflicts in the poem have all been settled when suddenly, in the last ten lines, a weary Charles is commissioned by God to undertake a new mission. Does this ending put what has preceded it in a new light?

Andreas Capellanus

It might seem as though, for college undergraduates, romantic love would be among the most accessible of subjects, but in fact it is very common for students of traditional college age not to appreciate its importance or even its nature. (Older, "non-traditional" students are often better attuned to the subject.) Many of the very young have never really experienced romantic love, and, of those who have, many assume half-consciously that it is just part of growing up, a developmental phenomenon available to people at a certain stage of life but eventually, and properly, put behind them. Will Andreas Capellanus throw any light on the subject for people who still need enlightenment? Therein lies one of the teacher's greatest challenges: to separate what seems quaint (or worse) in Andreas from whatever he has to say that is, more or less, permanently valid and illuminating. If students come to regard The Art of Courtly Love as little more than an interesting medieval convention, they will not simply have wasted their time, but one hopes that the work will turn out to be more meaningful for them than that.

1. The medieval period is often considered an age of misogyny. Is the seeming idealization of women in The Art of Courtly Love consistent with misogyny?

2. To some people (most of them male), Andreas's version of love seems to have a distinctively feminine flavor. How valid is this view?

3. In the dialogues of wooing dramatized by Andreas, the man seems always to take the initiative, the woman's role being the more passive one of accepting or rejecting the man's overtures. On the other hand, the man typically promises to be the woman's slave. If this account is accurate, which sex should be seen as having the greater power?

4. What makes the love described by Andreas "courtly"? Is love made more noble or less so when it is practiced and expressed through elaborate rules of style and etiquette?

5. Although Andreas apparently wishes to present love as, in some respects, a great leveler, his version of it is closely implicated with social hierarchy. To love well, for example, is one of the signs that one is a true aristocrat, and the dialogues are classified in terms of the relative social status of the man and woman. Is love, as Andreas presents it, a revolutionary force or a reactionary one?

6. Andreas's lovers often speak as if they were arguing legal briefs, or having a debate in a medieval university. Are we to take this tone and method as entirely serious, or is any humor intended?

7. The most notorious idea put forth in The Art of Courtly Love is the absolute impossibility of romantic love between people married to each other. Is this idea silly? Outrageous? Correct?

8. Courtly love is almost literally a religion; at the very least it borrows the terminology of religious devotion. Is this religiosity merely a convention? Is it blasphemous?

Students might profit from looking again at Shakespeare's Romeo and Juliet (most of them have read the play these days), which is full of religious imagery put to amatory uses.

At their first meeting, Shakespeare's lovers speak a sonnet in dialogue, based on the image of a religious pilgrimage.

9. Courtly love is obviously an expression of sexual desire. Is that fact compatible with the intense idealization that is also essential to it?

10. Compare Andreas's version of romantic love with sexual love as depicted in any of the following authors or works in Volume One of the anthology: Sappho, Catullus, Ovid, Virgil (the Dido episode), <u>Sir Gawain and the Green Knight</u>, Petrarch, Boccaccio, Marguerite de Navarre, Cervantes, Milton (Adam and Eve).

Marie de France

The problem in teaching Marie de France's lais is probably in getting students to slow down and take a close look. They are so easy to read and so apparently simple that students are likely to dismiss them. It is only when one starts taking them seriously that their subtlety and sophistication appear.

1. Marie opens "Bisclavret" by stressing the werewolf's savagery: "A werewolf is a savage beast; / while his fury is on him / he eats men, does much harm, / goes deep in the forest to live." Yet the story gradually reverses the expectations this opening establishes. The audience is likely to initially sympathize with the wife's revulsion and then gradually swing toward sympathy with Bisclavret. The question is thus finally posed of who the more savage beast is. Trace this irony through the story, as sympathy is distributed between Bisclavret and his wife.

2. Bisclavret has a "tragic flaw" (besides the lycanthropy, which he can't help): his inability to keep his secret from his wife, even though he knows that by telling her he risks losing not only her love but his "very self" (which indeed he does). Notice that this initial mistake is echoed and reversed at the end when he, as the wolf, refuses to put on his clothes before the court. A respect for privacy seemed to be a requirement of civilization. Trace this theme through the story. How do clothes function as an emblem of civilization?

3. Bisclavret's wife has a "tragic flaw," too: her inability to see her husband realistically, acknowledging his "animal" as well as "human" side. At first he is all good; after the confession he is all bad. Notice how her accusations double back upon her; she ends up being more "bestial" than Bisclavret.

4. Another irony of the story is that, while the human Bisclavret must periodically become a beast, the bestial Bisclavret behaves in a courteous and even courtly way. The king recognizes the human being in the beast, whereas the wife could see only the beast in the human being. What characteristics of civilized behavior does Bisclavret show while he is a wolf?

5. "Bisclavret" seems less a story of love than of its betrayal, and Bisclavret's wife, perhaps more than Bisclavret himself, is the central character. What statement is Marie making about the qualities necessary for loyalty in love?

6. "Yonec" draws upon the inclusa motif common in folktales: the situation of a woman kept in forced isolation by a jealous husband or father. Marie uses this motif as the basis for opposing images of enclosure and freedom throughout the story. Trace these images. What effect do they have on the story's meaning?

7. Notice that Marie presents the lady's adulterous affair with her bird-lover in wholly positive terms. What seems to make this a justifiable love and to make the marriage an unjustifiable one?

8. The fact that the lover comes in the form of a hawk is very suggestive. For one thing, the husband has him killed by sharp spikes like claws. Who is the more predatory of the two? For another, the fact reverses the familiar medieval equation of hunting with sexual pursuit. The lady does not range out with the hawk in pursuit of game; the hawk comes to

her prison-tower and is ultimately the victim rather than the predator. Are there other reasons for the lover to be a hawk?

9. The lady follows the fatally wounded lover into a magic castle under a hill, an example of the "other world" motif which Marie frequently uses. (Bisclavret's life as a werewolf is an "other world" of a very different sort.) What does the "other world" represent here?

10. Notice that the lady has the power to summon the bird; he comes only when she wishes for him. (Her yearning too often for her lover is an example of desmesure and leads to disaster.) Notice, too, that she is able to leap from the tower without injury after her happy love affair, although she was unable to do so before. Also, he gives her a magic ring that can keep her husband from remembering what has happened or imprisoning her again. What do these facts suggest about the status of the bird-lover? Is he partially an internal force in the lady?

11. The last episode, telling of Yonec's avenging of his true father upon his false one, introduces an unexpected element into the story, and yet Marie chooses to name the story after this secondary character. The doubling of fathers, the magic sword and ring, and the killing of the false father to avenge the mother and true father all sound like Oedipal fantasy. Is the story really Yonec's, rather than his mother's?

12. Robert Hanning and Joan Ferrante: "What Marie seems to be saying in the lai, as in several others, is that the world can imprison the body but not the mind, once the mind wills itself free." Does this seem an accurate interpretation of Yonec?

Saints Anselm and Thomas Aquinas

Besides addressing one of the most momentous of questions, the existence of God, the anthology selections from Anselm and Aquinas are valuable as illustrations of the workings of the medieval mind. We are thinking of the medieval style of reasoning but also of the rhetorical strategies deployed. It is interesting, in these respects, to compare the excerpts from Anselm and Aquinas with other samples of argument, strictly literary and not, in the book, notably in Plato, Aristotle, Andreas Capellanus, Chaucer, Dante, Marguerite de Navarre, and Montaigne. Such comparisons illuminate not just the ways in which language is used but also the metaphysical assumptions of different writers and periods, along with the relative weight given in different times and places to pure logic as distinguished from more affective strategies of persuasion.

1. If you did not know when the Anselm and Aquinas selections were written, could you have placed them in the medieval period, as in key ways akin to other medieval selections in the anthology?

2. Which argument for God's existence is most satisfactory (or, if you prefer, least unsatisfactory), Anselm's or Aquinas's?

3. Do Anselm and Aquinas use the same rhetorical style? The same rhetorical tone?

4. Both Anselm and Aquinas were Christian believers who considered faith in divine revelation to be essential. Is it necessary for such believers to compartmentalize their minds in order to attempt to prove God's existence by pure reason?

5. Is there something wrong, on the face of it, with any attempt to approach a transcendent and infinite God through limited human reason? To what extent are Anselm and Aquinas aware of this potential objection, and to what extent do they overcome it?

6. Anselm is famous for his dictum credo ut intelligam, "I believe in order to understand." Does this affirmation disqualify him for the purely logical task of proof he is undertaking?

One could get at this matter by way of analogy with less purely metaphysical questions. Could we properly reason out the proof of a theory of gravitation if we did not believe that objects do in fact fall to the ground? Or is this analogy not a valid one?

7. Anselm repeatedly defines God as a being than which a greater cannot be conceived. Could this not be a definition of an impersonal God--an ultimate source of cosmic energy, for example--rather than of the Judaeo-Christian God whom Anselm has in mind?

If this impersonal God lacks consciousness, though, is such a being not inferior not only to what we can conceive but to what we are ourselves?

8. Several of Aquinas's proofs depend on his assumption that an infinite regress, in time or causation, is impossible. Should he simply assume this impossibility? Is an infinite regress really inconceivable?

Many students will accept that, as a matter of fact, there is not an infinite regress, since the scientific consensus now ascribes a finite age to the universe. But that still leaves the question open as a matter of pure logic. On logical grounds, one could ask whether there could be any discrete now without a finite preceding series of then's. How, if one did not start from a unique point, could one ever reach any local point in time?

9. Part of Aquinas's standard method is to state objections at the outset and then, after adducing his proof, to answer the respective objections. In the case of his proofs of God's existence, are the initial objections he formulates the most powerful ones that could have been made? Should he have recognized other, more potent obstacles to theism?

Dante Alighieri

The <u>Divine Comedy</u> sets out to do just about everything, and so of course it can be approached from any number of directions. The introduction and footnotes in the textbook, along with the translator's interpolated summaries and bracketed glosses, provide some political and theological information, but the questions below play down these themes, since we are assuming religiously pluralist (and theologically naive) students who are uninterested in the details of medieval Italian politics and not greatly interested even in Dante's larger political ideas on Italian unity and the separation of civil and papal power.

Thematically, the questions address the moral and spiritual values of the <u>Comedy</u>, in themselves and as they relate to alternative, especially modern, value systems. It is important that students come to see the <u>Comedy</u> as perhaps the central literary embodiment of the medieval world-view, but some of the work's distinctive medievalism will inevitably emerge from discussions of what elements in it still hold good today and what elements don't.

In discussing Dante's artistry (often, perhaps always, inseparable from his themes and moral vision), the following matters seem important:

a) The total form of the poem, especially its status as allegory, epic, and sheer story. Hundreds of things in the poem stand for other things; the challenge is to show <u>how</u> they do and to discriminate where necessary between "pure" allegory and a more immediate, dramatic intention. (Clearly, the beasts of <u>Inferno</u>, Canto I, do not "mean" in the same way as the lovers Francesca and Paolo in Canto V.) In determining the poem's epic credentials one can emphasize its lineal indebtedness to the tradition (most obviously the <u>Aeneid</u>) or use more generic criteria such as the treatment of time or of heroism. In treating the poem as story, one can concentrate on the growth of the fictional pilgrim named Dante or on the progressive revelation to him of what the universe is like.

b) The architecture of Dante's cosmos. Its structure is endlessly analyzable in the minutest detail; time constraints may well dictate a more macrocosmic approach--for example, an analysis of gravitation as physical and moral principle.

c) Narrative method and characterization. These may pose teaching problems; to follow the one overarching personal story, that of Dante as pilgrim, requires alertness to subtle changes in him. For all omitted cantos of <u>Purgatory</u> and <u>Paradise</u> we provide summaries, which, it is hoped, will suggest the total narrative shape of the work if not the continuing development of the protagonist's character. Equally challenging, though for different reasons, is Dante's "small-scale" narrative method, since the inset stories such as those of Ugolino and Ulysses are never more than a few dozen lines long.

d) Imagery. Again, one can concentrate on macro-images (Hell as a cavity, Purgatory as a mountain) or on finer detail, as in the symbolism of punishments for the sins in Hell.

e) Language. This takes in Dante's use of rhetorical figures (especially similes), his vocabulary (is it plain or fancy?), and his sentence constructions (sometimes direct statements, sometimes elaborate circumlocutions). Since the Huse translation does not use rhyme or a regular meter, it can render Dante very literally while also preserving the integrity and cumulative rhythm of his tercets. One loses the sound effects, as in any translation, but on many aspects of language one can use this translation with pretty firm confidence that one is talking about Dante and not a translator's expedient.

Teaching Dante can be a touchy thing, and exploring reader response to him is especially important. Students are likely to find Hell engrossing as phantasmagoria, and they may well be awed by Dante's artistry, but some of them may find his moral vision sadistic or arrogant. However benighted this view may seem, it cannot be just dismissed, and in fact some famous and sophisticated people have shared it. One remedy, suggested in the Introduction, is to approach the Inferno not primarily as a depiction of the afterlife but as a timeless anatomy of evil and its relationship to the human will. In any event, it seems advisable to let students vent their feelings, not only for the students' sake but in order to focus more urgently on what, essentially, the poem is doing.

Although students' queries about what they are "responsible for" are often dispiriting, the queries need to be answered in connection with Dante. New readers, who cannot be expected to remember more than a small proportion of the hundreds of events and persons in the Comedy, will panic unless the teacher reassures them that they don't have to hold everything in memory. It does seem reasonable to expect--on, say, examinations--that students have taken in such things as the physical and moral shape of Dante's cosmos, the rationale and arrangement of the sins, and the half-dozen or so most memorable characters such as Francesca, Brunetto, and Ulysses.

Approaches to Teaching Dante's "Divine Comedy," ed. by Carole Slade (New York: Modern Language Assn., 1982), contains sixteen essays on teaching the poem to undergraduates, besides other useful material.

1. Analyze the symbolic appropriateness of the punishment for X, Y, and Z (several sins specified by the teacher).

Some of the punishments will be, essentially, re-enactments of the sins themselves; others may represent the compensatory opposites of the sins. Is this an important distinction?

2. Dante loves and reveres Brunetto Latini (Inferno, XV), although he is a condemned sodomist. How does one explain this? Does Dante distinguish between a person's inherent value and his or her eternal destiny among the saved or damned? What do such episodes tell us about Dante's conception of sin and of the human personality? Why, as with Brunetto, does Dante so often engage persons in talk about matters that have little or nothing to do with their sins?

3. Limbo is for the virtuous who lived outside the Jewish-Christian tradition. Does the existence of such a place undermine the poem's notion of justice?

4. The inscription over the gate of Hell says that Hell was made by Power, Wisdom, and Love. In what sense can it be true that Love helped create Hell?

5. In the Inferno (and the Purgatory too), lust is the least serious evil. How does this fact fit in to the poem's over-all moral vision?

6. If you were writing a revised version of the Inferno applicable to people today, what changes would you make? Would you make certain sins more serious, others less so?

Would new sins have to be added?

This question probably requires overnight thought; it could also be a paper assignment, geared either to the student's personal values or to what he or she considers the generally accepted values of the modern world. The assignment might seem to lead students away from the text into subjectivity, but at least implicitly they will be evaluating the universality of Dante's moral values. The question could be made more concrete in many ways--for example, by asking students to locate a certain sin lower or higher in the cavity of Hell and to defend their relocation.

7. If we define the epic tradition through the exemplars Gilgamesh, Homer, Virgil, Beowulf, and Roland, can the Divine Comedy be called an epic? Does it take the epic approach to history? to time? to narrative sequence? to the distinctive values of its age? to the idea of divine guidance? to heroism?

8. What role does Virgil play in the Inferno? Is it always the same? Does Virgil have significant limitations, and, if he does, what do they tell us? Does it help to have read the Aeneid?

9. What role does Beatrice play in the poem? Does her sex, and her identity as a woman Dante knew personally, contribute to or detract from her role?

Questions 8 and 9 invite a discussion of allegory, while leaving open the question whether Virgil and Beatrice are purely, or even mainly, allegorical.

10. Where does the water come from that is frozen into ice at the center of Hell?

11. The center of the earth and of the universe in Dante is ice; the uppermost terrace of Purgatory is fire. What do you make of this contrast?

Questions 10 and 11 are designed to explore the relationship between physical laws such as gravitation and moral laws.

12. Compare the last canto of the Inferno with the last canto of the Paradise, identifying as many parallels or contrasts as possible. What do these tell us about the values and total vision of the poem?

13. The story of the lovers Francesca and Paolo (Inferno, Canto V) is very short, only 71 lines long. Does Dante tell us all we want to know? All we need to know? Would it be relevant, for example, for us to know whether or not Francesca was happy in her marriage?

14. Is Ulysses (Inferno, Canto XXVI) recognizable as Homer's Odysseus? Is he sympathetic in Dante? Do we know enough about him to answer the question?

Questions 13 and 14 introduce the question of Dante's narrative method in the poem's episodes (most of the others are even shorter) and of his characterizations. One might want to compare the elliptical method used in folk ballads and to discuss whether the compression enhances or limits the power of Dante's episodes. (Incidentally, Tennyson's Ulysses also lies ahead in Volume II.)

15. In the last canto of the Paradise, Dante must try to express the Deity itself, a task he recognizes as impossible. How does he cope with it?

    This question can be linked to a discussion of the function of simile and imagery in other parts of the poem as well.

16. Examine lines 1-27 of the Inferno. Is the language plain or complex?

    The passage is given in Italian also. If students are given a glossary of the individual Italian words, they may focus even more intently on the diction and rhetoric here, and therefore also in later passages for which they do not have the Italian.

17. Is it as easy for a non-religious-believer to like or appreciate Dante as it is for a believer?

18. Someone once said that, if people today were assigned places in Dante's afterworld, they would almost all be among the trimmers outside Hell's gate. What does this statement imply, and do you agree with it?

    Questions 17-18 serve partly to let students get their feelings off their chests.

Sir Gawain and the Green Knight

The teacher preparing to teach Sir Gawain and the Green Knight for the first time (or the fortieth time) might well benefit from taking a look at the MLA volume Approaches to Teaching "Sir Gawain and the Green Knight," 1986. It is one of the best volumes in the useful series Approaches to Teaching Masterpieces of World Literature, and it contains a wealth of information, especially on such background matters as the romance tradition, Arthurian literature, chivalry, religion, law, and poetics. The questions raised here cannot substitute for these broad backgrounds but can only raise a few of the topics important in the poem.

1. How does Gawain, as a romance protagonist, compare with Odysseus, Aeneas, and Beowulf, as epic protagonists? The class might compare not only the protagonists but more generally the epic and romance worlds.

2. How do weather and the seasons figure in the poem? Gawain's two encounters with the Green Knight take place on successive New Year's Days. The cycle of the intervening year is traced in some detail (lines 500-535), and the bitter cold of Gawain's journey to the Green Chapel is also described vividly (lines 726-39). Are these references symbolic? Of what?

3. The poem is divided into four sections, or "fits." What happens in each section, and how does the division structure the action? What other structural features seem important? Notice the "envelope" construction, with Arthur's court at the beginning and end and the journey and Bercilak's court embedded between the two. And notice the many doublings and parallels—Arthur's court and Bercilak's court, the young woman and the old woman, the hunt and the wooing, etc.

4. The description and interpretation of the pentangle design on Gawain's shield is obviously a set-piece that encapsulates an important part of the meaning of the poem. What meanings does the poet find in the figure?

5. Bercilak's castle is paralleled with Arthur's castle, as another center of chivalry. But appearances are deceptive in Bercilak's castle, which turns out to be a trap for Gawain. What features are especially deceptive?

6. In Section 3, the Gawain poet does what a filmmaker would call "cross-cutting" between the hunt scenes and the seduction scenes. How do they echo and reflect one another? One scholar (D. W. Robertson, Jr.) has even suggested that the animals hunted on each day symbolize the potential weaknesses of Gawain that the lady appeals to. On the first day, Bercilak hunts does and gives Gawain venison, and the lady offers Gawain her body; both suggest the sin of gluttony (or lechery). On the second day, Bercilak hunts a boar (symbol of vainglory), and the lady appeals to Gawain's pride. On the third day, Bercilak hunts a fox, representative of avarice, and the lady tempts Gawain with gifts. (Gluttony, vainglory, and avarice were known in the Middle Ages as the "temptations of prosperity.") Can this idea be developed further?

7. Just before Gawain reaches the Green Chapel, the servant who has guided him there advises him to flee and then flees himself. What is the function of this scene? Is the

servant a foil for Gawain? How? (If the class has read Beowulf, a comparison with the cowardly kinsmen who abandoned Beowulf just as he encountered the dragon might be in order.)

8. In lines 2410 ff., Gawain, having learned the truth of the deception, bitterly denounces all the women throughout history who have betrayed men, from Eve on down. Is this just a piece of conventional medieval misogyny, or does the poem in general present women unfavorably?

9. What are the advantages and disadvantages of alliterative verse, with the bob and wheel stanza ending, as a verse form for a narrative poem? What would be lost if the story were in prose, or even in blank verse?

Geoffrey Chaucer

Like many other anthologists and people who have to classify literature, we have placed Chaucer earlier than certain Italian "Renaissance" writers who lived and wrote earlier than he did and, indeed, influenced him. Students may need to have this apparent time-warp, resting on the assumption that there was a Renaissance and that it arrived late in England, explained to them. The displacement of chronology is, of course, to some extent arbitrary and conventional, and that fact needs emphasizing too. On the other hand, there is some juxtapositional symbolism in having Dante and Chaucer back-to-back, since both poets created, in their very different ways, encyclopedic portraits of medieval life and culture. Students who read Chaucer right after Dante can be invited to compare the two writers and their world-views. At first glance, Dante will seem by far the more ambitious poet, but in some ways Chaucer has a wider range; for example, Dante's Divine Comedy is more divine than comic, while Chaucer is one of the greatest of all comic geniuses. Dante's intensity can be compared with Chaucer's leisureliness and seemingly easygoing open-mindedness. The problems in audience sensibility are almost opposite ones: the challenge may be, with Dante, to show students that he is more centered on earthly life than he seems to be, with Chaucer to show that his work has, in his understated way, moral and spiritual urgency.

All the Chaucer selections in the anthology can be regarded as comic pieces except the Pardoner's Tale, yet, curiously, this is the one that depends most on plot devices--incongruous juxtapositions, cross-purposes, inversions of role--that are normally the comic author's stock in trade.

Both poets' works can be presented as self-reflexive: for one thing, both appear as characters in their poems. This reflexive motif appears more clearly in The Canterbury Tales, however, a story that is overtly about storytelling. The poem is full of role-playing: the characters' tales are often extensions of their personalities and (as with the Wife of Bath and the Pardoner) of their Prologues. The Nun's Priest's Tale plays dazzling tricks with scale. The presence of inset stories, anecdotes, exempla, asides, exhortations, and sermons within tales that are themselves framed by prologues, within the larger framework of the General Prologue, puts The Canterbury Tales in the company of other great metaliterary works, obviously including many modern ones but also going back to The Odyssey, that play with our perspective on truth and illusion, reality and fiction.

1. If an author today were writing an equivalent of The Canterbury Tales, where might the modern pilgrims be going together? What thirty or so characteristic types of people or of vocations would be represented?

2. Like Boccaccio's Decameron (and, to look ahead in time, Marguerite de Navarre's Heptameron), The Canterbury Tales arises from a compact, made by individualized characters, to tell stories to one another in a systematic way. What other resemblances or important differences are there between the works?

3. Compare the degrees in which different characters know the Bible and the different ways in which they cite it. What do we learn from the biblical texts they choose and their methods of biblical interpretation?

4. In the General Prologue, what devices does the narrator use in order to pass judgment on the pilgrims?

5. Some of the pilgrims--the Prioress and attendant priests and nun, the Monk, the Friar, the Student (Clerk), the Parson, the Pardoner--are religious by professional occupation. What aspects of religion does each represent? How would you rank them in terms of their piety and integrity?

6. One widely-held image of Chaucer is as a cheerful, easygoing, tolerant man. How well does this image consist with the General Prologue?

7. In the Miller's Prologue, both the Miller, in addressing the resentful Reeve, and Chaucer as pilgrim/narrator, in addressing the reader, make variations of the same point: You won't be hurt if you don't look for trouble. Is this parallel significant? Trace other examples of the theme of dangerous knowledge in the Tale.

8. The Miller's Tale begins with successive portraits of Nicholas and Alison, both described with relish but with different emphases. Why does the tale begin in this way? Are the methods of characterization similar or not? Are Nicholas and Alison like each other? See also the characterization of Absolom in lines 126 ff. Like Nicholas, he has many accomplishments; do the two therefore resemble each other? Do they talk (declare their love for Alison, for example) in the same way?

9. Do you think the humor in the Miller's Tale is cruel? Do Absolom and John the carpenter get what they deserve? Note especially John's concern over Nicholas' condition when he is locked in his room and his similar concern over his wife when he learns that the deluge is coming. Are the carpenter's gullibility and Nicholas' cleverness intended to make us dislike and like them, respectively? Is this the kind of story where it matters whether we like the characters or not?

10. As the last five lines of the Miller's Tale emphasize, all three of the male characters in the tale come off badly, while Alison does not. Is this a significant point?

11. In lines 436-42 of the Miller's Tale, the sexual revelry of Alison and Nicholas is mentioned in the same breath with the reminder that the friars are praying in their chapel. Are there other such irreverent conjunctions in the Tale? Are they important to its effect?

12. Are we meant to admire the Wife of Bath? Are we meant to like her? Is she an effective voice of women's concerns? If she were alive today, would she be a feminist? Would feminists approve of her or disown her?

13. Are the Wife's arguments--on marriage versus celibacy, for example--persuasive? Does her own character give force to her arguments or weaken them?

14. What is the Wife's attitude toward her listeners? Is she interested in winning their approval or not? How would you compare her frankness with that of the Pardoner?

15. Is the Wife's Prologue comic or is it serious? If it is comic, at whose expense? If it is serious, in what respects?

16. The Wife's Tale seems to have a moral. What is it? Is it in keeping with the character of the Wife herself?

17. If the old hag in the Wife of Bath's Tale is really changed into a beautiful woman at the end, what happens to the force of her preceding argument that ugliness and age (along with poverty and social democracy) have their own value?

18. If the Pardoner is a greedy and scheming hypocrite, why does he confess his villainy so openly in his Prologue? Does he really think that, after all this, the other pilgrims will become customers of his?

19. The Pardoner says that, although his real motive is not to make people better, he does make them better. Is this true? For example, does he make them less greedy or does he encourage their greed?

20. The Pardoner inserts in his Tale a sermon against an assortment of vices. Does this interruption make his Tale more or less effective?

21. In the Pardoner's Tale, what significance has the old man who directs the three young sinners to the place where they can find Death? How does he contribute to the atmosphere of the story?

22. Taking the Pardoner's Prologue and Tale together, what sorts of irony do you discover?

23. The Nun's Priest's Tale contains grisly anecdotes (not to mention philosophical speculation) within a light-hearted mock-epic beast fable within a realistic setting (the widow and her daughters). What is the effect of this boxes-within-boxes structure? Which layer of meaning seems the most real?

24. The Nun's Priest's Tale, like the Wife of Bath's and the Pardoner's Tales, can be read as having a moral. What is it? Do the three tales have a moral in the same sense of the word?

25. What is there in the Nun's Priest's Tale that seems in keeping with the priest's situation?

26. Do you actually visualize Chanticleer and Pertelote as a rooster and a hen? As neither? Both? As different things at different times?

Christine de Pizan

Study of The Book of the City of Ladies should probably put the emphasis where Christine de Pizan herself put it: on feminist issues. But it has much to offer the student of the Middle Ages in other ways, too. Its allegorical method is worth close attention (and comparison with Everyman, perhaps). Its way of reasoning through appeal to authority and use of exempla is thoroughly medieval, as are its assumptions about history.

1. The opening section is, appropriately, somewhat different in tone from the allegorical sections that follow. It approaches psychological realism in its account of Christine's falling into despair and hatred of her femininity. How does this section prepare us for the rest of the book, and how does the appearance of the three ladies counter the "series of authorities" that seem to overwhelm Christine in the first section "like a gushing fountain"?

2. The three principal virtues in Christian doctrine are Faith, Hope, and Charity. Yet Christine makes her virtuous ladies represent Reason, Rectitude, and Justice. Why does she select these three qualities as her defense against despair? (Charity Cannon Willard: "Reason, Rectitude, and Justice are primarily secular Virtues come to offer lessons in prudence mondaine [worldly prudence], which they make clear in the course of The Book of the Three Virtues.")

3. The ladies carry symbolic scepters: Reason, a mirror; Rectitude, a ruler; and Justice, a cup. What is the appropriateness of each?

4. In the course of the book, Christine moves through conversations with Reason, Rectitude, and Justice, in that order. Do the topics of conversation fit the ladies? That is, is her conversation with Reason notably reasonable, etc?

5. What is Christine's view of history? In a section omitted here, she expresses a special affinity with the goddess Minerva because she, too, was "an Italian woman." Is there any "depth" to Christine's view of history? She methodically includes in her examples women from classical mythology, the Bible, ancient history, and her own day, but all are treated the same. Her sense of history is very medieval in that any sense of historical change is subordinated to timeless, universal categories.

6. Is the central metaphor of the City appropriate to the subject? What are its implications?

7. What is Christine's characteristic mode of argument? Take a typical passage, perhaps the passage in which she considers the question of whether women have any capacity for science, and analyze her reasoning. What does she accept as evidence?

8. What is Christine's tone in the argumentative sections? (Earl Jeffrey Richards: "Her view of women is not antithetically constructed; that is, her idealization of women does not represent an automatic antithesis to the demonization of women found in misogynist writers. She is not a prisoner of the literary cliches of her sources and of her opponents.")

9. The life of St. Christine which ends the anthology selection is likely to seem absurd to modern readers. And yet it occupies the same climactic place in the entire book that it does in the selection. What is the effect of giving the saint's life this emphasis? What implications does it have for Christine's argument?

Everyman

The content of Everyman is not difficult; it presents in a remarkably stark but thoroughly orthodox fashion the world-view of the medieval church: life as a struggle between good and evil, salvation as the central goal of life, the things of this world as fleeting and insignificant, and the church as a necessary guide to salvation. The complex and powerful theatrical realization of this content is more difficult to grasp, especially when the play is merely read rather than seen. A film of a production of the play is a valuable aid to teaching it; one such film (53 minutes), produced in conjunction with the medievalist Howard Schless, is distributed by Insight Media. Another option is to have the class act out scenes from the play. It's easy enough to rough out the basic areas of a medieval stage in the classroom and to have members of the class walk through a few scenes. Hearing the lines out loud will help the class feel the theatrical power of the rough, earnest verse, and thinking through problems of staging will help them understand the effectiveness of such physical elements as the long procession to the grave, behind the cross, which leads up to Everyman's descent into the grave. Such concrete experience will also make clear how the allegorical elements in Everyman work: not to reduce human experience to shadowy abstractions but on the contrary to give abstract concepts an earthy, urgent reality, as when death, for example, is represented in that memorable stage image of Everyman literally climbing down into a grave.

1. How is Everyman structured?

The surface naivete of Everyman conceals a quite sophisticated structure, which can be imagined as V-shaped. The play begins frankly in the theater with a presenter figure (the Messenger), progresses to Heaven and God's conversation with Death, moves to Earth and the main action of the play, then after Everyman's death moves back to Heaven with the Angel's speech, and ends back in the theater with another presenter character, the Doctor. The sequence of scenes thus forms a sort of envelope: Theater--Heaven--Earth--Heaven--Theater. The main turning point of the action--the point of the "V"--is in almost precisely the center of the play (lines 462 ff.), where Everyman, having been rejected by Fellowship, Kindred and Cousin, and Goods, begins to succeed in finding supporters to accompany him to the grave.

2. What is the verse form of Everyman and how is it varied to fit the dramatic action?

The basic verse form is irregular but predominantly iambic tetrameter lines, irregularly rhymed (AA, ABAB, ABBA, etc.) and usually with feminine endings. There are also a number of three-stressed lines, usually with masculine endings. These three-stressed lines tend to cluster at points of heightened dramatic interest. Compare the speeches of God and Death, for example, at lines 66 ff., where God speaks predominantly in the three-beat lines, Death in the four-beat ones.

3. How is Everyman characterized?

It is important to trace Everyman's gradual transformation in the face of death, from the shallow rationalizations of the initial scene with Death, to the crucial soliloquy beginning in line 463 in which he begins to repent ("Then of myself I was ashamed, / And so I am worthy to be blamed"), to the gradual recovery in the last half. The class might want to consider, among other questions of staging, whether Everyman should be presented as old or young. Has he reached his full allotment of years, or is he cut off prematurely?

4. How are the personified abstractions characterized?

The playwright does not rely upon loose identifications but carefully makes the companions illustrate what they represent, sometimes with only a brief, deft touch, as in Beauty's wonderful line (802): "I take my cap in my lap and am gone."

5. What other uses of allegory appear in the play, and with what effect?

Besides the personified characters, the class should note that sins are bonds which tie Good Deeds to the ground, Knowledge is Good Deeds' sister, penance is a literal whip, confession is a literal river as well as a "holy man," contrition is a garment, and death is a literal hole in the ground. All of these touches have unexpected implications that can be explored.

6. What is the significance of the order in which Everyman's friends drop out of the final procession?

The class should note, in addition to the order of the other friends, that Good Deeds can go into the grave with Everyman, a distinctly Catholic touch. Protestants would have Faith be the ultimate companion.

Francis Petrarch

Petrarch's poems, most teachers find, are very teachable. They are simple enough to be accessible and yet complex enough to offer plenty of material for close reading. The stance of the entranced, obsessed lover is familiar, too (though it may generate a little healthy, skeptical laughter), but the variations Petrarch works on that stance repay extended study. Translation, as always, drops a veil between poet and reader, but Anthony Mortimer's translations are so accurate and sensitive that the veil is exceptionally thin in the case of Petrarch. The translations are fine English poems in their own right and are worth close verbal analysis.

1. What is a Petrarchan sonnet? What variations does Petrarch work within the limits of the form?

Poem I can serve as a good example here, both for form (fourteen lines of iambic pentameter, rhymed ABBA♥ABBA CDE CDE), and for structure, the arrangement of the thought. The relationship between octave and sestet is especially worth noting. Here each is one long sentence, with the octave devoted to the past, the sestet to the present. This arrangement may be contrasted with other sonnets in the selection.

2. How does Petrarch present Laura in these poems?

The poems are short on physical description of Laura. Frequently, she is merely a shadowy presence, a daydream, or a memory. When she is described, it is often in fragmentary impressions, as in Poem CXXVI, where we glimpse only "the fair limbs," "the angelic breast," "those fair eyes," and other subjectively rendered parts of the whole. Similar representations are worth noting in the poems.

3. What does Laura mean to Petrarch?

Thomas Bergin's analysis of the "four Lauras," cited in the introduction, is a good starting point here. But Laura's role in each individual poem should be worked out carefully.

4. What kinds of self-revelation does Petrarch engage in in these poems?

5. Compare Poem XC with its source in Virgil's Aeneid, Book I.

6. How does Petrarch use imagery?

This question, of course, is relevant to each of the poems, from Poem III, with its dominant series of military images, to Poem CCCLXV, with its journey metaphors.

7. Analyze Petrarch's use of the canzone form in Poems CXXVI and CXXIX.

8. Trace the psychological progress of the speaker in Poem CXXVI. What retrospective light does the envoi throw on the earlier part of the poem?

9. Trace allusions to art in Poem CXXIX. What relationship between love and art is suggested? Compare the treatment of the relationship in Poem CXXVI.

10. Analyze the poetic rhetoric of Poem CXXXIV.

   This is the most extreme example of "Petrarchism" among the selections, especially in its stylized and artificial use of antithesis and hyperbole. The combination of high passion and extreme artificiality is worth analyzing as a recurring feature in Petrarch.

Giovanni Boccaccio

      Students may have heard of Boccaccio, if in no other way, as the author of "ribald classics." Without detracting from his reputation as a master of that kind of humor, which is represented in the anthology, teachers will probably want to emphasize his wider range and how that range helps put in perspective each of the individual tales. If time allows, it is desirable to assign all the tales included (even if one can't discuss them all), so as to preserve this sense of general context and tone; for example, the Petrarchan mood of the songs at the end of the day becomes more meaningful when posed against the earthiness of some of the stories. All the ones included, along with much of the framing, are variations on the theme of love and the related theme of the roles of the sexes, viewing these matters from a striking variety of angles. This common theme can provide continuity to class discussions. The selections later in the anthology from Marguerite de Navarre's Heptameron, which was inspired by Boccaccio's precedent, also deal with variations on love and therefore make an especially intriguing set of companion assignments.

1. Is Boccaccio's storytelling technique similar to that of modern short-story writers?

2. Besides being sexually bold, some of Boccaccio's stories are very irreverent about religion. Does this mean that he is anti-religious? Compare the tone in which people today tell ethnic or religious or racial jokes.

3. Does any general attitude toward women emerge from The Decameron?

4. Both The Decameron and Chaucer's Canterbury Tales are collections of stories told, by pre-arrangement, by fictional characters. The time of both is the fourteenth century. Is Chaucer's world the same world we see in Boccaccio? The occasion for Boccaccio's stories is a deadly plague, for Chaucer's a religious pilgrimage; how important is this difference?

5. The contrast between the horrifying setting of the plague and the serene, luxurious country retreat where the tales are told is extreme. Is the contrast too great? Does it make the young people's amusements seem too frivolous? Does it enhance our enjoyment of the setting and the tales? Are we to make any moral judgment on the young people's decision to escape from Florence?

6. While the women are discussing their planned departure from Florence, Filomena, who is called "prudent," says that the seven of them should have men with them, since women don't manage very well on their own. Is this opinion in keeping with what we see and read later?

7. In the story of Alibech and the desert hermit (Third Day, Tenth Tale), what role does the religious setting play? If the story were not somewhat blasphemous, would it have much point?

8. In the same tale, we find a situation common in bawdy stories and jokes: the inability of a man to satisfy the sexual demands of a lusty woman. Why should this situation be considered especially funny? Could the sexes be reversed in such situations?

9. The story of Friar Alberto and Madonna Lisetta (Fourth Day, Second Tale) also has a

religious context. Compare the Annunciation story in Luke, chapter 1. How does the context give point to the story? Does Boccaccio's intention correspond to Fiammetta's in telling the story?

10. In the tale of the sodomist Pietro and his wife (Fifth Day, Tenth Tale), why is it ironic that he calls down the fire of heaven against the "vile generation" of unfaithful wives?

11. In the same story, the old woman who provides Pietro's wife with lovers is a rather mysterious figure, and what she says seems important. What do you make of her and of her mixture of devotional piety and earthiness? In defining women's role in terms of sex, is she boasting or being bitter? How funny is this story?

Students can also be invited to compare her with Chaucer's Wife of Bath as an advocate for women.

12. What is the function of the songs that end the day? What is their tone? Note the ribald song that, at the end of the fifth day, Dioneo offers to sing before he chooses a more acceptable one. Compare this song with Petrarch's treatment of Laura and Dante's of Beatrice.

13. The story of patient Griselda (Tenth Day, Tenth Tale) has an obvious climactic place in the collection, as the very last of the hundred stories. The reaction of the listeners is understated; the ladies take "first one part and then another." The teller, Dioneo, introduces the tale ambiguously, condemning the "silly brutality" of Gualtieri and remarking that he did not deserve the "good" that came of his behavior in the end. What themes introduced earlier in The Decameron does the story treat? What does it say about the nature of love and the relationship between the sexes?

14. Everybody in the story of Griselda admires and loves her. Are we to take the same view of her?

15. In the Conclusion, Boccaccio defends himself against objections to the bawdy stories in the book. What is his tone? Are his arguments and analogies convincing?

Niccolò Machiavelli

Twentieth-century scholarship has gone a long way toward redeeming Machiavelli from his old image as the devil incarnate, but in many respects the text of The Prince as most students will read it seems to support the old image, and for that matter scholars are not at one in trying to launder him. Teachers whose minds are still open on this matter may face a difficult teaching decision, wanting to steer their students away from mere scandalized horror while not asking them either to disregard what the text seems to be saying fairly emphatically. Moreover, the "machiavel" is an interesting literary archetype to explore and define, whether Machiavelli really was one himself or not. One solution to these difficulties is to invite students to read passages for the different meanings that emerge if one makes different assumptions about Machiavelli--that he really was a black-hearted machiavel, that he was a virtuous ironist disgustedly "recommending" evil as outrageously as possible, that he was not immoral but a modern political realist, that he was an opportunist trying to regain office, and any other hypotheses that may seem plausible. Among other things, this method will alert students to nuances of tone that, in turn, may hold part of the key to Machiavelli's meaning.

1. Someone once said that certain great Renaissance writers, especially the humanists, had a peculiar ability to seal off hermetically part of their mind from the rest of it. Does this description fit Machiavelli?

2. Machiavelli is fond of saying that either such-and-such is true or such-and-such is true, sometimes subdividing each category into equally well separated options or possibilities. What quality of mind is implied by this habit of classification? Is the method appropriate in The Prince?

3. In the first paragraph of Chapter XV, Machiavelli contrasts the "real truth of the matter" with "its imagination," and "how we live" with "how we ought to live." This passage would seem to state a basic premise of The Prince. If we accept Machiavelli's premise here, are we bound to endorse his general attitude in the book as a whole?

4. To many readers, Machiavelli's statement in Chapter XVII that "men forget more easily the death of their father than the loss of their patrimony" shows the author at his most cynical. Much of The Prince seems to depend on assumptions about human nature similar to this one. Is this statement by Machiavelli true or false?

5. In Chapter XVIII, Machiavelli states that a prince needs to follow the animal in himself rather than, exclusively, the human in himself. To what extent is this a mere figure of speech? What is Machiavelli saying about human nature?

6. Does Chapter XXVI, on the liberation of Italy, put the earlier parts of The Prince in a new light?

Marguerite de Navarre

The Heptameron plays nicely into the instructor's hand, since discussion questions are built into the work itself, in the form of the post-mortem dialogues among the storytellers and their listeners. (Consequently, the discussion questions below raise general issues about the work instead of focusing on specific stories.) Moreover, the issues raised in these debates have a sure-fire human interest, raising questions about the psychology and ethics of love, about the relationship between the sexes, and about fundamental human values, that are perennially important. But questions of theme and value are not the only ones that are inherent in the text of The Heptameron; like The Divine Comedy, The Canterbury Tales,, and The Decameron, Marguerite's work is a self-reflexive one that at least implies strongly certain questions about the nature of fiction and of imaginative literature.

1. A number of the stories in The Heptameron are about cheating in sex, love, and marriage. Is this issue handled as Boccaccio would have handled it? Do Marguerite's stories have more "moral" morals?

2. Marguerite and her stand-in, Parlamente, seem to be Platonic idealists. How does their idealism fare in the work? Are the stories more concerned with worldly or with unworldly wisdom?

3. The Heptameron is often regarded, rightly, as a serious investigation of ethical, moral, and spiritual issues. Does the humor present in some of the stories interfere with these serious purposes or enrich them?

4. Which of the stories in the anthology could be most easily excerpted from the work and printed in, say, a short-story anthology as a self-contained artistic whole, without the accompanying discussion?

5. The stories in The Heptameron are supposed to be taken from real life, not from fiction. In fact, however, some of them have literary sources. What does the claim of factuality amount to? Does it make any difference to the reader whether or not the stories relate actual occurrences? Do the stories sound more like events in actual life than like invented stories?

6. The Heptameron has feminist implications. Is it possible to define the exact nature of Marguerite's feminism? Does it take the form of social protest? Is it rooted in religious or philosophical positions? Are men and women treated fairly by the author? Are any of the characters conscious and deliberate feminists?

7. Marguerite was Queen of Navarre, the sister of the King of France, and an influential figure in the political and public life of the sixteenth century. Is there anything in the stories that suggests these facts about her? Does her knowledge of human nature seem limited to the aristocracy?

8. In religion, Marguerite was a Roman Catholic with what some of her contemporaries considered a dangerous leaning toward Reformation principles. Does her religious position help us understand the stories?

9. The Heptameron, as far as we know, remained unfinished, never reaching the projected

length of a hundred stories. Imagine that you were asked to help finish it. Invent a plot and characters that you think would fit in with the kind of concerns the volume emphasizes. By what rules, if any, for plot, theme, structure, and characterization would you feel guided?

Michel de Montaigne

There are a number of pieces of non-fictional prose in Literature of the Western World up to this point--Plato's Republic and Apology, Aristotle's Poetics, specimens of philosophic thinking by Anselm and Aquinas, Machiavelli's The Prince--but Montaigne's work offers the first opportunity to teach the art of the personal essay. And what an opportunity! The main features of the personal essay are fully developed in these examples by the creator of the form: the loose structure, the attention to the ordinary and the everyday, the intimate tone, the self-revelation, and the tentative, unsystematic quality that gave essays their name ("attempts"). The class will probably be as interested in Montaigne and his new literary form as in the content of the essays.

1. Analyze Montaigne's consideration of the question of the origins of America in "Of Cannibals" as an example of his characteristic ways of speculation.

Note especially how he moves back and forth among "testimony from antiquity," homely analogies from his own experience, and common-sense speculation.

2. The key word in "Of Cannibals" is barbarism. How does Montaigne define and redefine this word?

3. What do you think of the values and customs of the cannibal society in the essay? How serious is Montaigne's praise of it? Does he use the cannibal society merely as a pretext to criticize his own society?

4. In studying the "Apology for Raymond Sebond," it is a good exercise to make a short outline of Montaigne's argument. If the bare bones of its structure are apparent, it is easier to see how Montaigne elaborates it and, in the process, to some degree undermines and subverts it.

5. What is Montaigne's tone in the "Apology"? For example, how seriously are we to take Montaigne's statement in the section headed "Second objection to Sebond and defense" that the best way to deal with those who find Sebond's arguments weak is "to crush and trample underfoot human arrogance and pride" and "to make them bow their heads and bite the ground beneath the authority and reverence of divine majesty"? Is there any irony in such a statement?

6. Montaigne studs his essays with quotations from other writers, especially classical ones. How does he use these quotations? Examine a few examples. Does the quotation always merely confirm Montaigne's point?

7. One of the most striking features of the "Apology" is the way it combines the most cosmic statements with the homiest of references. For example, in discussing "Human beings' place in creation," Montaigne suddenly asks, "When I play with my cat, who knows if I am not a pastime to her more than she is to me?" Find other such earthy references. From what areas does Montaigne draw them?

8. In the section headed "Human beings have no knowledge," Montaigne displays a great deal of knowledge. How does he use the word? (Knowledge is almost as important a word in the "Apology" as barbarism is in "Of Cannibals.") Trace the transformations this word

undergoes in Montaigne's hands.

9. In the entire essay, but perhaps especially in the section headed "We cannot rely on our senses," Montaigne develops what amounts to an informal theory of psychology. What is it? What mix of knowledge, ignorance, reason, passion, and instinct makes up human nature?

10. Examine Montaigne's conclusion, that "to hope to straddle more than the reach of our legs is impossible and unnatural" and that human beings can be raised above the human level only by God. What ambiguities are there in this conclusion? Is Montaigne advising us to throw ourselves into God's hands or to be content to "straddle" only what our legs can reach--or perhaps both?

Miguel de Cervantes Saavedra

It is always somewhat less than satisfactory to read a novel in an abridged version. But in the case of Don Quixote, the novel is so long and complex that a case could be made that a study of key scenes is a good first encounter with the book and can prepare the student to read the whole novel more intelligently, as we of course hope he or she will. The selection in the anthology has been made in such a way that it not only provides major scenes that can be studied individually but also suggests something of the novel's progression and overall shape.

1. Analyze the first paragraph of the novel carefully to define the narrative voice. Who is telling the story? What does he think of Don Quixote? Note that he says Quixote's name is reported as Quixada or Quesada, but "reasonably conjectures," on no evidence, that his real name was Quixana, and then asserts that in telling the story he will "swerve not a jot from the truth." What questions of art and reality does such a line of reasoning raise? How does Quixote's meditation on the number of wounds Don Belianis received raise the same questions, and what is the relation between Quixote's view of the subject and the narrator's?

2. Examine the events of the first sally (Part I, Chapters II-IV): the adventures at the inn, the encounter with the countryman beating his servant, and the encounter with the Toledo Traders. How is Quixote characterized in these initial episodes? Do we have any sympathy for him? Note that, like Belianis, he receives a great many wounds here and through the rest of the novel; what is the effect of all this violence?

3. As the novel progresses, a vivid sense of Don Quixote's world is gradually established. What is Spain like in Don Quixote--geographically, socially, and morally? What is the "reality" like to which Quixote opposes his idealism?

4. Cide Hamete Benengeli is first introduced, in this section, at the beginning of Chapter XXII. Trace references to him through the rest of the selection; see especially the ending of Part I, the passage at the end of Part II, Chapter II, and the ending of Part II. What is the function of this imaginary author? What is his relationship to the main narrative voice? What layers of fictionality does Cervantes suggest by introducing Cide Hamete?

5. The incident of the galley slaves (Part I, Chapter XXII) introduces a new moral complexity in Quixote's adventures. What questions does the episode raise?

6. Gines de Pasamonte (Part I, Chapter XXII) seems to be a foil to Quixote, and his book The Life of Gines de Pasamonte parallels Don Quixote in some ways. Explore these parallels.

7. Trace Sancho Panza through the novel. What is his attitude toward Quixote and how does it change? How do his conflicts echo those of Quixote?

8. Summarize the differences between Parts I and II. Which do you prefer? Why?

9. As the issues in Quixote's character are echoed and reflected in Sancho Panza, so are they also echoed in the minor characters. Analyze, from this point of view, the curate and the barber, Antonia Quixana, Don Diego de Miranda, and Sanson Carrasco. Pay special

attention to Carrasco. He has been called a "false Quixote"; is he? (Note especially his association with disguises, deceptions, and mirrors.)

10. What is the function of the adventure of the lions (Part II, Chapter XVII)?

11. Trace the conflict of realism and idealism through the episode of the Cave of Montesinos (Part II, Chapters XXII-XXIV).

       This is one of the richest and most suggestive episodes in the novel. Ironically, Cide Hamete is said to reject it as incredible (Part II, Chapter XXIV), though it is eminently believable: Quixote has simply fallen asleep and had a dream in the cave. In this dream within a multilayered fiction, some of Quixote's deepest characteristics emerge, especially his "Alonso Quixana" ones: the earthy skepticism and interest in prosaic fact that he represses when he is pursuing his "real" dream of knight-errantry.

12. What are we to think of Quixote's deathbed renunciation of knight-errantry? Now that he is "sane," why does Sanson Carrasco beg him to "come to his senses" and become a pastoral shepherd?

13. Explore the ironies and ambiguities of the last paragraph of the novel, including its attribution to Cide Hamete, its denunciation of the "false Quixote," and the insistence that the book's sole purpose has been to "arouse men's scorn for the false and absurd stories of knight-errantry."

William Shakespeare

It could easily be argued that Henry IV introduces students to a greater variety of Shakespearean modes than any other of his plays. Traditionally classed among his histories, it is also a comedy and a tragedy. (His eight plays on fifteenth-century English history are also considered by some critics to be Shakespeare's contribution to the epic genre.) The play's status as history is centered on the King, Prince Hal, and the Percies in their dimension as public figures; as comedy and tragedy it is centered on, respectively, Falstaff and Hotspur. Shakespeare's fabled gifts for creating character are brilliantly realized in these two men, and indeed Falstaff may well be the greatest of all comic figures. But virtually all the characters, major and minor, are fully realized: the King and the Prince, Hotspur's wife Kate, the Hostess, Glendower, Gloucester, Bardolph, the Douglas, and several others. Even characters who appear only through second-hand report are memorable, such as the foppish popinjay of a courtier who so maddens the battle-heated Hotspur. The construction represents Shakespeare's plotting at its best. His skill with double plots is nowhere more effectively realized: the high-political plot and the low-life tavern plot not only provide bracing tonal variety but also comment mordantly on each other, for both comic and serious purposes.

Especially for students newly acquainted with Shakespeare, it is supremely desirable that his plays come alive as performance, at least on records and preferably staged or (more likely) on film. Most of us can remember what a revelation it was the first time the rhythms, emphases, and nuances of Shakespeare's language came alive for us in this way, and moreover how thereafter our alertness to the printed versions even of plays we had not seen was enhanced by our trying to "perform" them in our own minds. Henry IV is especially valuable in this respect, since the voices of the characters--the literal sound of their speech--is so closely attuned to their personalities and to the various dramatic contexts.

One of the most valuable tools for teaching Shakespeare is a concordance. For example, to locate the references to honor in the play and then consider the passages where they occur makes one immediately aware of the multiple perspectives on honor and its thematic function.

1. Bear in mind that Shakespeare's plays were performed outdoors, by daylight, on a stage almost bare of scenery. Consider how the language creates the setting in such scenes as the nighttime robbery (II.1-2).

Scene II. 1 is also interesting for its earthy atmosphere. One can hardly help thinking of two modern semi-trailer drivers checking out their rigs and gossiping about their cargoes at a truck stop.

2. Henry IV is about half verse and half prose. Can we see why the prose scenes are in prose and the verse scenes in verse?

3. Look at the long speech with which the King opens the first scene of the play. What sound has his voice? What kind of rhetoric does he use? What is the state of his mind and conscience?

The blank-verse rhythm is stately (note the five consecutive unpunctuated lines 23-27). The images are bold, emphatic, and startling. On the other hand, the King's guilt over his treatment of the dethroned and murdered Richard II is apparent in his intention to make a penitential crusading pilgrimage to the Holy Land.

4. Shakespeare's stage had little scenery and thus was especially dependent on language for its effects. The quality of individual characters' voices is therefore especially important. Examine individual characters and describe how their voices sound.

The king's voice was discussed in connection with the preceding question. Glendower, in III.i., is sonorously vatic (which is part of what drives the anti-"poetic" Hotspur wild). Hotspur's wife Kate, in II.iii and III.i, is sometimes wheedlingly, playfully "feminine," sometimes impatiently downright rather in the manner of her husband. When she uses coy, delicate expressions like "in good sooth," Hotspur protests: "Swear me, Kate, like a lady as thou art, / A good mouth-filling oath . . . ." Falstaff has a variety of voices: the most typical seems short-winded, the staccato puffings of an old, fat man. At other times (in his "repentant sinner ruined by bad company" vein) he can sigh ruefully. In his anticipatory parody of the King's upcoming interview with Hal, Falstaff can sound mock-innocent and long-windedly euphuistic (to the delight of the Hostess). We learn from Kate's loving elegy for Hotspur in Part Two, II.iii, that his "blemish" was "speaking thick," which may mean that he had a speech impediment. When he is played that way, the tension between the impediment and his headlong, uninterruptible torrents of language (as in I.iii) can convey a powerful nervous energy. His dying phrase, in V.iv, "No, Percy, thou art dust, / And food for ---," can be heard as ending in a stammer: "for w--w--w--." With grave courtesy, the Prince completes the sentence for his dead opposite: "For worms, brave Percy." The pathos is piercing.

5. Look at Prince Hal's soliloquy at the end of I.ii, in which he reveals that in associating with his low-life companions he is merely biding his time, playing the dissolute ne'er-do-well so that his eventual adoption of his serious, royal role will have greater éclat. What light does this throw on his personality? Does the speech make him seem unattractively cold-blooded or attractively in control of his future? (It has sometimes been argued that this kind of question is on the wrong track, since the soliloquy is merely Shakespeare's way of conveying information and is not to be understood as psychological self-revelation.)

One might want to quote for the class the Prince's stern repudiation of Falstaff in Part Two, V.v: "I know thee not, old man. Fall to thy prayers . . . ." In any case, the Prince's prudence and calculation are to be contrasted with Hotspur's rash impetuosity; which man emerges as more attractive can be debated.

6. Consider the theme of honor in the play. How do different characters understand its meaning and importance?

One could start the discussion with Falstaff's skeptical speech about honor at the end of V.i.

7. Consider, near the end of III.i., the contrast between Hotspur's unsentimental brusqueness toward Kate and the (to Hotspur, sickening) soupiness of the newlyweds, Mortimer and Glendower's daughter. Are we to infer that Hotspur does not love his wife strongly?

8. In III.i., a quarrelsome Hotspur tells Glendower that he (Hotspur) hates poetry--"mincing poetry," as he calls it--and that it sets his teeth on edge. But is not Hotspur himself a poet?

See, for example, from his soliloquy opening II.iii, such lines as "out of this nettle danger we pluck this flower safety," and "I could brain him with his lady's fan."

9. Examine the ways in which the "high" action of the play, involving national politics and war, is echoed or parodied in the "low" action. What tone emerges from the juxtaposition? Do the "low" scenes undermine the gravity of the "high" action?

Of many cases in point, the most elaborate is the rehearsal (II.iv) staged by Falstaff and Hal of the latter's forthcoming interview with his father (III.ii). Note too that, at the very moment of high tragedy when Hal kills Hotspur, Falstaff saves his own life at the hands of the Douglas, by playing dead.

10. In III.ii, the King chides Hal not only for his immoral way of living but also for what the King considers bad political tactics: making himself too visible to the common people, in contrast with the King's careful rationing of his public appearances. Which of the two, father or son, seems the better politician?

11. Scene III.i shows the insurgents as dividing England among themselves, an immensely serious matter for Shakespeare's audience. Is it appropriate that this scene should also contain so much comedy?

12. The famous Shakespearean critic A. C. Bradley cited Falstaff as one of Shakespeare's four most marvelous achievements in characterization (along with Hamlet, Cleopatra, and Iago). What is marvelous about Falstaff?

Part of a conversation overheard by one of the anthology editors: "Falstaff is one of the most complex characters ever invented." "On the contrary, Falstaff's greatness lies, precisely, in his utter simplicity."

13. Several of the comic scenes involving Falstaff are displays of gamesmanship, on the most elaborate level. Comment on this aspect of the comedy in the play.

When someone is setting someone else up, it is often very hard to know how much awareness there is on both sides. In the long scene II.iv, set in the tavern, the proposed joke is to set Falstaff to lying about his desperate plight and valiant exploits during the robbery, then expose his lying. But Falstaff is much too smart to fall for this in any simple way, and it's clear (from his transparent self-contradictions about the number of his opponents, for example) that he is play-acting himself. The jesters intend to pin Falstaff to a lie, and to a certain extent they do, but they almost certainly expect him to land on his feet somehow and probably would be disappointed if he did not. Similarly, when, during the robbery itself, the aged rake Falstaff ludicrously cries out, "They hate us youth," we can't be quite sure for whose benefit this absurdity is uttered and at whom the comic barb is aimed.

14. In the latter part of the play, we see Falstaff in command of troops, in which capacity he is thoroughly corrupt and irresponsible. Is this a continuation of the comedy or do we have to revise our earlier impression of Falstaff?

John Donne

Literature courses are inevitably, among other things, courses in reading skills, and the skill that Donne's poems require is "close reading" or textual explication. It is paradoxical that the poems, whose effect depends so much on rapid thought, lightning associations, and sudden shifts of direction, should require slow, methodical analysis. But they do, at least for most of us; only after this kind of analysis can a second, less labored kind of reading capture the mercurial quality of the poems. A good starting point for reading a Donne poem is often dramatic situation: who is talking to whom and in what context? This leads inevitably into persona and tone. Consideration of form similarly leads to analysis of structure. Beyond that, the main task is careful line-by-line, sometimes word-by-word, analysis of syntax, diction, and figures of speech.

1. Who is the speaker in these poems? Is there more than one, or does it seem to be the same person in different moods and situations?

2. Love is the subject of most of these poems. What dimensions of love are treated? Compare, for example, "The Funeral," "A Valediction: Forbidding Mourning," and "Elegy XIX: To His Mistress Going to Bed."

3. Donne is famous for the range of allusions and specialized lore in his poems. "A Valediction: Forbidding Mourning," for example, uses the famous, unexpected image of two souls as a draftsman's compass, while "The Canonization" draws for references upon numismatics, medicine, law, medieval iconography, mythology, theology, linguistics, and optics. What is the effect of this bookishness? Does it seem cold and calculated? Or, on the contrary, does it make the speaker seem more real? Do the poems differ from one another in this respect?

4. A recurring theme in these poems is the relationship between the individual or the couple and a vaster world, as in "The Good-Morrow." On the other hand, Donne can achieve a microscopic diminishment, as in "The Flea," where a tiny insect becomes not only a marriage bed but a temple. It's as if--someone once said--Donne were a kind of physicist of love, alternatively imaging it as cosmological and as subnuclear. What is the effect of these shifts of scale in (and within) his poems?

5. Samuel Johnson disliked conceits (a term, incidentally, that many students will have to have explained for them) as used by Donne and other "Metaphysical poets": "The most heterogeneous ideas are yoked by violence together; nature and art are ransacked for illustrations, comparisons, and allusions; their learning instructs, and their subtlety surprises; but the reader commonly thinks his improvement dearly bought, and, though he sometimes admires, is seldom pleased." Do you agree with this judgment? Select a number of conceits from the poems and analyze the way they "yoke" ideas. Does Johnson miss some of the pleasures of the Metaphysical method?

6. Examine the Holy Sonnets X and XIV and the "Hymn to God the Father." What similarities do the religious poems have with the love poems?

7. Donne tends to use tight, highly structured verse forms and then to take great liberties within them. Look at the first stanza of "The Good-Morrow," for example, for the way he introduces pauses or caesuras into the pentameter line, or at the one-syllable feet in the

second line of Holy Sonnet XIV. The variations in the first example seem to give a personal conversational rhythm to the lines; those in the second example imitate the "battering" that is the subject of the poem. Explain the reasons for some of Donne's rhythmic variations in these and other poems.

8. Donne's poetry is a reaction against the Petrarchan tradition in poetry. Look back on Petrarch's poems and identify the elements in them that Donne rejects.

9. Donne is famous for treating religion as sex and vice versa. Which of these two strategies works best? Which is the more startling?

John Milton

Sometimes considered the gateway to much of subsequent literature, Paradise Lost also caps the traditions heralded at the beginning of Volume One in the Old Testament and Homer and refocused midway through the volume in the New Testament and Virgil. That a poem so vastly different from the Homeric epics as Milton's should have been considered by him to be in a direct line of descent can present students with a challenging, indeed mind-bending exercise in literary perspective.

People teaching Paradise Lost for the first time are often surprised at how well the work, so erudite and far removed from familiar speech (even of the seventeenth century), goes over with students, though perhaps the surprise should not be excessive if Milton really is one of the half-dozen or so greatest poets of the world. The fact seems to be that the grand style can and does appeal to students. The theological issues should probably be addressed; they are even more deeply intrinsic to the poem's message and effect than such issues are in Dante. Students are not bored by Milton's theology; the problem of foreknowledge, determinism, and predestination often interests them at least as an abstract problem in reasoning, and the theme of free will, authority, and rebellion can easily be translated, without cheapening, into other and more modern political and societal contexts. A number of other live issues of sensibility and values also suggest themselves, including the hoary arguments about the portraits of God and Satan and the feminist issue of Eve's status relative to Adam and God, a sore point at least since Mary Wollstonecraft joined battle over it in the eighteenth century.

1. Paradise Lost is full of references and allusions to ancient pagan literature. What various functions do they serve?

2. Much of the effect of Paradise Lost is achieved through its style. What are the characteristic marks of this style?

Among them are the inversion of normal word order (IX.41-43), omission of words normally necessary to the sense (I.141-42), the use of one part of speech for another (I.193), Latinisms (IX.328), the piling up of proper names (IV.268-85), the suspension of the thought and sentence construction (I.1-6), learned allusions (IV.210-14), extended similes, often in two or more parts (I.761-88), reflections of sense in sound (I.209), and tension between the verse paragraph and the pentameter line unit (III.40-55). In this last connection, note for example the verbal explosions at the beginnings of lines 52-54. It is a distinctive mark of Milton's blank verse that he so often places verbs and verbals (gerunds, participles, infinitives) at the beginning or end of a line.

3. Milton's handling of chronology owes something to the epic tradition, with its method of beginning in the middle of things, but some readers think his structure also foreshadows the twentieth-century modernists by his bends and loops in the time-line. Can you make a case for this position?

4. Paradise Lost is an epic, and epics are built on models and ideals of heroism. What is heroism, and who is heroic by Milton's standards?

5. It can be argued that the central theme of Paradise Lost is the nature of freedom. How

does Milton understand it? What modern definitions of freedom are closest to his and farthest from it? Is Eve's dependency on Adam consistent with a meaningful notion of freedom?

6. What role does external nature play in Paradise Lost? Is the landscape of Eden, for example, decorative and atmospheric or is it symbolic? What is implied by the changes in nature that take place in consequence of the human fall?

In connection with the last of these questions, it might be interesting to consider the view of many recent evolutionary psychologists, to the effect that human values are often rooted in the distant past in the opposite way, originating in evasive actions in response to the threat of death or extinction at the hands of the natural environment.

7. Milton is noted for the psychological skill with which he adapts the extended "epic simile." See, for example, I.761-92, where the fallen angels are compared to jousting medieval knights, bees, pygmies, and fairy elves. Why are these comparisons effective here? Find other such similes and analyze them for their psychological implications.

8. Satan is portrayed as a determined enemy of God's monarchy. Milton spent much of his life defending rebellion against political monarchy in England. Some people find these facts paradoxical. Do you think they should?

9. Trace the history of Satan from his earliest condition as we know it to the last we see of him in Paradise Lost, in terms of his outward appearance and the forms he assumes. If you have read Dante's Inferno, compare the depiction of Satan in Canto XXXIV.

10. Compare the epic opening formula as used in Paradise Lost (I.1-26) with the formula as used at the beginning of Homer's Iliad and Odyssey and Virgil's Aeneid. What attitude toward his predecessors does Milton imply in his opening and in IX.13-47? What source or sources does he look to for his inspiration? How do later parts of the poem give significance to his plea "what in me is dark / Illumine" (I.22-23)?

11. God allows the fallen Satan a certain amount of freedom, so that "with reiterated crimes he might / Heap on himself damnation . . . " (I.214-15). The Romantic poet Percy Bysshe Shelley argued that such motives in God made Him far more evil than Satan. Is this charge justified?

The lines quoted should be considered in the context of the entire passage (I.210-20) and of the theme of freedom in the poem as a whole.

12. "The mind is its own place, and in itself / Can make a Heaven of Hell, a Hell of Heaven" (I.254-55). This famous statement by the fallen Satan introduces a key idea in Milton's epic. How does the statement reverberate in other parts of the poem and other characters in it? In what senses does it prove to be true?

13. The speakers in the infernal council in Book II--Moloch, Belial, Mammon, and Beelzebub as Satan's spokesman and parliamentary leader--represent different varieties of evil. Can you relate them to corresponding classes of sin or types of sinners or memorable individuals in Dante's Inferno?

14. For at least two centuries a debate has raged over the allegation that, in moving from the Hell of Books I and II to the Heaven of Book III, Milton exchanges epic and dramatic power for insipidity, and that the characterization of God the Father in Book III is a disaster. What is your judgment on this matter?

15. What parallels and contrasts are there between the council in Hell in Book II and the council in Heaven in Book III?

16. Read the hymn to Light in III.1-55. What makes it appropriate and powerful at this point in the poem?

17. Compare the image of blindness and vision in Paradise Lost with the image as used in Oedipus the King.

18. Compare the descriptions of Hell, Heaven, and Eden in Milton and Dante. Which Hell better embodies evil and suffering? Which Heaven better suggests bliss and sublimity? Which Eden better suggests the perfection of earthly life?

(A wag has suggested that only an Englishman could envisage the state of perfect earthly felicity in terms of the details of yard work.)

19. Is God's argument (III.96-128) that His foreknowledge of the human fall is compatible with human freedom comprehensible? Is it presented as reasonable or as a mysterious article of faith? An astronomer knows well in advance when an eclipse of the sun will take place, but he or she has in no sense caused it to happen. Is this a true or false analogy with God's foreknowledge?

20. How much of Milton's story of Adam and Eve in Eden repeats chapters 1-3 of Genesis, how much is elaboration of what Genesis clearly implies, and how much is Milton's own invention? Consider, for example, the nature of male-female relationships and the role of sex before and after the Fall. Does Milton narrow the theological and religious teaching of Genesis by tying the Fall so closely to a male-female power rivalry? Does Milton portray Eve as weak even before the Fall?

21. Read the debate between Adam and Eve over whether they should work separately or remain together (IX.205-384), and try to ignore for the moment the fact that Adam's misgivings are borne out by events. Are Eve's arguments valid and convincing in themselves? Does she or Adam defend a loftier image of human nature? (You might ask somewhat similar questions about Satan's words tempting Eve in IX.692-703 and IX.725-28 and about Eve's words in IX.756-59.) Could it be argued that, in engaging in this somewhat heated dispute, Adam and Eve have already fallen?

22. Are we meant to apply familiar human criteria to the acts involved in the Fall? For example, when Adam eats the forbidden fruit, ought we to wish he had abstained and thus abandoned Eve to suffer alone the consequences of sin? Are we to wonder how and whether the human race would have been propagated if the man or woman, but not both, had fallen? Suppose Adam had not joined Eve in her sin; would original sin have been propagated? If not, would that fact have implied that the female sex is not important enough to have influenced the human future?

Most of these questions seem whimsical or scholastic, but in deciding whether or not they are worth asking, students can be led to the question on what plane of reality the poem is intended to work.

23. How do the quarrel and reconciliation of Adam and Eve in Book X affect the resolution of the poem, dramatically and thematically?

It has been suggested that the reconciliation is, on the human plane, an analogue of the theological solution outlined in Book XII.

24. Adam's words in XII.469-78, which imply that the Fall is a fortunate one, are central to Milton's goal of justifying divine providence. But, since theologically the original sin includes all other, later human acts of evil, can we infer that all acts of moral evil are in the last analysis good things we should be grateful for?

25. Michael promises Adam, and implicitly humankind, a "Paradise within thee, happier far" (XII.587) than the Paradise that has been lost. What kind of Paradise is now available to human beings? Would you yourself prefer this "higher" Paradise to the one described in Book IV?

Volume II

NEOCLASSICISM THROUGH THE MODERN PERIOD

Molière

In teaching Tartuffe, it is probably as important to think out what questions not to ask as to think of ones to ask. Questions about the psychological complexities of the characters, for example, will not get us very far. Molière's characters are the durable stock characters of the popular stage: buffoons, foolish old men and women, languishing young lovers, witty servants, and a few all-purpose confidantes and "Charles-his-friend"s--characters off the Roman comic stage which cropped up again in the Renaissance, endured through the "line characters" of the nineteenth-century repertory company, and still live a vigorous life in television situation comedy. Nor is there much use probing into the complexities of plot development; Molière's plots are as conventional as his characters--the attempts of a young couple to marry in spite of paternal opposition, the intrusion of a buffoon into a household and his expulsion, the machinations of witty servants in the service of love. The structure of Tartuffe, like that of most Molière plays, is a series of comic turns, some very broad, strung together on a conventional plot line (will Mariane get to marry the handsome Valère, or will she have to marry her father's choice, the slimy Tartuffe?). Molière generates brilliant drama out of such unpromisingly conventional materials by playing a series of variations upon a single theme, in this case the human propensity for self-delusion through projecting one's own needs or fears upon other people.

1. What is funny about the first scene?

The class will not miss the broad comedy of an old lady who says she must leave in a hurry, then talks for fifteen minutes about morality (meanwhile slapping the servant and calling her a slut), and then repeats all she has said at the door. This comic routine, though, conveys all the necessary information about the household and raises comically the theme of self-delusion; Mme. Pernelle accuses the family of "chattering on and on," while not letting them get a word in edgewise.

2. How is Orgon characterized at his first entrance (I.4)?

Dorine's speech (I.2) prepares us for Orgon's obsession, which is immediately demonstrated in one of the most famous scenes in Molière, in which Orgon responds to each piece of disastrous information about his wife with "And Tartuffe?"

3. How does Cléante function as a foil to Orgon?

Act I, scene 5, is crucial here. To Orgon's effusions about Tartuffe, Cléante responds with a cool, sensible moderation, and in the process comes close to articulating the theme of the play: "Is not a face quite different from a mask? / Cannot sincerity and cunning art, / Reality and semblance, be told apart?"(I.5.76-78).

4. How is Dorine characterized in Act II, scenes 1-3?

Dorine is a second "touchstone" character of good sense and temperance and is a foil to Mariane as Cléante is to Orgon. Mariane, for all her good instincts, lacks the courage to defy her father and stand up for true virtue against her father's obsession with appearances. It is Dorine who has to do this: "Must I play / Your part, and say the lines you ought to say?" (II.3.1-2).

5. How does the comic scene between Valère and Mariane (II.4) advance the themes of the play?

Valère and Mariane, in their lovers' misunderstanding, are neglecting reality in favor of appearances as much as her father does. It remains for the earthy Dorine, again, to bring them back to their senses.

6. How is Damis characterized in Act III, scene 1?

The students will note a certain family resemblance among Mme. Pernelle, her son Orgon, and his children Damis and Mariane in their tendency to be led by passions and appearances into extreme positions. Dorine has to moderate Damis's extremism here as she did his sister's in the preceding scene.

7. What ironies are involved in Tartuffe's character, as it is presented in Act III, scenes 2-3?

Tartuffe is the obligatory central obsessive character in a Molière play, the walking embodiment of hypocrisy. He is very funny and is likely to inspire some sneaking sympathy, of the kind we give to such other vital rascals as Richard III and W. C. Fields. But there are a number of ironies in his character. He would seem to be a clear-eyed Machiavellian, pursuing a straight course of self-interest. But when he tries to seduce Elmire, he misreads appearances as badly as Orgon does and almost wrecks his scam. The deceiver and the deceived have more in common than either does with the truly clear-headed people Cléante and Dorine.

8. How are Elmire and her son Damis contrasted in Act III, scenes 4-7?

Elmire here joins Cléante and Dorine as a representative of temperance and good sense. (See also her long speech to Orgon in Act IV, scene 3.) Elmire takes the attempted seduction coolly and tries to use it to blackmail Tartuffe not to marry Mariane, not a bad strategy in this dog-eat-dog world of self-interest. Damis, through his passionate idealism, only makes the situation worse.

9. What is the function of the Monsieur Loyal scene (V.4)?

It is a brilliant comic touch to introduce a completely new character, and such a deliciously absurd one, this late in the play. And Monsieur Loyal, with his fastidious, unctuous manner and the harsh, cruel content of his message, provides a test for the main characters on how well they have learned to restrain themselves and to look for the truth behind appearances.

10. How does Valère's behavior in V.6 contrast with Tartuffe's?

One of the many little balances and symmetries in the play is the fact that Valère repays the harsh treatment he has received from Orgon with kindness while Tartuffe repays Orgon's kind treatment with ingratitude.

11. What are the implications of the Officer's last-minute rescue of the family?

As pointed out in the introduction to Molière, the power of evil is so strong in Tartuffe that only this <u>deus ex machina</u> can avert tragedy and preserve the comic form of the play. But the scene also raises for one last time some of the recurring issues of the play. Louis XIV is a king to whom "all sham is hateful" and who "with one keen glance" has seen through Tartuffe's hypocrisy, in contrast to Orgon's and his mother's gullibility. But, on the other hand, they and the other characters have misunderstood the king, thinking of him as a stern punisher rather than a forgiving father. The play thus ends with one last twist of the ironic knife.

Marie de La Vergne de La Fayette

The Princesse de Clèves may seem to your students on first reading to be two novels: one a rather eccentric but clear French triangle novel and the other a historical novel crowded with confusing historical allusions. The editors have tried to provide as much help as possible in reading the historical sections, while acknowledging the delicate line between history and fiction in the novel, by annotating the historical material with unusual fullness. As study of the novel progresses, its doubleness may come to seem a strength rather than a weakness, an aid to understanding rather than a barrier. Not only does the split between fictional and historical material parallel the pervasive other splittings in the novel--between private and public life, between love and gallantry, between perturbation and repose--but themes are regularly reflected back and forth between the two levels of the novel, the Princess's experiences mirroring and being mirrored by the political situation. Tracing these reflections can help clarify the meaning of the novel.

1. Mme de La Fayette divided the novel into four sections. What is the function of this division? Each of the sections might be given a title--"The Education of the Princess," for example, for the first section. What titles might be appropriate for the other three sections?

2. The translator, Nancy Mitford, follows the original text by not using quotation marks to indicate direct speech. (Quotation marks, or their French equivalents tirets or dashes, were not used until the eighteenth century.) What is the effect of retaining this typographical feature? Does the occasional ambiguity or delayed recognition of speaker add to the fluid movement between public speech and private thought in the novel?

3. Mme de Chartres is presented somewhat ambiguously as a mother. On the one hand, we may admire her frankness with her daughter and her openness in warning her of the dangers of the court; she has been called a "modern mother." On the other hand, she tells her daughter that she can maintain her virtue only by "extreme mistrust of oneself" and by "following the one line of conduct which can make a woman happy, that is to say, loving her husband and being loved by him." She is "inordinately proud" and ambitious for her daughter, marries her off to a man of whom Mlle de Chartres says that "she was not particularly attracted by his person," and never realizes that "she was perhaps giving her daughter to somebody whom she could not love." What are we to make of this mother-daughter relationship? Is Mme de Chartres a good mother, and does she prepare her daughter sufficiently for adulthood and marriage?

4. The first meeting of the Princess and de Nemours at the ball appears to be a case of love at first sight. This scene deserves careful examination. Notice that it is appearance that creates the initial attraction. The Princess is "startled" by the sight of "this handsome Prince," and he is "much struck by her beauty." Notice too that the meeting takes place in public, in full view of the court, and is symbolically presided over and endorsed by the King, who "called to her to take the newcomer."

5. The first of the four controversial digressions in the novel--the story of Diane de Poitiers--occurs just after the ball scene. The others are the stories of Mme de Tournon, Anne Boleyn, and the Vidame de Chartres. Examine each of these digressions carefully. Are they really as digressive as they first appear? Notice not only the ways in which the digressions reflect the themes of the main plot but also the relevance of the narrative

presentation of each digression. Is the narrator important? (Mme de Chartres narrates the story of Diane de Poitiers, M. de Clèves the story of Mme de Tournon, and Mary Stuart the story of Anne Boleyn; the story of the Vidame de Chartres is partially narrated by him and otherwise presented directly.)

6. The character of M. de Clèves is almost as interesting as that of his wife, if less fully presented. He passionately loves and marries someone who he knows is not in love with him. He says, when he is telling the story of Mme de Tournon, that if his wife or mistress told him that she loved another he would "cast off the role of husband or lover in order to advise and sympathize with her as best I could." Yet, when his wife does make this confession, he is consumed by jealousy and dies saying that his wife's love for another has caused his death. Is M. de Clèves another "reflector" of the theme, in his wife's story, that passion is fatal? Is his behavior psychologically credible?

7. The confession scene, the most famous scene in the novel, is worth considerable attention. On one level, its central device of the accidentally overheard conversation is rather implausible and "stagy" (as are other, "fictional" scenes which turn around accidentally discovered letters and other melodramatic devices). On a less literal level, the scene has a considerable mythic power, involving a man and woman in a garden losing their innocence and metaphorically seeing each other's nakedness. (Is de Nemours the serpent in the shrubbery?) On a third, psychological level, the motives and reactions of each party are worth tracing in detail.

8. Looking and watching constitute a recurring motif in the novel; we are in a world where people are always observed, where malicious eyes are always on the watch for weakness and betrayal. Major events take place in full view of an audience, and scenes such as that in which de Nemours takes Mme de Clèves' miniature turn around complex patterns of gazing and being gazed at. One of the most complex is the pavilion scene in which the Princess gazes at a painting of de Nemours, unaware that de Nemours is gazing at her gazing, while M. de Clèves's servant is secretly gazing at de Nemours gazing, etc. What is the significance of this motif? Is there a difference between public displays (the ball, the tournament) and these private scenes of looking and spying? How are the gazing scenes related to the split in the book between appearance and reality, outer truth and inner truth?

9. A rather surprising feature of Mme de Clèves's final rejection of M. de Nemours is her reason for rejecting him. She drops her moral objections to marrying the man who caused her husband's death and instead argues that marriage would inevitably destroy the intensity of their love. He would go on to other women, and she would be unbearably jealous. M. de Nemours says that this is an imaginary barrier, and the Princess agrees that it may exist only in her own imagination. What do you make of this curious scene? Does its illogic reveal something about the Princess's psychology? Is it possible that both the exaggerated duty to her husband's memory and the fear of loss of love are rationalizations of a deeper reason for rejection, a fear of passion that will threaten perfect control and <u>repos</u>?

10. Is there anything generalizable from <u>The Princesse de Clèves</u> about women's experience? Women seem to wield great power in the world of the novel. The figure of Diane de Poitiers hangs rather sinisterly over the book, and the Queen first lures the Vidame de Chartres into a dangerous position and then easily crushes him when he makes a misstep. On the other hand, this power comes from women's sexual charms; it is acquired by their attaching themselves to powerful men. What about Mme de Clèves? What sort of power does she

exercise? She seems to have the fate of both her husband and de Nemours in her hands. Do the stories of powerful, dangerous women in the digressions serve as reflectors of Mme de Clèves's power? What about other issues of gender?

Jean Racine

Racine is as central to the French stage as Shakespeare is to the English stage; a comparative study of works by the two playwrights can tell us a great deal about different conceptions of theater. But even if the class has not read Shakespeare and cannot compare his work with Racine's, Phaedra can still be approached as the quintessential expression not only of Neoclassic drama but also of Neoclassic ways of thinking and feeling. As with any play, one problem is getting the class to imagine it in performance, and this problem is especially acute with Phaedra, whose dramaturgy is so alien to modern practice. Films and other visual aids are a big help. Talking through an imagined production of the play, reading key scenes, and analyzing the theatrical conventions they employ will also sharpen the students' sense of the play in performance. Understanding the assumptions behind theatrical conventions can lead into a useful discussion of the larger assumptions about human nature, society, and the cosmos which those conventions reflect.

1. What assumptions about drama underlie Racine's preface?

2. Racine says in his preface that "Phaedra is neither entirely guilty nor altogether innocent" and goes on to point out her guilty and innocent actions. Does your perception of Phaedra's degree of guilt correspond with Racine's?

3. In the preface, Racine also claims to have presented Hippolytus as perfect except for the "one weakness" of his passion for Aricia. Is Hippolytus more complicated in any way than Racine's statement would suggest?

4. How does Racine arrange his play to follow the three unities of time, place, and action? Does the Hippolytus/Aricia plot violate the unity of action? Why or why not?

5. Examine the relationships of the main characters with their confidants--Hippolytus with Theramenes, Phaedra with Oenone, Aricia with Ismene. What sorts of similarities and differences are there?

The confidant figures are important in Phaedra and do far more than just provide convenient ears for necessary speeches by the main characters. It is rewarding to examine them as foils or even doubles, expressing aspects of the main characters that have been denied or repressed.

6. Trace the imagery of the sun and of light and darkness through the play.

7. Trace references to monsters through the play. What functions do they serve?

8. A key concept in the play is order. Trace this theme through the various levels of action--personal, familial, social, and cosmic.

9. What is the relation of the political division in Athens, which would have been healed by the marriage of Hippolytus and Aricia, to the other themes of the play?

10. Phaedra can be read as a political allegory, a study of the behavior of people in authority. Where do both Phaedra and Theseus go wrong in exercising authority? (Note

especially the theme of false counselors.) Do Hippolytus and Aricia differ from Theseus and Phaedra in this respect?

11. The original French text of Phaedra is in rhymed hexameter couplets (alexandrines) in which the first line of each couplet expresses a complete thought, with another, balancing complete thought in the second line. John Cairncross translates the play into English blank verse; nevertheless, he preserves much of the symmetry of the balancing paired statements. Analyze some major speeches closely to see this underlying verbal structure.

12. It is hard to imagine two plays superficially more unlike than Tartuffe and Phaedra; yet they came out of the same society. What similar attitudes and beliefs do they express, one comically, the other tragically?

Jonathan Swift

Besides being a great writer in his own distinctive way, Swift is in several respects a representative figure. That Gulliver's Travels was written by a zealous clergyman is in itself a revealing fact about the unsqueamishness of eighteenth-century sensibility. The work also holds a central place in the utopia-dystopia tradition. Moreover, Gulliver and "A Modest Proposal," each on its own scale, are probably most teachers' definitive specimens of what satire is, and Gulliver is a compendium of almost all the possible strategies and tones satire can use. Neither the author nor Gulliver ever stands still long enough for readers to get a steady fix on what they are saying, and much of the fun--and value--in teaching Swift lies in tracking his reverses and zigzags of tone, target, and method. At some point in teaching him, it is a good idea to go through a few pages paragraph by paragraph, as an object lesson in readerly nimbleness.

The scholarly and critical storm over the meaning of Part IV, briefly sketched in the Introduction to Swift, is almost certain to find its way into most teachers' classrooms, because the controversy addresses the most fundamental questions about Part IV--the relationship to one another of the yahoos, Houyhnhnms, and Europeans--and because this is the question most students will be most interested in. Not many teachers will want to take the Thackeray position that Swift was a rabid misanthrope, but that view probably ought not to be simply dismissed out of hand; one doesn't have to be a Victorian to read (or misread) Swift that way. Anti-Thackeray readings that depend on a knowledge of local currents of thought in Swift's day may seem too heavy for introductory-level undergraduate classes, but such readings can also be supported by the text as any student can understand it. Gulliver's perverse reaction to Don Pedro de Mendez and the many comic touches in Part IV are good evidence that Gulliver's value judgments need not be exactly the same as ours.

Gulliver's Travels raises several questions that lie at the heart of myth, especially as it is embodied in the most significant science fiction. The most central of these questions are what it means to be human and where one should draw the line between what is human and what suprahuman or subhuman. Other questions recurrent in science fiction have to do with reason: Is pure reason a desirable and possible norm of individual virtue and social organization? What is the relationship between reason and possible higher sources of truth, such as religious revelation? One need not be a 1700-vintage theologian to investigate this last point; the Book of Genesis will take one at least part of the way.

1. To what extent are the yahoos identifiable with human beings?

2. Gulliver is careful to record the most minute factual detail. Does this concern with exactness serve the book's satiric purposes?

3. The Houyhnhnms are vegetarians, but the yahoos feed indiscriminately. Apart from zoological realism (horses are herbivores), does this fact have any significance?

One can compare the account in Genesis of vegetarian humankind before the fall.

4. Even after absorbing the Houyhnhnms' values, presumably including their lack of shame about nakedness, Gulliver continues to wear clothes. Why? Is there any significance in that fact, over and above Gulliver's wish not to be identified with the yahoos?

5. In the Houyhnhnms' language, their name means, etymologically, "perfection of nature." What do you make of this? Is the word origin a tip-off about Swift's values or a commentary on the Houyhnhnms?

6. The Houyhnhnms' language is limited; for example, all bad things are compounds with yahoo, and there is no word meaning "lie." Are these limitations consistent with the view that the Houyhnhnms represent rationality? Can anything be called rationality that seems aware of evil only dimly or not at all?

7. Gulliver is housed neither with the Houyhnhnms nor with the yahoos (Chapter II). Does this fact have symbolic importance?

8. In the second paragraph of Chapter IV, which describes how horses are treated in England, who or what is the butt of the satire? The English in general? The English upper classes? The Houyhnhnms?

    All three, of course. This is a good specimen of Swift's opalescent, rapidly shifting satiric focus.

9. In Chapter V, third paragraph, Gulliver identifies and briefly describes religious controversies that have caused wars. Granted that these descriptions of religious creeds are inadequate; but how would you describe the controversies in the same number of words?

    This exercise ultimately raises the question whether brevity forces honesty, stripping away obfuscatory circumlocution, or dishonest simplification.

10. Is the analysis of war and its motives in Chapter V still valid today? Have the two centuries since Swift made any difference in the satiric bite?

    Similar questions, about the structure of society, can be asked regarding Chapter VI.

11. The last paragraph of Chapter VI contains an analysis of social classes. Trace the shifts in tone and in the satiric target.

    Another specimen of Swift's transitionless, protean method.

12. Just as we have arrived at a point where we think of humanity as yahoo-like but better in some ways, Chapters V to VII reveal human evils the yahoos are incapable of. Is it possible that even the yahoos are less detestable than human beings?

13. Do the systems of marriage and child-rearing described in Chapter VIII have any parallels with twentieth-century trends in these areas? Is society today becoming more or less Houyhnhnm-like in these respects? Consider the transfer of parents and of parental functions, eugenics, marital fidelity, adultery, and birth control.

14. The Houyhnhnms have no written literature, and their oral literature has no room for conflict, tragedy, or pain. (See Chapter IX.) Is this what literature will be like in Heaven? If the world were perfect, would literature have to be limited in these ways?

15. At the end of the first paragraph of Chapter X, Gulliver catalogues several dozen evils

of civilization, some of which seem much more serious than others. Does this mixing together of grave evils with what seem merely pet peeves enhance or interfere with the satire?

16. Compare the attitude toward Gulliver of the servant sorrel nag appointed as his attendant with the attitude of his "master" toward Gulliver. (See, for example, the first paragraph of Chapter XI.) Does the difference imply any judgment on the Houyhnhnms' values and their society?

17. In making his boat to leave Houyhnhnmland, Gulliver uses the skins and fat of yahoos. How are we intended to react to this fact?

18. After he leaves Houyhnhnmland, Gulliver encounters various groups: the savages in Chapter XI, the Portuguese sailors, his family, horses in England. Is it possible to locate these groups on a spectrum defined by the yahoos and Houyhnhnms? Where does the captain Don Pedro de Mendez fit on such a spectrum?

19. Examine the last three paragraphs of Chapter XII (the conclusion of the work). What elements in this passage are serious, what elements are comic? At whom is the satire directed? Or has Swift dropped the satiric mask in order to make his point directly?

The attack on pride is considered by some interpreters central to Swift's message. The Houyhnhnms are not, however, without their own form of pride, and clearly Gulliver too suffers from a form of it.

20. In his "Letter . . . to His Cousin Sympson," Gulliver says he has been accused of "abusing the female sex." Has he been guilty of such abuse?

21. Write a "modest proposal," along the lines of Swift's pamphlet of that name, designed to "solve" in a similar way a current social problem. Try to use the same kind of tone and strategy of argument.

Swift's model is hard to emulate, and students may fall flat on their faces with this assignment, but it's one way to get them to analyze what Swift is doing and how he does it.

22. Does "A Modest Proposal" have any direct, literal relevance to current controversies over social morality? Which ones?

23. Does the joker in the last paragraph of "A Modest Proposal," about the projector's having no young children, enhance or interfere with the satire?

24. Would angry protest be more effective in producing social reform than the method used in "A Modest Proposal"? In practical terms, which method would be better? Do you think a method like Swift's would actually cause people to treat the poor better? If it did not have this practical effect, would the piece still have served any good purpose other than a literary one?

Alexander Pope

Metrics is usually not the topic with which teachers want to begin the study of a poet, but simply to ignore metrics in a literature survey is to do students a disservice. No verse form offers a better opportunity to explore the subject than the Popean heroic couplet, a form that challenges the reflex assumptions of many students about the relation between poetic "freedom" and expressiveness. To define the form is simple enough: "rhymed pentameter couplets, closed and endstopped." Next comes the real challenge: tuning one's ear to the almost unlimited variations a master like Pope can play upon the relation of the two lines, the relation of the rhyme words, the rhythmic possibilities of iambic pentameter, and the relation between syntactic and metrical form. The most accessible of these variations are probably those that achieve wit. After this effect has been recognized, one can go on to see the way Pope uses the possibilities of the couplet for other purposes.

Ultimately, an understanding of the tiny, verbal world of the heroic couplet can help us perceive the larger Popean world the structures and tensions of which the couplet mirrors. One of the tonal effects distinctively achievable in the Popean heroic couplet is confident assurance, a fact that makes this verse form an ideal vehicle for expressing gnomic wisdom. One might ask the class to consider whether the force and impact of An Essay on Man would not be seriously diminished if Pope had used a different metrical vehicle.

1. An Essay on Man is a theodicy, or attempt to justify the goodness of God in the face of the existence of evil in the world. The principle Pope appeals to is order, not a static, rigid order but, in Martin Price's words, "a system of interrelatedness, a field of forces in tension, a dancelike structure that preserves itself in constant movement." Trace Pope's treatment of order on various levels: the natural world, the human body, and the human personality.

2. Trace the traditional metaphor of the Great Chain of Being through the poem.

3. The moral values Pope celebrates in An Essay on Man are implicitly those of art: the ability to perceive order, a sense of proportion, and an ability to bring human invention and thought into harmony with the order of nature. Trace through the poem the theme of the human being as artist.

4. In other poems Pope uses the heroic couplet for various purposes, very often for comic satire. In An Essay on Man he uses the form for philosophical exposition. How does he adapt the couplet here for that particular purpose?

5. The last line of Epistle I--"One truth is clear, Whatever is, is right"--is sometimes taken as an expression of a myopic optimism, rather like that of Dr. Pangloss in Candide. Is this a fair judgment?

One approach to this question is to note how Pope, unlike Pangloss, squarely faces various sorts of evil in the world. His response, however, is neither bland denial nor romantic despair, but a tough realism, a sense of proportion, and a faith in an underlying order that makes working for personal and social goals possible--a position closer to that of the chastened, mature Candide than to that of Pangloss.

Voltaire

Candide is so funny and so easy to read that teachers are unlikely to have to do much proselytizing on its behalf. But it's also rich and ironic enough to repay extended study. One problem that should be faced right away is what Candide is. Is it a parody of romances of adventure, a spoof of eighteenth-century "philosophical novels," a satire on Leibnitzian Optimism? It is all of these things, of course, but none of these approaches does much to explain why we continue to find it funny and telling. Little, if any, time need be spent on the long-forgotten specific works Voltaire parodies; their general nature is clear enough to anyone who goes to movies or watches television. Neither should the teacher worry too much about Leibnitz; the footnotes in the text probably provide as much information as students need. The ultimate butt of Voltaire's wit in Candide is not Leibnitz and his Panglossian followers but all those who retreat into easy, slick answers to hard questions about the meaning of life. The trouble with Pangloss is not that he's a Leibnitzian but that he's a fool, as suggested by the fact that Pope, no fool, could defend similar ideas in the Essay on Man and draw from them a complex, almost existentialist realism rather than Pangloss's bland escapism.

A more useful way of looking at Candide for teaching purposes is as a theodicy, an attempt to reconcile God's goodness with the presence of evil in the world. This approach can suggest links with other works, especially with the prototype theodicy: the Book of Job. We can place Pangloss, for example, among Job's "Comforters," as someone who is too quick to explain away evil with glib, conventional answers, and we can profitably compare the chastened, initiated Candide of the end of the story with the chastened, post-whirlwind Job, who can acknowledge the inadequacy of human reason to resolve such questions. The element of theodicy in Candide can also point us forward, linking Candide with the existentialist heroes of modern literature who turn from the big, imponderable questions to take care of their own gardens. This link between the centuries may have been a factor in the success of Leonard Bernstein's musical version of Candide in 1956. The class will probably enjoy a performance of that work, on a recording or videotape.

1. The castle of Thunder-ten-tronckh is described (Chapter I) as "the most magnificent and most agreeable of all possible castles." Is it?

   This question can lead into an analysis of Voltaire's persona and his use of comic irony, through a study of the gap between what he says and what he implies about the castle.

2. After Candide leaves the castle, he is plunged immediately into various evils of the world among the Bulgarians and in Holland (Chapters II-IV). What categories of evil are represented here?

3. Lisbon is the next of the societies Candide encounters (Chapters V-IX). What new kinds of evil does he encounter here?

4. The old woman who tells her story in Chapters XI-XII is a foil to Pangloss. What philosophy of life has she adopted as a result of her sufferings?

5. What sorts of evil are illustrated in the Paraguay episode (Chapters XIV-XV)?

6. Cunegund's brother is a foil to Candide. What ironies are involved in his story (Chapter XV) and the conclusions he draws from his experiences?

7. The next society Candide encounters is that of the Oreillons. What sorts of evil are illustrated here?

8. Cacambo is another foil to Candide. How is he characterized?

9. The El Dorado episode (Chapters XVII-XVIII) provides the only genuine utopia in Candide. What makes it so perfect? Compare it with the society of the Houyhnhnms, if you have read Gulliver's Travels.

10. How does Martin contribute to the developing theme of Candide? See Chapters XX-XXI.

11. The episode in France (Chapter XXII) is full of topical as well as more general satire. How does Voltaire represent his own country?

12. What is the function of the Pococurante episode (Chapter XXV)?

13. The episode of the dervish (Chapter XXX) is important to the meaning of the ending of the book. How?

14. What does Candide mean in the final line: "Let us take care of our garden"?

Jean-Jacques Rousseau

It may be hard for students to credit Rousseau's claim that the Confessions inaugurates a bold new genre, since self-revelation for its own sake is a commonplace mode in our time. Depth and abnormal psychologies, not to mention literature, have prepared us for quirks in human character at least as odd as Rousseau's, and plenty of people, especially celebrities, undergo psychoanalysis or other forms of introspective therapy almost as a matter of course. This does not mean, however, that students will yawn over Rousseau's disclosures; many of them find it exciting to discover that current commonplaces originated at certain times and in certain circumstances in the history of culture. As the Introduction to Rousseau intimates, quite a few modern habits of mind started with or were most memorably formulated by him. Moreover, jaded though many people today may be about the perverse, Rousseau remains a distinctive, challengingly enigmatic personality, and analyzing this personality can be a stimulating classroom experience.

Rousseau is good preparation for many Romantic themes, including individualism and the importance of childhood, and for certain later authors including Wordsworth and Whitman. If students have also read Montaigne, in Volume I, they can make fruitful comparisons with the self-revelations in the Essays.

1. Is Rousseau modest or vain?

2. Is the honesty Rousseau claims for himself really honesty or is it something else?

3. Rousseau makes much of his fetish for spankings and of its effect on his adult personality, although he admits to extreme embarrassment in addressing the subject. Is this fetish laughable? Contemptible? Understandable? If all people told the truth about themselves, would most of them have similar skeletons in their closets?

4. Compare Rousseau's loves for Mlle de Vulson and for Mlle Goton, both of which he says were very powerful. In what tone does he describe these loves? Can the love of an eleven-year-old boy for a woman twice his age be taken seriously, by Rousseau or by his readers?

5. For Rousseau, the incident of the damaged comb marked a departure from Eden. In what way? Had everything been happy until that incident? Is the loss-of-Eden metaphor applicable to his childhood and adolescence as a whole?

6. What inferences can we draw from Book I about Rousseau's ideas of education?

7. Is Rousseau troubled much by feelings of guilt?

8. At the end of Book I, Rousseau says that if circumstances had been a little different he could have lived an uneventful life of quiet contentment as a Genevan craftsman. In light of what he says about his temperament elsewhere in Book I, does this seem likely?

9. Rousseau says he is singling out the episode of the tree and the "aqueduct" from among many he might have inflicted on the reader concerning his childhood at Bossey. Does the story have any point? Are we in fact interested in it?

Johann Wolfgang von Goethe

Faust, Part One is so complex a work--in genesis, content, form, and aesthetic strategy--that teachers, having only a limited amount of time to spend on it in a survey course, have to make some hard decisions on how to approach the work and which of its myriad aspects to emphasize. To begin with, should one approach it as a stage play or as a philosophical poem? How important, and how profitable, is it to get the story line and chronology straight? For example, the sequence and timing of events in the Faust-Gretchen love affair and her subsequent pregnancy and infanticide are in many respects problematic, but ironing out such wrinkles (if, indeed, that can be done) will assume a greater or lesser importance depending on whether one wishes to stress issues treated symbolically or realistic depiction of people and events. One solution is to spend some time at the outset determining just what interests students most in the work and then following up on the issues they themselves raise.

1. What is the relationship between the Prologue in Heaven and the Prologue in the Theater? Do these two introductory frames point us toward different modes of interpreting the work that follows?

2. What is the importance of the parallel between the Prologue in Heaven and the Book of Job? Can we understand God in the same way in Goethe's work and in the biblical book? Does Faust raise the same issues as in Job?

3. Faust is often regarded as one of the archetypal representatives of Western humankind over the last few centuries, along with such figures as Don Quixote and Don Juan. Why is Faust so central and representative?

4. In most versions of the Faust legend, Faust sells his soul to the Devil by sealing a contract with him. Interpreters of Goethe's Faust tend to insist that Faust makes a wager rather than a contract with the Devil. What, specifically, is the wager? What is the difference between this wager and a contract, and why is the difference important?

5. The traditional versions of the Faust story usually present Faust as a quester for suprahuman, often forbidden, knowledge. Is it knowledge, ultimately, that Goethe's Faust is seeking, or something else?

6. Does Faust make any progress toward the goals he has set for himself? (After all, at the end of Part One he seems overshadowed by the transfigured, "saved" Gretchen, in a sense dwarfed by her.)

7. Someone--we wish we could remember who--once said, in effect, "In Goethe's Faust, Faust sells his soul to the Devil and, in return, is empowered to seduce a simple young woman of modest social station--a feat that has been achieved by others without supernatural assistance." Is this a fair account of what happens in the play?

In a way it is, as least as regards Part I of Faust taken in isolation. But this answer raises further questions, some of them important. How much, for example, of what Faust does under the tutelage of Mephistopheles could Faust not have done on his own? And if he often would seem not to need Mephistopheles, should the latter be regarded less as a character or external agent than as a symbol, presumably of something within Faust? Another question that arises: Is a romantic love affair inherently a more minor form of self-realization than, say, involvement with public projects or the plumbing of metaphysical mysteries?

8. Could Faust have been written in such a way as to leave out all supernatural incidents and effects? Could Mephistopheles, for example, have been conceived as an influential, resourceful, worldly-wise, and immensely cynical human acquaintance of Faust's? Would the play have been more powerful, especially for a modern audience, in this more naturalistic guise?

9. Which episodes of Faust seem to you least effective in light of what the work as a whole is doing? Is Mephistopheles' interview with the freshman student functional? The scene in Auerbach's tavern featuring Mephistopheles' magic tricks? The Walpurgis Night's Dream scene? (This last scene has often been criticized as inappropriate and easily dispensable.)

10. Can you reconstruct the sequence of events in the love affair between Faust and Gretchen, from their first meeting through the final dungeon scene? Is everything explained as it should be, and in a realistically intelligible way? For example, how has Valentine learned the news, which he describes as common knowledge, of Gretchen's affair with Faust? How has Faust learned, at the beginning of scene XXIII, that Gretchen has been imprisoned and condemned?

This is a difficult and time-consuming task, especially for students, and the teacher may have to help by pointing out some of the many anomalies in the plot. (Almost all the commentaries address these problems.) Most of the anomalies would seem to arise from Goethe's having drawn, for his final version of Part One, on material, less than completely revised or reconceived, that had been part of his Urfaust and the intermediate-stage Fragment he had published earlier. The point of bringing up these problems in continuity and chronology is to get students to consider the relation between two different goals: realistic story-telling and psychological or symbolic development.

11. What is the significance of Mephistopheles? In what ways is he like the traditional Devil, in what ways different? In creating Mephistopheles, does Goethe trivialize the Devil? Should the Devil be given traits such as lechery and a penchant for practical jokes? Should he be more titanic in defiance of God? Is Mephistopheles at all like Milton's Satan in Paradise Lost?

12. Is Marguerite too lightweight a character to be convincing in the play? Does her naivete and small-town-girlishness help us understand why Faust is drawn to her, or does it seem incompatible with his vast aspirations?

13. What makes the final dungeon scene effective? Does Gretchen's madness make her more poignant than she would have been if she had remained fully sane and conscious of her situation and surroundings?

14. If you were writing your own version of Faust, would you make the protagonist a professor? Would some other occupation or profession be more likely to produce a man (or woman) who has exhausted the possibilities of knowledge and become jaded with it?

15. If you were writing a modern version of Faust and were adhering to the old formula in

which he sells his soul to the Devil, for what might he most believably sell his soul today?

16. The number and variety of scenes in Goethe's <u>Faust, Part One</u> makes its text look more like a screenplay than like a stage play. Would the work play better as a movie than on the stage? In addition to practical matters like changes of setting and scenery, what issues are involved? How important is sheer language? How important is spectacle? How important is realistic action? How important is dreamscape?

William Blake

Blake's rootedness in the eighteenth century is worth dwelling on: in some ways he is closer to Voltaire and Swift than to Wordsworth and Keats. But in most ways Blake is not only a Romantic but the hardest-core of the Romantics. <u>Visions of the Daughters of Albion</u> and <u>Songs of Innocence and of Experience</u> are central expressions of the Romantic idea that imagination shapes the world, not vice versa. At the same time, Blake is one of the most powerful social critics ever to write lyric poetry (or any other kind of literature, for that matter). This double focus, on the psyche and on society, creates one of the more interesting challenges in literary interpretation, and therefore also in teaching. "London" and "The Garden of Love," for example, are hard-hitting protest poems, but both can be reasonably interpreted as proceeding from damaged personalities. (The word <u>of</u> in the title <u>Songs of Innocence and of Experience</u> is a heavily-freighted pun, meaning both "concerning" and "proceeding from.") Even <u>Visions</u>, arguably, is readable in that way. Much that is fundamental to Blake can be approached by examining the way in which his treatment of the individual psyche blends into social psychiatry. Some of the following questions, especially on the <u>Songs</u>, assume the importance of identifying the speakers and understanding their subjective states of mind, at the same time that one considers the comments the poems make on what the world is "objectively" like.

A fair amount of teaching time is required to satisfy students' curiosity about Blake's larger ideas--about religion, about sex, about the senses and imagination. For this reason, the Introduction to Blake in the anthology tries to break ground for the teacher by advancing common--though by no means universally accepted--interpretations of Blake's views on these matters. But most teachers will want to concentrate mainly on close explication, especially of the <u>Songs</u>, some of which are among the best-crafted gnomic masterpieces in all literature. It helps to have students read all the <u>Songs</u> (they are included complete in the anthology), since they are synergistic. To have read them all, even if one can discuss only a few, facilitates explication and can even, paradoxically, save classroom time; "The Little Black Boy," for example, puts in a new perspective the plight of the white little black boys of the two "Chimney Sweeper" poems, not to mention the ventriloquist motifs present in all three poems.

1. <u>Thel</u> and <u>Visions</u> both open with the heroine in solitude, then move to dialogues with, respectively, a lily and a marigold. What do the two flower-dialogues tell us about the protagonists and about the issues to be explored in the poems?

2. Compare the images of marriage in plate 4 of <u>Thel</u> and plate 5 of <u>Visions</u>. Which view is more convincing? What do the two views of marriage tell us about the heroines and the issues in the poems?

3. Some readers take Thel to be the voice of Innocence and Oothoon to be the voice of Experience. Are these identifications consistent with the pictures of Innocence and Experience in the <u>Songs</u>?

4. How should the questions in plate 1 of <u>Thel</u> ("Thel's Motto") be answered?

This question broaches the theme of knowledge earned at first and second hand; passages pertinent to the answers elicited include Thel's subterranean descent at the end of

Thel and Oothoon's reference to the eagle and mole in Visions 5:39-40.

5. Is Thel about death or about sex?

6. What does Thel learn from her visit to the underground world in the last plate? Is she still listening mainly to herself or is she learning a new lesson? Does she shriek and flee because she is a coward? If so, does her flight have implications for what we might forecast about her later life? Or does she have good reason to run away? Has she progressed in her sexuality or not?

7. Visions has usually been regarded as a feminist poem. In what ways is this true? Is the feminism in the poem the best kind of feminism? Is Oothoon truly a liberated personality? Does the sex-saturated quality of her mind ("there my eyes are fix'd / In happy copulation"; 6:23-7:1) demonstrate or undermine the notion that she is a feminist? What do you think of her offer to Theotormon to "catch for thee girls of mild silver, or of furious gold" (7:24)? In what sense does she mean this?

8. The "daughters of Albion" are, among other things, Englishwomen, and Oothoon is the "soft soul of America." What do we learn from the political allegory about Blake's method and values? Does the political allegory have any application to Oothoon's rape? to conditions today?

9. Compare Bromion and Theotormon in Visions. How do their values (especially about sex) compare or contrast?

10. Would you rather be regarded as innocent or as experienced?

One can take an actual poll of the students. Usually a large majority will prefer to be regarded as experienced. The question can be useful in a) identifying a bias toward "experience" that--some teachers may feel--needs to be neutralized in discussing the Songs; and b) introducing the special senses in which Blake uses the words innocence and experience.

11. Consider the two poems called "The Chimney Sweeper," in Innocence and Experience. Which is the more effective as social criticism?

The Experience poem is sweeping rhetoric, while the Innocence version is full of heartrending physical and circumstantial detail. Students can be invited to generalize from this difference to see part of what the Songs are doing.

12. "The Lamb" in Innocence opens with a question, then gives the answer; "The Tyger" in Experience is made up entirely of questions, unanswered. What do you make of this?

One can broach questions about good and evil or discuss point of view in the Songs--trust versus fear, assurance versus doubt, and similar contrasts.

13. What kind of innocence is revealed in the Innocence "Holy Thursday"?

We get one kind of answer if we concentrate on the children observed, another if we concentrate on the adult speaker. Some readers find the poem a rather dark one, with hints of the sinister (of which the speaker is unaware) in almost every line. Comparison with the Experience version can begin with the concrete question whether "harmonious thunderings" or "trembling cry" is likely to be a more accurate description of the sound of singing children.

14. "My Pretty Rose Tree," "Ah! Sunflower," and "The Lilly" were all engraved by Blake on the same plate. What idea about love emerges from this group of poems? Do "The Lilly" and The Book of Thel elucidate each other?

The questions are designed to explore the synergistic relationship between different works by Blake.

15. "'My Pretty Rose Tree' shows how women, especially wives, fail to appreciate the sacrifices their men make for them." Is this a fair summary of what the poem says?

Many scenarios are possible besides the one the speaker wants us to assume, some of them comic.

16. What do "The Garden of Love" and "A Little Girl Lost" have in common as statements about sex?

Besides the motif of tyrannical repression, some complicity in their own repression on the part of the victims may be detected.

17. In "The Clod & the Pebble," which of the two views of love is preferable? Does this poem belong clearly in Experience?

This is a good question to use in exploring point of view. Instead of concentrating on the points of view of clod and pebble, one can concentrate on the person who is speaking the whole poem. What are we to make of a person who seems to think that, between the clod-attitude and the pebble-attitude, it's a toss-up?

William Wordsworth

Someone once said that it is impossible for anyone under forty to appreciate Wordsworth adequately. Fortunately, many students seem unaware of their impediment. Their attraction to the poet is hard to define, since his poetry is not highly colored, having no sex appeal literally or figuratively. Emotionally, students probably respond best to his treatment of childhood, one of the few things about which most of them are old enough to feel Wordsworthian nostalgia. They are often skeptical about Wordsworth's claims in his major poems that, whatever he may have lost, something better has replaced it--a skepticism that, on an elementary level, reflects the tendency in modern Wordsworthian criticism to read his poems as dark and problematical. Teaching Wordsworth has its difficulties; one of them is students' proneness to formulate too simplistically the poet's view of childhood and of nature. The first four poems in the anthology are good warming-up etudes for reading Wordsworth, showing how much he can do with simple language and situations, but they need to be put in the context of the greater lyrics if the students are not to over-sentimentalize the poet.

On the other hand, many students are intrigued by Wordsworth's combination of elusiveness and directness. As with Keats, they feel that in exploring the subtler reaches of Wordsworth's mind they are at least starting from a clearly comprehensible meaning. (The "Intimations" ode is a special case.) And they have a clear enough awareness of modern sensibility, though perhaps in an unsophisticated form, to recognize that there is something modern in the problems explored in "Tintern Abbey" and the "Intimations" ode, particularly the problems of making sense of one's own personality and of turning personal introspection into public matter.

1. Memory is a central theme in Wordsworth, but so is forgetting. Trace these twin themes in as many of his poems as are pertinent.

2. What similarities and differences are there between Wordsworth's picture of childhood and Blake's in <u>Songs of Innocence and of Experience</u>? Do both poets value the same thing in the child's view of the world?

3. Identify two passages in Wordsworth that Blake might have written and two that he could not have written. Justify your choices.

A paper or examination-essay question. Besides thematic matters--the dynamics of perception, the role of nature, and the like--students can be encouraged to examine style, imagery, and tone. Could Wordsworth have written "The Lamb"?

4. At the end of "Anecdote for Fathers," the little boy gives an apparently absurd answer to his father's question. What in the father's mind or behavior has prompted his son's answer? Might the little girl in "We Are Seven" have given such an answer?

5. Compare the ways in which child and adult use numbers in "We Are Seven."

The adult's subtraction problem and the child's kinesthetic "twelve steps" provide an introduction to the poem's theme of indirect versus direct knowledge.

6. Lines 21-24 of "The Tables Turned" say that one impulse from the woods in spring can teach us more about man and about moral evil and good than all the sages can. Think of some great sages--Socrates, Aristotle, Confucius, the Old Testament prophets, Jesus. Is one touch of spring really more instructive, and more instructive morally, than the sum of their wisdom? Do the tone and arguments in the poem and in "Expostulation and Reply" make such a case?

7. Both "Tintern Abbey" and the "Intimations" ode admit to a loss but say that what has replaced it is better and spiritually higher. Do you believe Wordsworth? Do you base your answer to that question on what you believe about life or on the text of the poems? Is the speaker himself confident of what he says?

8. Wordsworth thought of "Tintern Abbey" as a kind of ode, partly because of its "transitions," or movement back and forth. Trace this movement in the poem and show what it has to do with the theme.

9. "A Slumber Did My Spirit Seal" describes the deceased girl or woman as one with nature, to use a phrase often associated with the Romantics. Does her kind of oneness with nature mean what the phrase usually means?

10. An often-noted fact about Wordsworth is that his longer poems deal with intimate, private experience, while his sonnets take on very large subjects in their fourteen lines. What do you make of this fact?

11. "Composed upon Westminster Bridge" is unusual among Wordsworth's poems in celebrating not nature but the city (London). Does Wordsworth use the same poetic methods to celebrate city and countryside?

12. "Composed upon Westminster Bridge" and "It Is a Beauteous Evening" both celebrate tranquility. Is the effect produced by similar means?

13. In "I Wandered Lonely as a Cloud," some form of the word dance occurs in each of the four stanzas. Why is this significant?

14. "The Solitary Reaper" is a poem about sound. What poetic techniques does Wordsworth use to underline that fact?

15. In strophe VI of the "Intimations" ode, Wordsworth calls nature ("Earth") a "homely nurse." Nature is also called a nurse in "Tintern Abbey," line 109. Does the word have the same force in both poems?

16. The image of a "glory," that is, a halo, appears in several forms in the "Intimations" ode. Show how it reflects the poem's theme and helps pull the poem together.

Similar questions can be asked about other images and image-patterns: heavenly bodies, light, sound imagery, clothing, flowers, seeing and blindness.

17. In the "Intimations" ode, lines 141-50, Wordsworth gropes toward expressing the exact quality of the childhood remembrances that lift him out of the despair of strophes V-VIII. The language is imageless and abstract. Why is this so, and what is Wordsworth saying?

Wordsworth once said that he was referring to an "abyss of idealism" that he experienced in childhood, his sense of reality as mental becoming so strong that he had to clutch at material objects to bring him out of the trance. The last two paragraphs of Melville's Moby-Dick, Chapter XXXV ("The Mast-Head"), make an excellent correlative to the Wordsworth passage and idea.

Samuel Taylor Coleridge

Coleridge's "Dejection" is the classic companion piece to Wordsworth's "Intimations" ode, to which "Dejection" is, in part, a response. "Kubla Khan," in turn, is a contrasting companion piece to "Dejection," in a number of ways. "Dejection" is in the mode of Coleridge's "conversation poems," while "Kubla Khan" represents his exotic vein. Both Coleridge poems can be read as explorations of the sources of art and, more generally, of creative power. "Kubla Khan" is also a piece of virtuosity in sound effects. Note, for example, the palindromic arrangement of sounds in the first line, the alliteration in the final feet of the first five lines, the internal echoes in the first seven lines ("pleasure" and "measureless," "fertile ground" and "girdled round").

1. Both Coleridge's "Dejection" ode and Wordsworth's "Intimations" ode confess to a loss of mental or spiritual power. Do they describe the same kind of loss? Which of the two poets is worse off?

2. The phrase "There was a time," from line 1 of Wordsworth's "Intimations" ode, is repeated in line 76 of "Dejection." What is the function of this echo? What other echoes of the Wordsworth poem, linguistic or imagistic, do you find in "Dejection"? The image of a "glory" (halo), for example, occurs in both poems; for what purposes?

3. Does the storm in the seventh strophe of "Dejection" herald something beneficial or the opposite?

4. Compare the casual phrasing ("Well! If . . .") with which "Dejection" begins with the assertive tone of the opening of "Kubla Khan." How does this difference reflect the basic difference between the two poems?

5. Kubla Khan decrees a pleasure dome (line 2); the speaker desires to "build that dome in air" (line 46), with music. What is the point of this contrast between decreeing and building?

6. "Kubla Khan" can be read as a poem about the sources of creativity in the unconscious. Can you work out such a reading?

John Keats

Keats is most students' favorite among the English Romantic poets, and he is probably the most teachable of them. Young people are drawn to Keats partly by the pathos of his death in his mid-twenties, but his fundamental appeal for the young goes deeper, reflecting at once their penchant for sensuousness and their skeptical insecurities, their need both to affirm and to question. Despite the inexhaustible suggestiveness and complexity of his symbols and language, his basic meaning is almost immediately clear, and therefore teaching him by way of close explication is especially rewarding, since the deeper levels of his meaning enrich but do not betray students' initial understanding of him. This section on Keats in the Manual focuses more on broad issues than on particular poems or their elements, because it seems idle to focus on a dozen or so details from among the hundreds that merit attention in Keats's poems and will occur to teachers without prompting. Almost every line in the poem announces itself as worth explicating.

1. Is Keats an escapist or a realist?

This question is a bald version of the perennial question about Keats. It is sometimes posed by students (but also in some published criticism of Keats) in strange ways: for example, whether it is better to be a living human being than to be a painted figure on an urn, or than a nightingale, or whether it is better to fall in love with the goddess of the moon than with a human woman--as if one actually had such choices. One of the teacher's main jobs is to bring home the authentic human questions raised by Keats's symbolic action: for example, how much happiness it is reasonable to demand of life, the extent to which we can exert such "reasonable" control over our aspirations, wherein the best happiness is to be found, and how valid the Romantic ideal of the imagination is.

2. Which image in Keats's poems seems to you to capture best his meaning and method?

The best suggestions will reflect as many as possible of the Keatsian motifs: tensions between lushness and harshness, stasis and movement, positive and negative connotations (sleep, death), mortality and immortality, and so forth.

3. Taking Keats's poems as a group, is it possible to formulate from them his view of the value and function of art?

4. Keats's odes are sometimes considered an organic group. What evidence or justification is there for this view?

5. Is <u>The Eve of St. Agnes</u> a celebration of love or a warning about cynical seductions?

6. A number of Keats's poems move from outside to inside and then back, or from detachment to intensity and then back. What does this typical movement tell us about Keats's ideas or the quality of his response to life? Do different poems use such movement for different purposes?

The questions can be asked about the "Nightingale" and "Grecian Urn" odes, "La Belle Dame Sans Merci," and <u>The Eve of St. Agnes</u>.

7. What special significance do women or other feminine figures have for Keats?

8. What importance does the image of sleep have for Keats?

9. Is Keats the best friend of Romanticism, its severest critic, or both?

Mary Shelley

Frankenstein is one of those books that are interesting not just for what is in them but also for the history of their reputation. The work has never sunk into oblivion, but its high repute as a major contribution to literature is relatively recent. One is tempted to wonder whether the author's having been the wife of a major canonical poet helped Frankenstein by keeping it before the public eye or, conversely, hampered its reputation by encouraging unhelpful or invidious comparisons with Percy. A similar question is posed by the status of Frankenstein as an item of sensational popular culture in the twentieth century: did movies help the novel by expanding awareness of it or did they trivialize it in the eyes of serious readers?

The foregoing just might generate entry questions for teaching Frankenstein, speculative though their answers must necessarily be. More suggestive, probably, are the reasons for the novel's enhanced reputation over the last generation or two. The vogue of archetypal myth criticism is one of these reasons; Frankenstein re-explores the Prometheus myth, the Faust myth, and the Paradise Lost myth. Another reason is the increased interest in women authors and feminist approaches; in this connection, Frankenstein can be read as a commentary on male and female roles in creating and nurturing human life. Above all, the increasing popularity of science fiction, and the growing recognition of its status as a cultural telltale, suggest fruitful fields of classroom inquiry. Frankenstein asks the questions science fiction tends most often to ask: What does it mean to be human? Where does one draw the line between what is human and what is not? Is there a firm boundary between what is naturally possible and what isn't? If so, what is the role of science and technology in manipulating that boundary?

1. The critic Harold Bloom has argued that the Monster is more human than his creator, Victor Frankenstein. What are the various meanings this statement could have?

2. Walton, the explorer who finds Frankenstein on the Arctic ice floe, almost worships him. Why does he do so? In light of what we learn about Frankenstein in the course of his autobiography, is the worship justified?

3. Frankenstein could be read as a version of the Faust story, in which a mere human attempts things that should properly lie beyond human power and aspiration. As such, the novel would seem to point a moral. Do you find this reading satisfactory?

4. One of the most disturbing things some readers find in Frankenstein is the suggestion that physical ugliness is so powerful a force that nothing can compensate for it, even among high-minded people like the cottagers. What do you make of this motif in the novel?

Students often reply that tastes in beauty and ugliness are socially conditioned, not innate. But note that the Monster, himself relying on that assumption, finds it contradicted when he approaches Frankenstein's younger brother, William, and discovers that the "unspoiled" child is just as repelled by him as adults are.

5. One of the most curious things about Frankenstein, the novel and the movies made from it, is the tendency people have to call the Monster himself Frankenstein. Is this mere careless usage, or does it reflect something telling about the story?

6. The major female characters in Frankenstein tend to be innocent and ethereal, their role being mainly to instill the gentler virtues in people around them. Is this fact important?

7. Frankenstein's creation of the Monster would seem to usurp the creative prerogative of God. A similar motif may seem to underlie the Prometheus model (emphasized most obviously in the novel's subtitle). Is this religious perspective a valid way to approach the book?

Instructors not averse to biographical applications may wish to remind students that both Mary and Percy Bysshe Shelley were militantly distrustful of Christian religion, and that the latter's greatest poem champions Prometheus' heroic defiance of the cosmic ruler.

8. Clearly, Frankenstein derives partly from Milton's Paradise Lost and is some kind of commentary on it; both explicit references and clear allusions to Milton's poem are everywhere in the novel. How do you work this out? The Monster seems a stand-in for both Milton's Satan and his Adam, and by that logic Victor Frankenstein would seem to be a stand-in for God. If Frankenstein has that role, and if we regard him as unsympathetic (as we easily can), does that make the novel an attack on God, or at least on God as Milton and Christians understand God?

9. The creation of the Monster by Frankenstein can also be understood as a usurpation of gender: the usual role of the mother in bringing life into the world is negated. Especially in light of the general treatment of women in the novel, do you think this motif is important?

10. Is Frankenstein a condemnation of science? Victor Frankenstein's own reflections on his career would seem to imply as much. Is he right? Is this what the author wants us to think?

11. The youthful Frankenstein is caught up in the writings and theories of outdated, mystical pseudo-scientists such as Cornelius Agrippa and Paracelsus. This phase of his intellectual development seems wholly unnecessary to the sheer plot of the novel, since Frankenstein's professors at Ingolstadt soon set him straight. Why is this youthful misguidedness included in the novel at all?

12. Mary Shelley is careful to outline the progression of the Monster's awareness, beginning with his earliest sense impressions, and this progression seems to duplicate the stages of infant, child, and general human development. Does this account tell us anything important about what it means to be human?

13. Frankenstein may seem to endorse the common modern sociological premise that anti-social or criminal behavior is conditioned by rage, which in turn is induced by society's rejection of its marginal members. Does the novel give clear support to this sociological premise?

14. The first thing Frankenstein does after bringing his Monster to life is to flee, first to sleep in his bed and then to wander through the streets. Is this behavior consistent with his later behavior? What does it tell us about him?

15. After Frankenstein's decision not to create a female mate for the Monster, the latter vows to avenge himself on Frankenstein on his wedding day. Through all the long months during which Frankenstein broods over this threat, it never occurs to him that Elizabeth, and not he

himself, may be the intended victim. What do you make of this rather incredible lapse of imagination?

16. Much of Frankenstein takes place in austere or forbidding natural settings, many of them in regions of ice and desolation. Is this fact symbolically important?

   It may be pertinent to remember that both Victor and Elizabeth were born in Italy.

17. What function does the frame story, of Walton the explorer, have in the novel?

Alexander Pushkin

Perhaps the first challenge in teaching "The Queen of Spades" is to get students to take it seriously. Tolstoy called it a "masterpiece" and Dostoevsky thought it was "the height of artistic perfection." But the student reading it quickly for the first time may wonder what all the shouting is about and dismiss it as an entertaining but shallow piece of supernatural melodrama. The problem may lie in Pushkin's deliberately cultivated technique of "detached narration": understatement, implication, and irony. Beneath the neat twists of the plot lie considerable depths of psychological and even political meanings.

1. Is this really a tale of the supernatural? The main "supernatural" elements of the plot are the secret of the three cards, the Countess winking at Hermann from her coffin, her appearance to him with the secret, and the Queen of Spades laughing at him after his loss. Can any or all of these be explained naturalistically?

2. Hermann is characterized from outside; we are told primarily what he does, not what he thinks and feels. What motivates him? What are his weaknesses? He is characterized at the beginning by another character as "a Teuton, and therefore cautious," and a little later he rather piously says that "caution, moderation, and diligence--these are my three faithful cards." And yet within a few days he is wagering his father's precious legacy on a single turn of cards and in a few more days he is mad, muttering over and over, "Three, seven, ace. . . three, seven, queen!" Is he really a motiveless villain, a Napoleon or a Mephistopheles with "at least three crimes on his conscience," as Tomsky describes him to Lisaveta? Or can he be understood in more ordinary terms?

3. Describe the point of view and the narrative voice of the story. The scene in the bedroom between Hermann and the Countess is a particularly fruitful one for analyzing Pushkin's rapid shifts between a neutral, third-person point of view, a skeptical, ironic third-person, and the various points of view of the characters, a technique that has been called "cinemagraphic."

4. Weather and time of day figure as important symbols in "The Queen of Spades." Notice, for example, that on the evening of the ball in section 3, "the weather was atrocious, the wind howled and snow fell in moist flakes." The Countess wears a heavy sable cloak, but Lisaveta wears only "a thin wrap, with flowers in her hair." Trace such details through the story and comment on their effect and meaning.

5. Several of the many night scenes in "The Queen of Spades" are linked by the presence of dim, flickering lights. Identify these and show significant links between the scenes.

6. Paul Debreczeny has commented that "The Queen of Spades" is "as full of numbers as any scientific treatise." The most obvious of these are the threes and sevens which chime throughout the story, anticipating the secret cards. Trace these through the story. Why is the secret anticipated or recalled at each point?

7. Twos are equally important, if less obvious than threes and sevens. In the Countess's bedroom, for example, Hermann must choose between two doors, one to Lisaveta's room and one to the Countess's study, a choice that perhaps is linked to the fateful right and left cards of faro. Trace other such binary elements in the story.

8. Time is given considerable emphasis in "The Queen of Spades," not only in the precise times that are given for each event but in the kind of "double time" evoked most vividly by the simultaneous presence of the appallingly decayed old Countess and her youthful portrait, "a young belle with an aquiline nose, her powdered locks, brushed up from the temples, adorned with a rose." What significance does time have in the story? Is Hermann torn between the dead hand of the past and the promise of the future? Which does he choose? Does the choice have a political or historical significance in terms of Pushkin's period?

9. Note carefully the references to cards, especially at the beginning of section 6. The obsessed Hermann associates the Three of Hearts with young girls and "an enormous flower," the Seven with time and "Gothic portals," the Ace with paunchy men and "a huge spider," and the Queen, of course, with the Countess. Do these associations function as images, recalling other details in the story? In the light of the association of the Ace with portly men, for example, is it significant that on his first visit to Chekalinsky's, Hermann has to reach around "a fat general" in order to play?

10. Each of the six sections of "The Queen of Spades" is headed by an epigraph, and there is another epigraph to the entire story. The relationship of these epigraphs to the content of the story and its sections is sometimes rather oblique. Can you explain the relevance of each? Do the epigraphs suggest an ironic, "outside" interpretation of the action?

11. In light of the prominence of older women (the Countess, the Queen) and older men (Chekalinsky, the Ace) in the story, it might be argued that Hermann is locked in a struggle with parental figures, basically an Oedipal struggle. Examine the ambivalence with which parental figures are treated in the story, in connection with Hermann's rejection of Lisaveta. What does it mean?

Alfred, Lord Tennyson

Literally and figuratively, Tennyson seems in many ways an insular poet, definitively a Victorian Englishman; yet he reaches out in a surprising number of directions to other ages and other writers in the anthology. The three dramatic monologues in the book can be profitably compared with the three by Browning included in it; the methods have interesting similarities and differences, while the theme of striving and quietude, for example, is central in "The Lotos-Eaters," "Ulysses," and "Andrea del Sarto." Comparisons with Keats are perhaps even more instructive. Ancient myth as well comes newly alive in Tennyson, and students who have read the Odyssey (not to mention Dante's Inferno) will have a foil with which to contrast Tennyson's portrait of Ulysses.

1. All the poems by Tennyson included in the anthology examine the theme of quiet retirement versus active striving. What differences in treatment of this theme strike you?

2. Keats influenced Tennyson, and both poets are noted for the sensuousness of their descriptions and of their language. Do they use this sensuousness in similar ways? If you were to read a lush passage written by one of the two, how would you try to decide who wrote it?

3. Keats's "Ode to Psyche" and "Ode on a Grecian Urn" have ancient classical subjects; so do Tennyson's "The Lotos-Eaters," "Ulysses," and "Tithonus." Do the two poets use classical material in similar or in different ways?

4. Do "The Lotos-Eaters," "Ulysses," and "Tithonus" make moral statements, or are they mainly neutral descriptions of mood, atmosphere, character, and situations?

5. The ocean is a central image in both "The Lotos-Eaters" and "Ulysses." How does it reinforce the contrast between the two poems?

6. The first five stanzas of "The Lotos-Eaters," before the Choric Song begins, use the Spenserian stanza, the same stanza form used in Keats's The Eve of St. Agnes. Can you see why the two poets might use this stanza form in these works?

   The stanza is used in a number of poems, by Spenser and others including the Byron of Childe Harold, which combine vignette descriptions with a leisurely narrative.

7. Line 47 of the Choric Song from "The Lotos-Eaters" refers to "Portions and parcels of the dreadful past." What line or lines in "Ulysses" does this remind you of? How does the contrast point up the general contrast between the two poems?

8. Tennyson's "Ulysses" is based partly on Homer and partly also on Dante's Inferno, canto XXVI. In what ways does Tennyson's portrait resemble or differ from the earlier ones?

9. In what tone does Tennyson's Ulysses describe his son Telemachus? Are we meant to admire one of them more than the other? Which one? Why?

10. In what ways does "Tithonus" blend physical description of the dawn with physical description of the goddess of the dawn?

Robert Browning

The most obvious way to teach Browning, and surely one of the best, is to work through the poems, to "solve" them, bringing out along the way the salient features of the dramatic-monologue form. The questions below are mainly pump-primers; almost every line of each of the poems provides a handle by which theme, setting, and character may be grasped. Students will find much in the poems obscure at first, but Browning apparently expected this to be true, and the difficulty can be turned into profit as, piece by piece, the lines, action, and motives become clear.

One of many reasons why the Browning poems are interesting and valuable is that they are a kind of double exposure, reflecting the values of Victorian England and also the values of the Renaissance as filtered through English Victorian sensibility. Students who have read Boccaccio and Machiavelli can be asked whether the impressions they got from these writers square with what they read in Browning. His poems help explain how the nineteenth-century mythos (still alive) of the Renaissance came about. Looking ahead, students can be led to understand one of the sources for the form of poems like Eliot's "Prufrock."

1. All the Browning poems in the anthology have something to do with painting or sculpture. How does the theme of art work in each of the poems? Do the attitudes toward art in the three poems have anything in common?

2. What picture of Renaissance Italian religion emerges from the Browning poems? Is the picture attractive or repulsive?

3. What techniques does Browning use to create the effect of a distinct, individual speaking voice?

4. In "My Last Duchess," why does the speaker show his late wife's portrait to the visitor?

5. In line 13 and again in line 113 of "The Bishop Orders His Tomb," the Bishop asks, "Do I live, am I dead?" What meanings do these words have in each context?

6. In "The Bishop Orders His Tomb," lines 81-83, the words "hear," "see," "feel," and "taste" are used emphatically, in parallel. What do they suggest? Why are they ironic? What theme in the poem do the words reflect?

7. In line 93, the Bishop refers to "the life before I lived this life." What two lives does he mean, and why is the mention of them significant?

8. In lines 85-90, the Bishop describes how, on his deathbed, he imitates a statue. Does the Bishop want to be alive or dead? What is the difference from his point of view? How does life relate to art in the poem?

9. In "Andrea Del Sarto," we are meant to get a distinct impression of Lucrezia and what she is doing while Andrea speaks the words of the poem. Trace her actions and reactions at different points in the poem.

10. Is Andrea a sympathetic or an unsympathetic character? Is he, for example, arrogant or

apologetic? If he is both, how do you account for the paradox?

11. Life-versus-art is a theme in "Andrea Del Sarto"; see, for example, lines 178-179: "The Roman's is the better when you pray, / But still the other's Virgin was his wife." Does the theme mean the same thing it does in "The Bishop Orders His Tomb"?

12. Andrea Del Sarto suggests at times that he is satisfied with the decisions and choices he has made and with his present situation. To what extent is he telling the truth?

Frederick Douglass

Frederick Douglass's <u>Narrative</u> lends itself to a variety of teaching approaches and emphases. As a slave narrative, it follows certain conventions of the genre: a polemical purpose, white sponsorship, a series of cruelties, sections of direct excoriation of slavery, final attainment of freedom, etc. But it also belongs to the larger genre of autobiography and can be studied, along with Rousseau's <u>Confessions</u>, perhaps, in terms of the critical issues raised by autobiography. And it can be related to other works in the anthology in terms of such themes as freedom, individualism, and nature.

1. The Preface by William Lloyd Garrison and the Letter by Wendell Phillips that precede Douglass's text are interestingly related to it. How? You might consider not only content (the parallel accounts of Douglass's speech to the Abolitionist convention, for example) but also style and the contrast between the white Abolitionists' flowery rhetoric and Douglass's own directness and simplicity.

2. Douglass's first three paragraphs, on his age and his parents, introduce immediately the theme of identity and the way the slave system operates to deny slaves an identity. Explain.

3. Alfred E. Stone has commented that the incident of the flogging of Aunt Hester, with its metaphor of "the blood-stained gate, the entrance to the hell of slavery, through which I was about to pass," though "traditionally Christian on one level, also communicates more private and inchoate feelings about birth, sexuality, violence, dark mothers and white fathers." Discuss these themes, both in this passage and in the rest of the book.

4. Douglass, throughout his narrative, keeps us simultaneously aware of his past and present selves. Trace this awareness through representative passages, perhaps his accounts of slave songs in Chapter 2 and of his treatment as a child in Chapter 5.

5. Occasionally, Douglass breaks the pattern of his simple, strong style for sentimental, purple-passage set-pieces: the description of his grandmother's imagined death in Chapter 8, for example, his apostrophe to the ships in Chapter 10, and his evocation of his loneliness in New York in Chapter 11. Examine these passages carefully. How do they contrast with Douglass's dominant style?

6. Trace Douglass's use of names through the <u>Narrative</u>. Notice that he retains Frederick as his first name throughout, but has three last names: Bailey, Johnson, and Douglass. Notice, too, that some of the whites' names seem real (Lloyd, Auld), while others seem invented and allegorical (Severe, Gore, and Freeland). In other cases, the matter is ambiguous; is Sophia Auld's first name significant?

7. Trace references to writing through the book, and discuss how it functions as a sign of Douglass's mature identity.

8. Ships are a complex, recurring image in the book. Discuss the image, with reference to the trip to Baltimore (Chapter 5), learning to write in the shipyard (Chapter 7), the apostrophe to the ships (Chapter 10), the fight in the shipyard (Chapter 10), and the escape (Chapter 11).

9. In the 1846 edition of his book, Douglass defended its truth by writing: "Frederick the

Freeman is very different from Frederick the Slave." Freeman vs. Slave is one obvious opposition in the book. Identify other basic oppositions that complement this one.

10. Waldo E. Martin, Jr.: "The guiding assumption unifying Douglass's thought was an inveterate belief in a universal and egalitarian brand of humanism. His seemingly innate commitment to the inviolability of freedom and the human spirit best exemplified this overarching assumption. This grand organizing principle reflected his intellectual roots in the three major traditions of mid-nineteenth-century American thought: Protestant Christianity, the Enlightenment, and romanticism." Discuss the appearance of these traditions in the Narrative.

Walt Whitman

Of the many revolutions in American literary taste, none is more dramatic than that which in the twentieth century overthrew the titans of mid- and late-nineteenth-century poetry--Bryant, Longfellow, Whittier--and set in their place Emily Dickinson and Walt Whitman, one unknown in her own time, the other known until late in life only as a faintly disreputable versifier. Even now, a century after his death, Whitman has not lost his power to shock and outrage his readers, and the more thoughtful your students are and the more carefully they read, the more likely they are to be outraged. One possible teaching approach to Whitman takes its starting point in this very outrageousness, the term being defined as a flamboyant defiance of received ideas of poetic form, conventional conceptions of appropriate subject matter, orthodox religion, and even ordinary standards of good taste. Such outrageousness makes sense, though, only when measured against the traditional; once the class defines Whitman's rebellion, it can turn its attention to the way the poetry achieves traditional poetic goals, though in non-traditional ways. Whitman's nature poems, love poems, philosophical poems, and elegies are not wholly unlike earlier poems in these genres.

1. In "I Saw in Louisiana a Live-Oak Growing," Whitman tells us that the live-oak "made me think of myself." Why? Identify links between Whitman and the tree. He also tells us that the twig he broke off reminds him of his "own dear friends." Is there any contradiction here? Explore the tension between the individual and the group and between human beings and nature in the poem.

2. The boy in "Out of the Cradle Endlessly Rocking" hears two voices, one of the mockingbird, the other of the sea. What does each say?

3. "Out of the Cradle Endlessly Rocking" is a memory poem, a poem about a mature man recalling an incident from childhood that, he says, made him a poet. How does the speaker describe himself as a poet, and how does "Out of the Cradle Endlessly Rocking" exemplify the sort of poem he writes?

4. What does the title of "Out of the Cradle Endlessly Rocking" mean? What is the cradle? Why is it endlessly rocking? (Note the next-to-last line, in which the sea is compared to "some old crone rocking the cradle.")

5. How does Whitman organize his free verse? Notice especially the following:

   1) the varying line lengths and rhythms
   2) the absence of end rhyme
   3) the use of parallelism and repetition (as in the string of prepositional phrases that opens "Out of the Cradle....")
   4) the use of lists or catalogues
   5) the recurring imagery (like that of the moon in "Out of the Cradle....")
   6) the use of initial or internal rhyme (as in the "long"/"prong" of l. 56)
   7) the use of occasional metrical regularity (as in the opening line).

6. The italicized lines are, of course, the song of the bird. What is the effect of Whitman representing a bird's song in human language? Note that while Whitman says that the bird gave him a voice as a poet, in writing the poem he himself gives the bird not only a voice but a human voice. What does this suggest about the poem as a genuine memory or as an artful construction of a past that will help explain the present?

7. The contrast between astronomy and actual stars in "When I Heard the Learn'd Astronomer" is enriched by a remarkable number of parallel contrasts in this eight-line poem. The lecture-room, for example, is loud with "much applause," while outside there is "perfect silence." Identify other such contrasts and comment on their effect.

8. Analyze the symbolism of the lilac, the star, and the bird in "When Lilacs Last in the Dooryard Bloom'd."

9. Like most elegies, "When Lilacs Last in the Dooryard Bloom'd" deals less with the dead person than with the survivor and his attempts to come to terms with his grief. Trace Whitman's response to the death of Lincoln through the poem. How does he finally come to at least a partial reconciliation with the fact of death?

10. "When Lilacs Last in the Dooryard Bloom'd," like "Out of the Cradle Endlessly Rocking," deals with the great Romantic theme of the relation between the poetic imagination and the objects of its contemplation. Compare the treatment of this theme in the two poems, and compare both with Wordsworth's treatment of the theme.

11. In "A Noiseless Patient Spider," the speaker's soul is compared to a spider spinning a web. How does this metaphor work? Take it apart and analyze its elements: spider, promontory, space, filaments, spheres, web.

Herman Melville

One of the editors once had a student who, asked to write an essay on "Bartleby the Scrivener" on an exam, merely wrote politely but firmly across the page, "I would prefer not to." The student got an A; he was so bright, industrious, and generally unBartlebian a student that the editor knew that his reconstruction of the "Bartleby" situation was far from casual or uncalculated. The competitive, achievement-oriented classroom suddenly took on the atmosphere of the shallow bustle of nineteenth-century Wall Street, the student's usually repressed Bartlebyism had a healthy airing, and the editor, an optimistic, liberal academic, was rather uncomfortably forced to confront the "Bartleby" narrator within himself (an inner presence probably confirmed by his grading of the non-essay). Critics have had a hard time with "Bartleby the Scrivener." (Some especially dubious readings are mentioned in the Melville introduction.) An alternative to realistic or allegorical readings is an absurdist one; perhaps we can understand the story better by looking back on it through the work of Beckett, Ionesco, and Kafka. Bartleby may be less a realistic character than an enigmatic intruder, like the Matchseller in Pinter's "A Slight Ache," whose mere presence becomes a screen upon which the narrator projects his own deepest anxieties and with whom he builds up a complex, ambivalent identification.

1. Examine the narrator's self-characterization in the first three paragraphs of the story. Why is he especially vulnerable to Bartleby's baffling but firm assertion of his own desires? Trace his attempts to deal with Bartleby through the story. What do they further reveal about himself?

2. The names of Turkey, Nippers, and Ginger Nut all suggest food, and the three are associated closely with eating and drinking as well as with rather infantile self-indulgence. How do these associations suggest the characters' function in the story?

3. The subtitle of "Bartleby the Scrivener" is "A Story of Wall Street," and a great many walls appear in the story: the walls outside the window, the office walls, screens, prison walls, etc. What do these walls symbolize?

4. Why is copying an ideal occupation for Bartleby? What does it come to represent?

Note the line "I cannot credit that the mettlesome poet, Byron, would have contentedly sat down with Bartleby to examine a law document of, say five hundred pages, closely written in a crimpy hand."

5. After Bartleby has announced that he would "prefer not to," the narrator and his other assistants find the word "prefer" cropping up frequently in their own speech. Why?

6. The narrator at one point says of Bartleby that "He was more a man of preferences than assumptions." Does this line define an important difference between Bartleby and the narrator? In what ways is the narrator a "man of assumptions"?

7. The ending of the story, in which the narrator tells of Bartleby's earlier career in the Dead Letter Office, has been widely criticized as gratuitous and inconsistent in tone. Do you agree? Does it add anything to our sense of what Bartleby represents?

Emily Dickinson

Dickinson's poems can be approached from the point of view of the history of ideas. Her views on nature, God, death, the self, and other crucial topics can be placed within the broad context of Romanticism and within the narrower ones of Calvinism, Transcendentalism, etc. But a more personal approach is also possible, one that sees the poems as a progressive revelation of aspects of a complex personality, haunted by deep fears of isolation, loss, and madness, and defending itself against those fears through varied strategies--irony, denial, trivialization, confession, rationalization--strategies which are transmuted into the methods of her art.

1. Poem 67 is made up of three sentences: a general statement, a brief example, and a more extended one. Both generalization and examples suggest a characteristic Dickinsonian stance toward life. What is it, and how does it reappear in the other poems in the selection?

Note the ambivalence with which Dickinson treats the recurring theme of separation. On the one hand, it is the source of understanding and insight; on the other, it is the ultimate terror, leading to madness.

2. Analyze closely the metrics and diction of Poem 67. The form of the poem is basically hymn-tune quatrains of iambic trimeter lines. Where does Dickinson stretch the limits of the form through radical variations? Comment on the poem's diction, especially "comprehend a nectar," "purple Host," "forbidden ear," and "agonized and clear." What is the effect of these metrical variations and this diction?

3. What is the dramatic situation of Poem 199? Explore the words "wife," "Czar," "Woman," and "Girl" in the poem. What ironies and paradoxes are involved?

4. Poems 258 and 214 contrast sharply, expressing as they do ecstasy and despair. What are the sources and nature of the two states of mind in the poems? Are there any similarities between the poems despite their contrasting subjects?

5. Dickinson frequently writes of madness. What sort of madness does she fear? Note especially Poems 258, 280, 303, and 435.

6. What is the tone of poem 303? Is the isolation of the soul behind "valves of stone" represented as desirable? Undesirable? Both at the same time?

7. Poem 328 seems to change sharply in tone, the first fourteen lines being comparatively light and whimsical, the last six gravely musical and almost visionary. What is the meaning of this shift? Does the bird represent a general force in life?

8. The last words of Poem 341 are "letting go." What do these words mean, in connection either with the person freezing to death or with the poem's actual subject, the person living in the aftermath of grief? For the freezing person, does "letting go" mean abandoning life or, perhaps, relaxing into the comfort that is supposed to supplant pain in the last stages of freezing? For the person living in the aftermath of pain, does "letting go" mean recovering from the grief or abandoning oneself to it, without "formal" restraint, as in a flood of tears?

9. What is Dickinson's attitude toward death? See especially Poems 465, 470, 712, and 1732.

10. In Poem 829, consider what the difference would be if, instead of the last two lines, "Let no Sunrise' yellow noise / Interrupt this Ground," Dickinson had written, "Let no morning's golden light / Violate this ground."

Several palindromic patterns of accent in the poem are also notable; for example, the accents in the first two lines run X x X X X / X X X x X.

11. In Poem 1732, is there any internal evidence of what events made the speaker's life "close twice before its close"? Trace the theme of parting through the other poems.

12. Trace the following images through Dickinson's poems: small animals, eating and drinking, the sun, elements of the landscape, kings and other rulers, and doors and keys.

13. The critic Richard Chase finds the central symbolic act in Dickinson's poems to be "the achievement of special status" through such crucial experiences as love, marriage, death, poetic expression, and intense intuitive experiences. Can you identify this pattern in several Dickinson poems?

Gustave Flaubert

A natural starting point for the study of "A Simple Heart," for both teachers who want to teach the story for its own sake and those who want to stress Flaubert's technical contributions to the development of fiction, is point of view. The narrator of "A Simple Heart" is the textbook Flaubert narrator, coolly building up from concrete detail the elements of Félicité's world, while withholding explicit judgment or interpretation and even the thoughts and emotions of his characters, for the most part. The result is a complexly ironic work, which leaves a great deal for the reader to do. He or she must sense the levels of irony with which the multiple worlds and value systems of the story are presented. There is, first of all, Félicité's "simple" world of self-denial and frustrated yearning for something to love. Then there is the world of her employer, who remains, like Félicité, oblivious to its meanness and vulgarity. And finally there is the world of idealism and romance, itself presented ironically and yet providing a standard against which to measure the other worlds.

1. Examine the first two short paragraphs of the story. How do they establish the narrative tone and point of view? Is the observation that Félicité was "the envy" of the ladies ironic in any way?

2. Analyze the story of Félicité's abortive love affair at the beginning of Part II. Note its objectivity; Flaubert reports what she said and did but seldom what she thought or felt. What is the effect of this objectivity? What do you make of Flaubert's remark that Theodore proposed marriage out of frustrated passion, "or perhaps quite artlessly"? Shouldn't the author know?

3. What ironic associations do the names Paul and Virginie have?

   The class will need some help here. Paul et Virginie (1788) was an enormously popular novel by the Rousseauvian Bernardine de Saint-Pierre. Paul and Virginie are two children reared on an island who have an idyllic love affair which is ruined when civilization intervenes. The contrast with the real children is obvious, but the names contribute to the world of idealism and romance of which the saint's-legend elements and the church rituals are also a part.

4. Periodically through the story Félicité is dazzled by spectacular displays of various sorts: the assembly at Colleville where she is nearly seduced, her first experience in church, etc. Are these scenes linked in any other ways?

5. Félicité is initially attracted to the parrot because he comes from America and thus reminds her of Victor. Are there any other reasons for her exaggerated attachment to the bird?

6. Examine the detailed descriptions of rooms and furniture in the story. What do they tell about their inhabitants?

7. "In church [Félicité] was always gazing at the Holy Ghost in the window, and observed that there was something of the parrot in him." Is this line wholly facetious or does Flaubert mean it in a partially serious way?

8. Is Félicité really a saint? Is there a suggestion in the story that the lowest and the highest are linked in a blessedness to which the middle (Madam Aubain's meanness and selfishness) can never be admitted?

Fyodor Dostoevsky

Notes from Underground and "The Grand Inquisitor" are both highly didactic works, and a good bit of class time will probably have to be devoted to analyzing and clarifying Dostoevsky's ideas. But both are wonderfully dramatic works, too, and equal attention should probably be paid to the ways in which Dostoevsky brings his ideas to life by embodying them in complex characters and action.

1. Notes from Underground is a long dramatic monologue; Dostoevsky intrudes upon the speaker's voice only twice, in the long initial footnote and in the final note. What is the effect of these two intrusions? Do they reinforce the dramatic situation by adding another layer of narrative to the story's complex, nested structure?

2. What is the relation of Parts I and II?

   The class should note the time scheme; the Underground Man is forty years old in Part I and looks back upon events when he was in his twenties in part II. The three episodes of Part II appear to account for his beliefs in Part I and to illustrate them.

3. To whom is the Underground Man's monologue addressed? (See I.xi.)

4. The Underground Man describes himself as motivated primarily by "spite." What does he mean by this word, and how does he develop its meaning throughout the story?

5. Discuss what the Underground Man means by the following statements:

   a) "Every sort of consciousness is, in fact, a disease" (I.i).

   b) Petersburg is "the most theoretical and intentional town on the whole terrestrial globe" (I.ii).

   c) "I admit that twice two makes four is an excellent thing, but if we are to give everything its due, twice two makes five is sometimes a very charming thing" (I.ix).

   d) "Reactionary as it is, corporal punishment is better than nothing" (I.ix).

   e) "I swear to you, gentlemen, there is not one thing, not one word of what I have written, that I really believe" (I.xi).

6. Summarize the Underground Man's comparison of French, German, and Russian "romantics" (II.i). Does he mean something special by "romantic"? Is there anything "romantic" about his own views?

7. How are the three episodes of Part II--the officer, the farewell party, and Liza--related? Do they represent progressive stages in the Underground Man's self-destructiveness? How?

8. The incidents in Part II are apparently intended to illustrate the Underground Man's assertion in Part II that a person will sometimes do irrational things against his own interest in order to assert his own freedom of will or his own "identity." This is a philosophical

explanation of his behavior; are materials provided for a complementary psychological explanation?

Notice the speaker's various brief accounts of his childhood and school days, especially in II.iii. A position of "moral masochism" much like the Underground Man's is described in Bernhard Berliner, "On Some Psychodynamics of Masochism," Psychoanalytic Quarterly, XVI (1947), 459-471.

9. The Underground Man says of his plea to Liza (II.vii) that "It was the exercise of my skill that carried me away; yet it was not merely sport." What are his motives? Note his own analysis in II.ix. How does he contradict himself in explaining why he tried to "save" Liza?

10. Analyze the Underground Man's relation with his servant Apollon. How do they echo his relations with other people?

11. The Underground Man says that the impulse to humiliate Liza by giving her money was "not an impulse from the heart, but came from my evil brain" (II.x). Does the distinction illuminate the Underground Man's psychology and his idea of himself?

12. The Underground Man, in the concluding section, says that we all "feel a sort of loathing for real life." What does he mean by "real life," and how does the remark constitute an interpretation of what has gone before?

13. Ivan calls "The Grand Inquisitor" a "poem in prose," and it is framed by Ivan's conversation with Alyosha. What is the effect of this emphasis upon the story's fictionality?

14. What is the effect of having Christ remain silent? Of the final kiss?

15. How does "The Grand Inquisitor" express fundamental social and political issues of Dostoevsky's time? Of ours?

16. What themes link Notes from Underground and "The Grand Inquisitor"?

Leo Tolstoy

"A Simple Heart," Notes from Underground, and "The Death of Ivan Ilyitch" offer many points of comparison and good opportunities to explore the possibilities of realism. All three explore the meanings of ordinary, commonplace lives, described in great detail. But what differences there are among the three works! "A Simple Heart" is a realist's saint's life, in which a lush romanticism nevertheless hovers just outside the frame of Flaubert's realistic portrait of Félicité. Realism for Dostoevsky is psychological realism; "ordinary life" for his Underground Man is a twisted and yet paradoxically rather noble struggle to hang on to his own human freedom in the face of highminded but inhuman nineteenth-century meliorism. For Tolstoy, Ivan Ilyitch's life--"the simplest, the most ordinary, and the most awful"--is given meaning by the tenets of primitive Christianity. Inevitably, the differences also appear in narrative technique, in Flaubert's pervasive detachment and irony, in Dostoevsky's intense dramatic monologue, and in Tolstoy's deceptively simple straightforward narrative.

1. "The Death of Ivan Ilyitch" is a simple chronological narrative, except for section I. Why does Tolstoy begin with this episode after Ivan's death as a prologue to the story of Ivan's life? Why is this section told largely from the point of view of Pyotr Ivanovitch, a minor character?

2. Why is it important that Ivan Ilyitch be an unusually capable and successful man, by ordinary standards? Would the point be different if he were a failure?

3. Dante, in the Inferno, placed the "trimmers," those who had remained noncommittal and had done nothing either particularly good or particularly evil, in the vestibule of Hell, denying them entrance even to that place of torment. Would Ivan Ilyitch fit in this group?

4. Analyze carefully the account of Ivan's early career in section II. How does Tolstoy suggest the origins of his later character traits?

5. Who tells Ivan's story? What is the narrative voice like? How is our perception of it affected by the first sentence in section II and such passages as the paragraph in section III, beginning "In reality . . . ," telling us what Ivan's house was like?

6. Ivan Ilyitch deals with the early problems of his marriage by working out for himself "a definite line, just as in the government service" (section II). Is this strategy representative of his general approach to life? Give examples of how he deals with other problems.

7. The words "easily, agreeably, and decorously" become a sort of refrain in descriptions of how Ivan Ilyitch lived. Do they define both the virtues and the limitations of his life? Are the adverbs ironic?

8. Ivan's wife Praskovya Fyodorovna is the chief secondary character in the story. How is she a foil to Ivan Ilyitch? Is she a sort of female version of Ivan?

9. Tolstoy, in Part III, describes Ivan Ilyitch's sharp compartmentalization of his personal and his official life. How does this account of inner division compare with Dostoevsky's treatment of the same theme in Notes from Underground?

10. How do the recurring references to card games figure in the story?

11. What is the role of the peasant Gerasim in the story? Why does Ivan become so attached to him? Does he represent peasant values as opposed to Ivan's bourgeois ones? If so, what are they?

12. What is the role of Ivan's youngest son Volodya in the story? Note especially that Ivan feels that, except for Gerasim, "Volodya was the only one that understood and was sorry" (section VIII), and pay particular attention to his role in the death scene. Do the repeated references to Volodya's masturbatory habits have any organic function in the story, or is Tolstoy lapsing into crankiness in these passages?

13. Trace the spiritual changes that come over Ivan Ilyitch in his last days (sections IX-XII). What thought brings about his deathbed illumination?

14. When does the "death" of Ivan really occur? Can it be argued that it is only with the near approach of his literal death that he begins to live, most of his existence having been a figurative state of death?

15. Tolstoy wrote, in **What is Art**?, "If a man is infected by the author's condition of soul, if he feels this emotion and this union with others, then the object which has effected this is art: but if there be no such infection, if there be not this union with the same author and others who are moved by the same work--then it is not art." Is "The Death of Ivan Ilyitch" art by these criteria?

Henrik Ibsen

As, in the anthology, Flaubert, Dostoevsky, and Tolstoy form a sort of triptych of nineteenth-century realistic fiction, so Ibsen and Chekhov constitute a diptych of early realistic drama. And the house of realistic drama, like that of realistic fiction, has many rooms. The main features of the realistic method in drama having been established, the class would do well to ask, with each of these playwrights, "What kind of a realist is he?" For Ibsen, the answer might be to call him a "subjective realist," or by some such term that captures Ibsen's constant emphasis upon the inner, spiritual struggles beneath the external details of the plays and the way each detail is colored by those struggles. A simple exercise such as tracing references to the weather through A Doll House will demonstrate vividly the difference between a neutral photographic realism and Ibsen's artful, painterly realism (to use a metaphor he employed repeatedly himself).

1. Read the initial description of the setting carefully, and then follow changes in it carefully through the play. Is there anything symbolic about the room's having so much furniture in it and being overheated? Trace through the play references to the stuffiness of the room and to the temperature outdoors. Do they prepare us for the symbolism of the slamming door at the end?

2. Why does the play take place at Christmas?

3. Nora lies to Helmer in the opening scene about eating macaroons. Trace the theme of lying through the play. What moral ambiguities are involved?

4. The story of Kristine Linde amounts to a subplot in the play. What is the relationship between Kristine's story and Nora's?

5. A Doll House, like Oedipus the King, has a revelatory plot, in which revelations of past events are major actions. It is also, partially because of this structure, full of dramatic irony, a result of the disparity between what characters and the audience know at particular points. Note for example the issue of whether Nora is a spendthrift or not. Helmer calls her that in the opening scene, but Nora's scene with Kristine forces us (but not Helmer) to revise this judgment. Identify major revelations in the play, identify gaps in knowledge between characters and audience, and analyze the ironies involved.

6. What is the function of Dr. Rank in the play?

Note that Rank is hardly needed at all for the development of the plot. But his presence enriches the play thematically and symbolically, especially his relationship with Nora (which clarifies her relationship with Helmer), his carrying a fatal, buried secret, and his status as a solitary figure outside the domesticity of the Helmers' world.

7. The servant Anne-Marie, in her short scene opening Act II, provides the story of another woman's life to compare with Nora's and Kristine's. How does it compare with theirs?

8. Nora's character is a study in the bad effects upon women of traditional marriage and traditional sexual roles. Is Helmer's character a comparable study of their bad effects upon men?

9. What is the relationship between Kristine Linde and Krogstad? (See especially the opening of Act III.) Is it intended as a contrast to the relationship between Nora and Helmer?

10. A number of playwrights and novelists have written "sequels" to A Doll House. What would a credible sequel be like?

Kate Chopin

The Awakening is a beautifully crafted novel, and students' keen interest in its feminist theme ought not to preempt class time to the extent of wholly ignoring the work's craftsmanship. Like the nearly contemporary Heart of Darkness, though in a very different style, it successfully blends the methods of realism and symbolism, creating an intriguing web of interconnected images and leitmotifs. The feminism in The Awakening nevertheless does call for rather extensive discussion, not only because feminism is timely today but also because its exact quality in Chopin's novel is problematical. Edna Pontellier's suicide is troubling, even offensive, to some current feminists, and therefore its elusive motives warrant careful exegesis. That her liberation is identified so strongly with a romantic love interest is another aspect of her story that feminists may find controversial. Much of the feminism in the book is undated, but some of it has a period quality colored by turn-of-the-century aestheticism. This fact is dramatized by the striking similarities between The Awakening and Harold Frederic's The Damnation of Theron Ware, both of which were written by Americans at about the same time, were almost forgotten for half a century and then rediscovered, concern respectively a woman's and a man's hope to find sensuous beauty and erotic fulfillment outside of married propriety, draw a contrast between Protestant earnestness and a slightly decadent Catholic aestheticism, and even use as central vehicles emotional intoxication by the Preludes and other piano works of Frederic Chopin. Not that many, if any, of your students will have read Theron Ware, but alerting them to these and similar motifs will help them understand something of the sensibility of the period and part of the mood of a phase in the evolution of feminism.

1. What meanings does awakening have in the novel? How does it relate to the implications of sleep and dreaming? Consider this question both in general and in connection with concrete instances in the book.

2. The arts, especially music and painting, are often mentioned in The Awakening. How do different characters regard the arts? Is art, for example, a pleasurable escape into freedom or a painful act of heroism?

3. What similarities or differences are there between the feminism of The Awakening and present-day forms of feminism?

4. Is the narrative voice in The Awakening a neutral reporter? Is it sympathetic with Edna and her campaign for self-realization? Is it ever ironic? If so, at whom or what is the irony directed?

This is not an easy question; the rapturous description of Mme. Ratignolle's beauty in Chapter IV, for example, may be irony, but very possibly it is not.

5. Edna feels confined in her marriage. Is this because her husband Léonce is the kind of man he is, or is it marriage in general that she bridles at? What are we readers supposed to think of Léonce? Should we, for example, take at face value the statement (Chapter III) that Edna is "the sole object of his existence"?

6. Adèle Ratignolle is a foil to Edna, most obviously in their attitudes toward their domestic roles but in other ways too. But Adèle seems much more than a caricature of the dutiful wife

and mother; in Chapter IV the author waxes lyrical about her beauty and likens her to a "bygone heroine of romance." She is also a warm friend and a expressive pianist (Chapter IX). Should Chopin have presented her instead as a colorless and unglamorous drudge?

7. What role does Alcée Arobin play in The Awakening? Does he contribute to Edna's spiritual liberation or is he a distraction from it? How does what he means for Edna compare with what Robert Lebrun means for her?

  See, for example, Chapter XXVIII and Edna's reflection on Arobin in the last chapter.

8. How essential is Robert in Edna's awakening to her new self? Is he the cause of her awakening or is her love for him rather a symptom or result of it?

9. During the first part of the novel, at Grand Isle, we catch frequent glimpses of two unidentified young lovers and an equally mysterious religious woman in black. What function do these figures serve?

10. The Awakening is largely about Edna's discovery of her sensuousness, but in some respects she seems more strait-laced than the French Creoles she lives among. Note, for example, their easygoing attitude toward flirtations with other men's wives (Chapter V) and toward risqué literature (Chapter IV). What do you make of this? Which would be more accurate, to call Edna an emancipated woman or to call her a puritan?

11. Look at the passage in Chapter X about Edna's difficulties and fears in learning to swim. What is the analogue with her inner development?

12. Edna's conversation with Dr. Mandelet in Chapter XXXVIII is a difficult passage, but it seems central. What is each of them saying, and what bearing do their statements have on the meaning and conclusion of the novel?

13. The theme and imagery of children and childbirth run through The Awakening and become especially insistent in the last three chapters, XXXVII-XXXIX. Note, for example, that as Edna stands naked at the edge of the waves she feels "like some new-born creature, opening its eyes . . . ." Why so much emphasis on birth as the story leads toward death?

14. When Edna last sees her children, in Chapter XXXII, she seems especially close to them. Yet in the last chapter she considers them as "antagonists who had overcome her." How do you account for this seeming paradox? Also, in this last chapter she reaffirms her earlier-stated conviction (Chapter XVI) that she would sacrifice the "unessential" for her children but not sacrifice herself. Is her suicide an act of self-sacrifice or of self-preservation?

15. Just before her death, Edna recalls a number of episodes from her earlier life, including the seemingly endless meadow she had walked through as a child and the cavalry officer for whom she had had a childhood passion. (These are described earlier, in Chapter VII, which also sketches other romantic crushes Edna had felt while growing up.) These, clearly, are important symbols. Of what?

16. The passage at the end of Chapter VI beginning "The voice of the sea is seductive" is repeated almost verbatim in the last chapter as Edna arrives at the beach. Why the echo?

17. Is Edna's death a defeat or a victory? If a victory, over what? If a defeat, by what? Society? Some flaw in herself? Something inherent in human life?

18. Could The Awakening be made more easily into a play or into a movie? Note that the chapters vary a great deal in length, that some are mainly dialogue while others are mainly summary, analysis, and commentary, and that some describe the inner Edna and some see her from outside.

19. We are occasionally admitted, at least briefly, inside the minds of relatively minor characters such as Dr. Mandelet and Mariequita, but we are seldom if ever admitted inside the mind of so important a character as Robert. Does this seem appropriate? Does or does not our understanding of the ending depend in part on knowing how Robert sees things?

Anton Chekhov

The gentle serenity of the surface of Chekhov's works masks a great inner complexity, a complexity that is the delight of actors but often a source of bafflement to students. Chekhov's war against predictable formulas is still not won, and students reared on the easy formulas of television drama sometimes find it hard to deal with a play in which a tragic cry from the heart is immediately followed by somebody mooing like a cow. Tone is everything, especially in the plays, and a good way to begin the study of The Cherry Orchard is to assign parts and have the class read through the opening scene of the play, getting the delicate and realistic shifts in tone firmly in their ears.

1. "Gooseberries" is a frame-tale; the story of Nikolay Ivanovitch and his gooseberries is told within the frame of Ivan Ivanovitch and Burkin's visit to Alehin. What does the story gain by this frame structure?

2. Nikolay Ivanovitch's rural dream is epitomized by gooseberries. What is the effect of this absurd detail?

3. At the beginning and end of Ivan Ivanovitch's story, Chekhov mentions the ancestral portraits which look down as if listening to the story. What added dimension do these references provide?

4. "Gooseberries" begins with a shower of rain and ends with the rain "pattering on the window-panes all night." What does water symbolize in the story?

5. Ivan Ivanovitch is humane and idealistic; are his views undercut in any way? Is Alehin a foil to Ivan? How?

6. The four acts of The Cherry Orchard take place, respectively, in the nursery, in the open country by a roadside shrine, in the drawing room, and again in the nursery, now empty. Examine the descriptions of these settings carefully. How do they reflect the themes and imagery of the play?

7. The Cherry Orchard covers about six months, beginning in May and ending in October. How is this time scheme related to the meaning of the play?

8. What sense do we have of the neighborhood of the Ranevsky estate? How has it been organized economically and socially? How is it changing?

9. The Cherry Orchard is named after its central symbol. What does the orchard symbolize? Note especially the discussion of the orchard in Act I. What view of the orchard does each character express?

10. Each act of The Cherry Orchard is built around some social or domestic occasion. What are they, and how does Chekhov use them to generate dramatic action?

11. Love is generally frustrated or unreciprocated in The Cherry Orchard. Analyze the following attachments and discuss why they don't work out: Lyubov and her Paris lover, Varya and Lopahin, Trofimov and Anya; and Dunyasha, Epihodov, and Yasha.

12. Chekhov called The Cherry Orchard a "comedy." What comic elements does it contain? What tragic elements?

13. In Act I, Lyubov thinks she sees her dead mother walking in the orchard. Trace the theme of motherhood through the play. Are all the characters searching for a lost security associated with maternity?

14. Images of life (spring, cherry blossoms, the nursery) and images of death (guns, gravestones, axes) run throughout The Cherry Orchard. Identify the images and discuss their meaning.

15. Trofimov's long speech beginning "All Russia is our garden," near the end of Act II, seems a major thematic statement. How is it undercut? What ironies are implied?

16. Examine the attitude of each character toward work. Does any of them have a happy, productive working life? Why not?

17. The quarrel between Lyubov and Trofimov in Act III reveals a number of parallels between the two. What are they?

18. The ending of The Cherry Orchard is rather open and indeterminate. What do you think will happen to each of the characters?

19. What themes and techniques do The Cherry Orchard and "Gooseberries have in common?

French Symbolist and Modernist Poetry

Not all aspects of Modernism are anticipated in the anthology selection of French symbolist poets (defined, as the Introduction in the book indicates, rather broadly), nor are all the aspects evident in the two poets, Apollinaire and Valéry, who can themselves be considered Modernists. Quite a few of the roots of Modernism, however, can be traced in the poets included--the dissatisfaction with bourgeois life, the obsession with the possibilities of art accompanied by an ironic sense of human limitations and of the dissolution of certainties, the rejection of the past and of faded conventions, the concern with the psychology of perception. At the same time, certain symbolists sustained aspects of Romanticism--a taste for the exotic, for the gorgeous, for the ideal and suprahuman (the "azure"). The symbolists tended to reject the Realism contemporary with them, but even some of these Realist concerns are apparent in them--for example, in Baudelaire's unflinching description of human and animal decomposition, and in Corbière's lesson to Victor Hugo in how sailors really talk and think.

This heterogeneity of ingredients in the poets represented would make it hard to teach them for their own sake while covering them all. Users of the anthology will probably choose wisely by opting to single out certain strands to be examined for specific purposes--to concentrate, for example, on the element of irony, or on redefinitions of the goals of art, in connection with the transition from Romanticism to Modernism.

It isn't a bad idea to show that one recognizes the comic elements in certain of the poems included. The comedy is really there, and to respond to it may help students feel more at home with the poems.

1. What is Baudelaire's attitude toward sin? Does it nauseate him or allure him or both? Is his treatment of lust and sex in "A Voyage to Cythera" characteristic of him?

2. Does the view of the poet in Baudelaire's "The Albatross" reappear in other poems by him? Can the albatross symbolize human beings other than poets?

3. The epigraph of Corbière's "Paris by Night" reads, "It's not a city, it's a world." Is this poem, and its companion "Paris by Day," about Paris or about the world?

4. Corbière's "The End" comments ironically on a poem about sailors by Victor Hugo, cited as an epigraph. Which tribute to the sailors, Hugo's or Corbière's, makes them seem more heroic?

5. Consider the lyrics of Verlaine in light of his brief manifesto "The Art of Poetry." Does he practice what he preaches there?

6. Does Verlaine fit comfortably with the other seven poets in this section of the anthology? Are his delicacy and tenderness not simply romantic?

7. How does Rimbaud's "The Drunken Boat" mean? Should we study it intently, hoping that with close analysis it will become more coherent? Or should we simply abandon ourselves to its phantasmagoric wash of images?

8. Rimbaud's sonnet "Vowels" is one of the most famous poems of the nineteenth century. Are the connections he makes with the five vowels merely impressionistic or do they make any kind of objective sense? Are the effect and meaning of the poem the same as in Baudelaire's "Correspondences"?

9. Contrast the "Here-below" ("Windows," line 33) with "The Azure" in the poems of Mallarmé.

10. The poems by Laforgue in the anthology include elements of both seriousness and flippancy. Can these elements be reconciled with each other in the poems by him?

11. The poems of Apollinaire too seem both jaunty and painful. Can these elements be brought together to define a consistent attitude?

12. Consider Apollinaire's "The Pretty Redhead." What does the poem say about the future and the modern? Does Apollinaire imply a poetic manifesto such as we have seen in some of the other poets in this group? Does the image of the pretty redhead make sense? Why should Apollinaire have chosen it?

13. What is the subject of Valéry's "Helen"? The Trojan War? Beauty? Time? Life and death? Does the "azure" of line 1 mean what it meant in Mallarmé?

14. What does "Song of the Columns" say about beauty? Is the idea of beauty in this poem too remote and mathematical to have appeal? Or is the poem really, in its way, sensuous?

Sigmund Freud

Teachers with a Freudian bent may want to use "Dora" as the occasion for introducing some basic psychoanalytic principles in the course, especially the unconscious, infantile sexuality, and the symbol-making of dreams. Such concepts may prove useful later in the course, especially with such authors as Pirandello, Kafka, Lawrence, and Joyce. But "Dora" is well worth close study for its own sake, for its fascinating characterization of Dora (and of Freud himself), its complex narrative structure, and its tantalizing problems of interpretation, several never solved, as Freud was the first to admit.

1. What brings Dora to Freud? Notice that Dora's motives and her father's are not the same and are even in conflict.

2. What is Freud's theory of hysteria? Notice that Freud, in diagnosing Dora as a hysteric, lists three "determinants" of hysteria: "a psychic trauma," "a conflict of affects," and "a disturbance in the sphere of sexuality." A short history of hysteria might be in order here, from its attribution to a "wandering womb" in ancient times to its recent removal from the list of mental illnesses recognized by the American Psychiatric Association.

3. Perhaps the most controversial interpretation that Freud makes in the case study is that Dora's negative reaction to Herr K.'s first sexual advance to her when she was fourteen was "already entirely and completely hysterical." What assumptions seem to lie behind this judgment? Do the other characters in the study seem to agree with Freud that the normal reaction to such an incident would have been merely a pleasurable "feeling of sexual excitement"? Note that Freud reflects here both the sexual assumptions of his Vienna and his own belief that sexual feelings should be relieved of their burden of guilt and repression.

4. How does Freud go about interpreting dreams? Both the first and second dreams offer abundant materials for tracing Freud's methods.

5. The editors of the standard English edition of Freud provide the following chronology for Dora's story:

1882	Dora born.
1888 (Age 6)	Father ill with TB. Family move to B---.
1889 (Age 7)	Bed-wetting.
1890 (Age 8)	Dyspnoea.
1892 (Age 10)	Father's detached retina.
1894 (Age 12)	Father's confusional attack. His visit to Freud. Migraine and tussis nervosa.
1898 (Age 16)	(Early summer:) Dora's first visit to Freud. (End of June:) Scene by the lake. (Winter:) Death of aunt. Dora in Vienna.
1899 (Age 17)	(March:) Appendicitis. (Autumn:) Family leave B--- and move to factory town.
1900 (Age 18)	Family move to Vienna. Suicide threat. (October to December:) Treatment with Freud.
1901	(January:) Case history written.
1902	(April:) Dora's last visit to Freud.
1905	Case history published.

Compare the order of events in Dora's life (the "story") with the order in which they appear in Freud's narrative (the "plot"). What is the effect of this rearrangement?

6. Freud is as important a character in the case study as Dora is. How does he come across in the study? What does he think of Dora as a person? Which people in Dora's life does he seem to identify with himself? Notice especially his reflections after the case has ended on how he dealt with Dora and things he might have done differently.

Joseph Conrad

No more than any other important literary work was Heart of Darkness written so that it could be taught in college courses, but it might as well have been. It has all the elegance of design, the considered richness and coherence of imagery, the intricacy of narrative method, and the thematic counterpoint that distinguish great teachable works from certain others that may be equally great but leave one wondering what to do with them in the classroom. On top of its formal teachability, though, Heart of Darkness is a key historical document, not just of the 1890s but of modern politics and culture in general. (The Norton Critical Edition of the work, edited by Robert Kimbrough, 1971, is an excellent teaching tool, including important documents and biographical information as well as interpretive essays.) Nor will the novel be killed by the microscopic analysis it invites; its final meaning remains hauntingly indeterminate. And, unlike many other works that dazzle us when we are young by their melodrama or virtuosity, Heart of Darkness is not a work one outgrows.

Apart from its inherent interest, the work can also be treated as part of the history of literature, poised as it is between the values, methods, and sensibility of the nineteenth century and those of the modernists. There are, in addition, fairly explicit echoes or anticipations of particular works, including Dante's Inferno and the poems of T. S. Eliot.

The biggest teaching problem is that there is so much to teach. It may be that the novel itself is a little musclebound, but in any event it can make the teacher feel that he or she is. Rather than try to cover, or even touch lightly on, everything, teachers would be wise to single out three or four passages for close analysis and examine only four or five themes/images (the two often blend with each other). If, after that, one still feels that the work has been done less than justice, one can assign a paper; no mere week or so of attention in the classroom will exhaust the opportunities students have to read closely or to venture opinions about the over-all meaning.

For other discussion questions besides those that follow, see the last paragraph of the Introduction to Conrad in the anthology.

1. Open Heart of Darkness at random, read half a page, and make a list of the key words, images, and themes you find in the passage.

   Students can all be asked to do this at the same time, during a class session. Then have a student volunteer read his or her list, one word, image, or theme at a time. For each item on the list, ask the other students to supply echoes in the passages they happened on. The game will bring home to them how dense the texture of the novel is and stimulate alertness to both detail and general patterns on further reading or re-reading of the work.

2. The title Heart of Darkness is a complex pun. What different meanings does it have? Anchor it in a few concrete details of the work.

3. The theme of truth and lies is central in Heart of Darkness. What meanings does truth have? How important is it to Marlow? Do his actions support his principles on the subject?

4. List some physical objects in the novel that are light, or white, and some that are dark,

or black. How do these objects correspond to the metaphorical meanings of darkness and light? What ironies or ambiguities are there?

5. A striking technique in Heart of Darkness is the presentation of corresponding scenes, sometimes widely separated in time or place--for example, grass growing in Africa between a dead man's white bones and in Europe between the paving stones of a "sepulchral" city. Cite other examples of this technique and show how they in particular, and the technique in general, serve Conrad's purposes.

6. Work is a key theme in Heart of Darkness. What kinds of work do different people in it do? What makes some forms of work good and some bad? Is it the spirit and motive underlying the work? Its practical effect on the world? Its psychological value for the worker?

7. The first two paragraphs of the novel describe the Thames river and the "mournful gloom" brooding over London. How do these images reverberate in other parts of the novel? Compare the narrator's vision of the English past in the sixth paragraph with Marlow's vision of it.

8. In the ninth paragraph of the novel, the narrator says that for Marlow the meaning of an episode was not inside it but outside it, "enveloping the tale . . . as a glow brings out a haze." What does this mean? How is the statement borne out by Marlow's, and Conrad's, story-telling method?

9. Before he leaves for Africa, Marlow's aunt tells him that "the labourer is worthy of his hire." She is quoting Luke 10:7. Look up the passage in Luke and find out how the context there enriches the meaning. While you're looking in the Bible, see Matthew 23:27, on "whited sepulchers"; what is the connection of that biblical passage with Conrad's story?

10. Marlow's relationship to the forces of African and other kinds of "darkness" is complex; he seems drawn to and respectful of it and also determined to resist and oppose it. How do you account for this mixture of feelings?

11. Marlow seems both to admire and to abhor Kurtz. How do you account for this ambivalence?

12. Probably the most salient thing about Kurtz is his voice. Why is that important?

13. Kurtz's last words are "The horror! The horror!" What does he mean by that?

14. Study the scene between Marlow and Kurtz's "Intended" near the end of Heart of Darkness. What links to and contrasts with other parts of the novel emerge from this scene?

This is probably the most obvious of the scenes we had in mind in recommending the close study of a selected few. Any key episode such as this will provide a node of important motifs in the work as a whole.

15. The Europeans in the book seem to have two motives: the spiritual advancement of the "savages" and commercial greed. Are these motives antithetical or opposite sides of the same coin? How do they compare with Marlow's motives in going to Africa and then penetrating

the dark continent?

16. Journeys are archetypes of spiritual experience, and their meaning in particular works is sometimes related to concrete aspects of the particular journey. Is it straight-line or winding? Is it one-way or round-trip? Does it move outward or inward? Is it undertaken alone or in company? Is it vertical or horizontal? What do the answers to such questions reveal about Heart of Darkness?

For some analogues and comparisons, see the journeys listed in the formal index of this manual.

William Butler Yeats

Teachers have many options with Yeats; the dozen poems in the anthology contain a rich variety of ingredients that can be mixed in several ways and added in many different sequences. "The Second Coming" and "Leda and the Swan" will seem to many teachers good for openers; they have the characteristic Yeatsian diction, magical yet limpid, do not require laborious explication before their over-all artistry and significance can be appreciated, and suggest a few fundamentals of Yeats's mythic system without being highly arcane. After that, "Sailing to Byzantium" might be introduced--a poem that is rich in meaning and artistry but, like Keats's odes (which make excellent foils for it in several ways), is fairly accessible in its basic meaning. Thereafter, several groupings by theme are possible--the theme of Ireland, for example, in "To Ireland in the Coming Times" and "Easter 1916." Some of the numbered questions below suggest still other thematically related groupings. Pairings by contrast provide another option--the colloquial but brilliant "Crazy Jane Talks with the Bishop" posed against the lush dreaminess of "He Remembers Forgotten Beauty," for example, or any of the early poems against a late one. A few of the poems are pretty difficult; "Among School Children" and "Lapis Lazuli" will probably require help from teachers, but we think students will find the effort rewarding. Yeats is a spellbinding poet, and in introducing students to his work one sometimes makes lifelong converts of the kind who meet to celebrate him on St. Patrick's Day.

1. Read the Introduction to Modernism in the anthology and then, after reading Yeats's poems also, decide to what extent and in what ways he is a true modernist. For example, what is his attitude toward the past? Is the past in vivid contrast with the present? Does Yeats long for it nostalgically? Does he find the contemporary world threatening? Exhilarating?

2. A frequent topic in Yeats's poetry is art, including poetry. How does Yeats regard poetry and his role as poet? In "A Coat" poetry is embroidery and nakedness; in "Easter 1916" poets are people who ride "our wingèd horse"; in "The Circus Animals' Desertion" poetry can originate in a foul rag-and-bone shop. Which of these seems the aptest description of most poems by Yeats?

3. Is the spirit of "The Lake Isle of Innisfree" the spirit of Romantic nature poetry, that of, say, Wordsworth or Keats? How does the refuge of nature in the Romantics compare with the desired place of retreat in this poem and with Byzantium as a retreat in "Sailing to Byzantium"?

4. In "To Ireland in the Coming Times," how does the poet see his relationship to his country? Compare this relationship with the one he describes in "Easter 1916."

5. In "To Ireland in the Coming Times," the word "measure" or a variant of it occurs six times. What meanings does the word have, and how do they elaborate the theme of the poem?

6. Compare the conception of beauty in "He Remembers Forgotten Beauty" with the "terrible beauty" described in "Easter 1916." How do the two poems differ in vocabulary and imagery?

7. "A Coat" contrasts two kinds of poetry, one represented by an embroidered coat and the other by nakedness. Classify the Yeats poems in the anthology according to this distinction.

8. The third section of "Easter 1916" (lines 41-56) contrasts changing things with an unchanging stone. What is this section doing in the poem? How does it relate to the repeated refrain "changed [or 'transformed'] utterly"?

9. What judgment does "Easter 1916" pass on political activism?

10. What attitude does "The Second Coming" take toward violence? Is change progress? Does the fact that Christ's cradle "vexed to nightmare" the preceding age mean that the arrival of the Christian age was a calamity? If it in turn is about to yield to another age, will that change be good or bad?

11. Like Keats's "Ode to a Nightingale," Yeats's "Sailing to Byzantium" uses a singing bird as an emblem of immortality and of the escape from time to timelessness. What crucial differences are there between the birds in the two poems? Along similar lines: Like Keats's "Ode on a Grecian Urn," the Yeats poem contrasts the "sensual" world of the living (the word is used in both poems) with the world of an inorganic work of art. Do the poets use these symbols in similar or different ways?

12. "Leda and the Swan," based on a myth Yeats used to help express his view of history, is built on images of activity and passiveness. Trace these images, noting especially the verbs and participles, and show how they express the poem's theme of the transfer of power.

13. "Among School Children" brings together a number of Yeats's central concerns and images, including youth and age, ideas and their material embodiments, sensuousness and asceticism, love and knowledge, the decay of the body and the pangs of birth. How can so many large themes emerge from a humdrum scene in a schoolroom? Compare the way the themes and images are used in this poem and in other Yeats poems where they appear.

14. The last six lines of "Crazy Jane Talks with the Bishop" include at least six words on which elaborate puns are built. A number of these puns have sexual meanings or have to do with filth. Show how such overtones and puns are necessary if Crazy Jane is to make her point in reply to the Bishop's words about abandoning the sty for the heavenly mansion.

15. Line 17 of "Lapis Lazuli," in connection with actors performing Shakespearean tragedies, refers to "Gaiety transfiguring all that dread." This is apparently meant to answer the complaint in lines 1-8 about the frivolity of artistic gaiety. Is this a real answer? Isn't it true that actors are only pretending, while war is real? By way of comparison, what, if anything, transfigures dread in "Easter 1916"?

16. In "The Circus Animals' Desertion," two sources or kinds of poetry are contrasted, one represented by the circus animals, one by the "foul rag-and-bone shop of the heart." What does this contrast mean? Can this distinction be used to classify elements in the other poems by Yeats in the anthology? Compare the distinction with the one drawn in "A Coat."

17. Section II of "The Circus Animals' Desertion" has three stanzas, and in each of them a certain key word reappears. What is the word, and how does it relate to what the "heart" stands for in the poem?

Luigi Pirandello

<u>Six Characters in Search of an Author</u>, Pirandello's "play in the making," recalls other "works in the making" such as the <u>Canterbury Tales</u>, the <u>Heptameron</u>, <u>Don Quixote</u>, and "Tlön, Uqbar, Orbis Tertius"--problematic works which raise questions of the boundaries between life and art. An excellent filmed production of the play is in the Films for the Humanities series (see Media Guide). Eric Bentley's essay on Pirandello in <u>Theatre of War</u> (1970) is highly recommended for its provocative and teachable reading of the play.

1. What would the audience's response be to the beginning of <u>Six Characters</u>?

   Notice that there is no signal that the play has begun; the impression is that the spectator has stumbled by mistake into a real rehearsal. The only inconsistency is that the auditorium, which is treated as empty by the actors, is really full. The boundary between life and art is thus brought into doubt almost immediately.

2. What is the effect of having the company rehearsing a fictional Pirandello play named <u>The Game As He Played It</u>?

3. The Characters' story is a play within a play. What is the relationship between their story and the story of the company's rehearsal? What is the central action of <u>Six Characters</u>? The Characters' story? The attempt to make a play of their story? The debate between the Father and the Producer?

4. Summarize the Characters' story. The author has abandoned it half-finished. Which incidents are well worked out and which only sketched in? Which characters are developed and which are incomplete?

5. Notice that there are really seven "characters" in <u>Six Characters</u>, Madame Pace being the seventh. Examine the way in which she is brought into the action. What does it tell us about artistic creation? Why does she speak with an absurd Spanish accent, and how does the Producer react to it? Her name means "peace" in Italian; why is this ironically appropriate?

6. Throughout the play, the Father defends the proposition that he and his family are more "real" than the Producer and the actors. What are his grounds for asserting this? Are any paradoxes or contradictions involved in his definition of "real"?

7. The Father argues that "real" people have no fixed identity but only a series of roles they assume in different situations. The Producer vehemently denies this. Is there any irony in the fact that the Producer is a member of a theater company?

8. Is the Boy dead at the end of the play? What does it mean for a "character" to be dead?

9. Explore the basic equation of life and the theater in <u>Six Characters in Search of an Author</u>. How is life like the theater? How is it unlike it?

Thomas Mann

"Disorder and Early Sorrow" is one of the most frequently reprinted and reread of short stories, and deservedly so: it is one of the great modern stories, almost dizzying in the way it opens up depths of profound and far-reaching meaning in a small incident of domestic life. Inevitably it will seem prophetic in the way it foreshadowed, in 1926, the disorder and sorrow of the next twenty years of German history. But its implications are not limited to Germany; the class will no doubt find many parallels with present conditions, an appropriate way of studying a story that deals with historical continuity and change.

1. What is the tone of "Disorder and Early Sorrow"? It is written in the third person, though from the point of view of Dr. Cornelius. Is there any gap between Cornelius' attitudes and the implied attitudes of the narrator? The narrator uses present tense; does this affect our perception of tone?

2. The story focuses tightly on the Cornelius household, and yet hints of the outside world of Germany in the 1920's constantly slip in. What elements of the revolution in society especially disturb Cornelius?

3. The Cornelius household is in effect a microcosm of German society, with what amounts to three generations of Corneliuses (the parents, the older children, and the younger children); "blue-faced Ann," the nurse; the servant Xaver; and the Hinterhofer sisters. What signs of social disruption and pressure appear in this family microcosm?

4. Dr. Cornelius thinks that he is typical of history professors in disliking the disorderly present and preferring the "coherent, disciplined, historic past." Examine carefully his feelings on this subject. Are they ambivalent? Is there any irony or self-deprecation in his self-analysis?

5. Dr. Cornelius thinks that there is something "not perfectly right and good" in his love for Ellie. What is it? What paradox is involved?

6. Dr. Cornelius thinks that "father love and a little child on its mother's breast" are "timeless, and thus very, very holy and beautiful." What light does the ending of the story throw upon this view? Is childhood really timeless?

7. Most of the young people in "Disorder and Early Sorrow" want to be artists of some sort. Ingrid wants to be an actress, Bert would like to be a dancer, Xaver dreams of being a film star, and most of the guests at the party have artistic interests. Professor Cornelius, in thinking about the makeup Herzl, the actor, wears, thinks that it demonstrates the "abnormality of the artist soul-form." What is the significance of the theme of art in the story? Is art balanced against Professor Cornelius' version of history in the value-system of the story?

8. Another important strand in the story is sexual identity. The "big folk" have a fluidity of sexual qualities that disturbs Dr. Cornelius, while Snapper and Ellie have stereotyped "little boy" and "little girl" characteristics. What is the significance of this theme?

9. "Disorder and Early Sorrow" contains a number of images of life and a number of other

images of death. Certain values are aligned with each set of images. Can you make parallel lists of the images and values, clarifying the conflicts of the story?

10. What is the significance of Ellie's "early sorrow" at the end of the story? Does it bring about any change in her father's attitudes? Or does it merely confirm them?

James Joyce

"The Dead," the culminating story in Joyce's <u>Dubliners</u>, has sometimes been acclaimed as the finest piece of short fiction in the English language. Like Conrad's <u>Heart of Darkness</u>, it also belongs to that group of works that, on top of their excellence, are also immensely teachable. It would be hard to think of any major aspect of the art of fiction that is not handled masterfully in "The Dead": plot construction, the management of point of view, characterization, setting, diction and dialogue, symbolic imagery used both structurally and thematically, emotional resonance, and ultimate visionary power. This story will help students understand why Joyce's stories have, along with Chekhov's, provided the dominant models for short fiction through most of the twentieth century. "The Dead" also invites speculation on the problem, widely discussed these days, of topicality versus universality. The Irishness of the story extends to almost every aspect of it, yet (as its last words imply) it also comments on humanity defined as universally as is possible: "the living and the dead."

1. What is the narrator's tone in "The Dead"? How does it change in the course of the story?

2. Gretta tells Aunt Kate that whenever it's wet out Gabriel wants her to wear newfangled goloshes from "the continent." Gabriel, listening, "laughed nervously and patted his tie reassuringly." How does this little exchange express a major image in the story and a major aspect of Gabriel's character?

3. Trace references to death and images of death through the Morkan sisters' party. What do they suggest about Dublin society?

4. Examine Gabriel's scene with Molly Ivors. What does it reveal about Gabriel?

5. "The Dead" is full of references to songs and singers. What is the function of music in the story?

6. Read Gabriel's speech carefully. What does it reveal about his attitudes toward his aunts, Miss Ivors, the present, Ireland, and himself?

7. What does Gabriel's story about Patrick Morkan's horse reveal about him? What similarities does the story have with "The Dead"?

8. Just before they leave the party, Gabriel sees Gretta standing on the stairs, listening to something. He feels as if she were "a symbol of something" and imagines a painting of her called "Distant Music." How is this response typical of Gabriel? What echoes does the incident raise of other details in the story?

9. Read carefully the passage about Gabriel's thoughts as he walks with Gretta to the cab. What incidents does he think of, and why? Why does he think of the time he asked the man making bottles if the fire was hot?

10. Examine Gabriel's response to the story of Michael Furey, especially the conflicting attitudes toward himself it triggers. What is his attitude toward Michael Furey as a double of himself?

11. Michael Furey, like Gabriel, has an angel's name: Michael is the angel of the Last Judgment, while Gabriel is the messenger angel who brought to Mary the tidings of Jesus' conception. How is this relevant to the story? Have other names in the story been symbolic? Lily? Mr. Browne? Constantine?

12. How do the incident in the hotel room and the story of Michael Furey force us to revise our attitude toward the dead, as they have been presented in the story? Are the dead really more vital than the living, as old Parkinson and Michael Furey are? Or is this view merely a continuation of Gabriel's nostalgic sentimentality?

13. In the last paragraph, what is the meaning of the line "The time had come for him to set out on his journey westward"?

14. Note that Gabriel is falling asleep in the last paragraph of the story. What is the significance of the last images that drift through his mind before sleep?

15. What is our final judgment of Gabriel? Do you think the revelations of the evening have brought about any permanent change in him? What will his future life with Gretta be like? Will he go to the west of Ireland for his holidays?

16. Joyce's stories usually culminate in an "epiphany," or revelation. Gabriel seems to have two epiphanies in the last episode: one having to do with Gretta and his marriage, one with the human condition. Clarify these two epiphanies and show how they are related to each other.

Virginia Woolf

Special kinds of writing require special kinds of reading, and Virginia Woolf's project of capturing a "luminous halo" of "a myriad impressions" demands a willingness on the part of the reader to pay close attention to detail and to open himself or herself to the ebb and flow of another consciousness. Some direct discussion of "how to read Virginia Woolf" might be a good way to begin (or end) the study of Woolf. Comparisons with other writers--Conrad, Mann, Joyce--who use some version of interior monologue might be useful, too.

1. What is the function of the mark on the wall in "The Mark on the Wall"? It is tempting to say that it's a sort of Rorschach blot that triggers a series of associations for the narrator. But a Rorschach blot's shape presumably serves as the focus of the test-taker's projections. Sometimes that is true here, as when, perceived as a small hump, it triggers a meditation on funeral barrows. But at other times the shape seems to be irrelevant; the connection between the mark and the associations seems rather abstract. It is worthwhile going through the story analyzing as closely as possible the connection between the mark and each association.

2. Are the narrator's associations completely random or do they form some sort of pattern? Notice, for example, how many of the associations have to do with time and loss: the memory of the previous occupants of the house, who will never be seen again, and the list of "the things lost in one lifetime."

3. The historical past as well as the personal one also preoccupies the narrator: the seed sown in the reign of Charles the First, prehistoric burial mounds, Shakespeare. How does the narrator regard the historical past? Is her attitude ambivalent, at times wondering at the majesty of the past and at other times feeling it to be a burden and a constriction?

4. One of the oddest and most provocative fantasies in the story is that of being blown through the London Tube and "shot out at the feet of God entirely naked," as an infant. This seems to be a highly ambiguous thought, either a fantasy of rebirth or a fantasy of "unbirth"--reversing the process of birth in order to recover some edenic state in "the fields of Elysium." This wish may be connected with the desire stated shortly afterwards "never to have to rise from my chair, to slip easily from one thing to another, without any sense of hostility, or obstacle. . . . to sink deeper and deeper, away from the surface, with its hard separate facts." Trace similar images of regression through the story. What do they mean? Do they suggest that the realm of art is the realm of reverie and fantasy, far from "hard separate facts"? Or is the impulse more individual and personal?

5. In the self-referential passage on "the novelists of the future," who will "explore the depths of reflections" rather than the "description of reality," an opposition is set up between the real and the unreal. And the passage is immediately followed by one in which the narrator remembers discovering that the "realities" of Victorian domestic life--"Sunday luncheons, Sunday walks, country houses, and tablecloths"--were "not entirely real, were indeed half phantoms." Trace the "real" and the "unreal" through the story. What does each come to mean?

6. One of the "realest" things in the story is Whitaker's Table of Precedency, which has nevertheless become "since the war, half a phantom to many men and women." What does

the Table of Precedency represent in the story?

7. The last association is with a tree. What values does the tree suggest? (There may be some significant points of comparison here with another famous tree in modern literature: the "great-rooted blossomer" at the end of Yeats's "Among School Children.")

8. The person who enters and breaks the reverie at the end of the story says, "Curse this war; God damn this war!" Why? Has the story in any sense been about the First World War and its social and moral impact?

9. One of the classic questions feminists confront is why women have produced so little of the world's art. Summarize Woolf's answer to this question in "Shakespeare's Sister."

10. The fundamental opposition between the "real" and the "unreal" that appeared in "The Mark on the Wall" reappears in "Shakespeare's Sister," especially in a passage like this: "What one must do to bring her to life was to think poetically and prosaically at one and the same moment, thus keeping in touch with fact--that she is Mrs. Martin, aged thirty-six, dressed in blue, wearing a black hat and brown shoes; but not losing sight of fiction either--that she is a vessel in which all sorts of spirits and forces are coursing and flashing perpetually." Trace the opposition between the "poetic" and the "prosaic" through the essay. How is it related to Woolf's feminist theme? Is one of the oppressive forces that have kept women back men's tendency to idealize them, to see them as unreal?

11. How would you characterize Woolf's tone in A Room of One's Own? How does she achieve it?

12. In describing why women have been barred from literature, Woolf says a good bit about what writing is, whether by men or women, especially in the section in which she describes the artist's mind as "incandescent, unimpeded" (with Shakespeare as the best example). How do these observations relate to her other pronouncements on art and her own practice?

13. Would Woolf's portrayal of the disadvantages of women authors in the past be more powerful if, instead of inventing an imaginary sister of Shakespeare's, she had written about some real woman in the past whose literary aspirations ended tragically?

Franz Kafka

The teacher seeking links between "The Metamorphosis" and other works of modern literature will not have far to look. Despite the monstrousness of its central metaphorical action, its basic thematic concerns--the self, the family, society--appear pervasively in other works in the anthology. To be transformed into a gigantic insect differs formally but not substantively from feeling oneself to be a doll in a doll house (Ibsen) or a character in an abandoned play (Pirandello). As the class progresses, they will probably be concerned less with the surreal premise of the story than with Gregor's very real human dilemmas.

1. How would you describe the narrative voice in the story? What is the narrator's attitude toward Gregor? Note that the story follows Gregor's point of view until he dies and then describes the family's activities after his death. What is the effect of this shift?

2. Summarize everything the narrator tells us about Gregor's job. Note that the chief clerk in Gregor's firm is in the habit of "sitting on high at a desk and talking down to employees." May his job have triggered Gregor's metamorphosis?

3. Summarize everything the narrator tells us about Gregor's family. What are the father, the mother, and the sister each like? What has the attitude of each been to Gregor?

4. Does Gregor ever come to any understanding of the way he has been exploited in his job and at home? Note his reaction to learning that his father has been secretly withholding money. Is our reaction different from Gregor's?

5. What are we to think of Gregor's sister's treatment of him after his transformation? Is she blameworthy for her final betrayal of him? Or is it healthy and inevitable?

6. What happens to the family after Gregor can no longer earn their money? Notice that at the end their prospects are "not at all bad." What does this tell us about the unintended effects of Gregor's exaggerated sense of responsibility when he was in human form?

7. Food plays an important role in "The Metamorphosis." How does this motif function? How do you explain the bizarre scene in which Gregor's father throws apples at him?

8. Gregor's transformation is often said to be a symbol of his guilt. Do you agree? Is Gregor guilty of anything, or is he the victim of others' exploitation and selfishness? Or are both possibilities true?

9. What is the function of the three lodgers in the story? Notice that they, along with the chief clerk and the charwoman, represent society outside the family. What do we learn about that society and about the family in these scenes?

10. Gregor has a picture hanging on his wall of a woman in furs holding "a huge fur muff into which the whole of her forearm had vanished," and the picture is the item he chooses to protect when his mother and sister are clearing his room. What is its significance?

D. H. Lawrence

The contrast between Lawrence and Joyce suggested in the anthology Introduction to Lawrence might well be developed in the course of studying "Odour of Chrysanthemums" and "The Horse Dealer's Daughter," if the class has read Joyce as well. For example, both "The Dead" and "Odour of Chrysanthemums" involve the exposure of the "truth" about a long-time marriage, and both Joyce and Lawrence in both of his stories deal with varieties of love. As in Joyce, the Lawrence stories build up to intense, epiphanic moments of insight. But these similarities are qualified by fundamental differences of artistic technique and world view, which might well be explored in class.

1. Read the first paragraph of "Odour of Chrysanthemums" carefully. Does this realistic description of setting also establish key metaphoric conflicts in the story? Note especially the locomotive and the colt, the wagons and the hedge, and the coppice and the pit-bank.

2. Explain the story's title. What do chrysanthemums come to represent?

3. What is the function of the short scene between Elizabeth Bates and her father?

4. What impression of Walter Bates is given in the early part of the story? How does Elizabeth view herself as wife and mother? How are these impressions revised at the end?

5. What is the function of the scene with Walter's mother?

6. Read the section in which Elizabeth, over her husband's body, reviews their life together. What views of love, intimacy, marriage, and parenthood is Lawrence implying here?

7. What influences have contributed to the failure of the Bateses' marriage? Consider social conditions, conventionalized sexual roles, parents, etc.

8. Trace the successive points of view from which "The Horse Dealer's Daughter" is told. What is the effect of the changing viewpoint?

9. A major motif in "The Horse Dealer's Daughter" is enslavement. How is Mabel a slave? Her brothers? Jack Fergusson?

10. Mabel's brothers are identified with their horses. Trace the analogies through the early part of the story. What do they mean?

11. Mabel Pervin and Jack Fergusson are balanced against each other in the story. What do they have in common? How do they differ?

12. Mabel seeks death in the pond but finds a sort of rebirth, as Jack does also. Examine the scene in the pond closely. What imagery is used? What does it suggest about the symbolism of the pond?

13. How are we to interpret the encounter between Mabel and Jack after the rescue? What happens to them? Is Mabel tricking Jack into marriage? Are their feelings reasonable? Does Lawrence suggest that they are valid?

Isak Dinesen

The existence of a first-rate film version of "Babette's Feast" inevitably suggests a way of teaching the story: simply reading the story, watching the film, and comparing the two. The film is so faithful to the story that comments about one usually apply quite well to the other. But inevitably there is some gap between the words that carry the story and the images that carry the film, principally in the story's narrative voice. And in that voice is implied much of the meaning of the story.

1. In the first paragraph of the story, the little town of Berlevaag is compared to "a child's toy-town." How does the comparison anticipate key themes in the story? Does Berlevaag turn out to be in some ways rather unreal, compared to, say, Paris?

2. Work out the time-scheme of the story. It begins sixty-five years ago when Martine and Philippa are already elderly and Babette has been working for them for twelve years. But with Part II: "Martine's Lover," we go back to 1854, when Martine was eighteen and Philippa was seventeen. Part III takes place a year after Part II, when "Philippa's lover" arrives in Berlevaag, but Part IV jumps forward fifteen years to 1871 and Babette's arrival at the sisters' house. Why these departures from chronological order? Notice that at the end of Part I, we are told that the reason for Babette's presence was to be found "further back in time and deeper in the domain of human hearts." Does this correlation of the past with human emotion illuminate the way the story presents time?

3. After the feast, Babette tells Martine and Philippa, "I am a great artist, Mesdames." What does she mean by "artist"? There are a number of definitions of art in "Babette's Feast." What are they? Which seem valid? Notice especially what General Loewenhielm remembers Colonel Galliffet telling him in the Cafe Anglais in Paris: "This woman is now turning a dinner at the Cafe Anglais into a kind of love affair--into a love affair of the noble and romantic category in which one no longer distinguishes between bodily and spiritual appetite or satiety!" Does what Colonel Galliffet says about a love affair apply also to art?

4. Babette has fled Paris because of the defeat of the 1871 Commune of Paris, which, at the end of the Franco-Prussian War, opposed the peace settlement with Prussia and called for a new government and for economic reform. The defeat of the Commune was followed by harsh reprisals, including the execution of over 17,000 people. The class might profit from doing a little research into this historical background; it illuminates the story. Notice that Babette has been a <u>communard</u> (supporter of the Commune), but that she mourns the loss of her political enemies:

> "You see, Mesdames," she said, at last, "those people belonged to me, they were mine. They had been brought up and trained, with greater expense than you, my little ladies, could ever imagine or believe, to understand what a great artist I am. I could make them happy. When I did my very best I could make them perfectly happy."

Comment on this surprising passage. Is Babette implying that only the wealthy and privileged can appreciate "art"? Is her view presented with any irony?

T. S. Eliot

Little need be said about teaching "Prufrock"; students tend to be fascinated with it, unlikely though that may appear to people who have not taught the poem. Whether students find its rather sorry protagonist interesting or not (many do, in fact), they delight in the poem's verbal bravura, especially its epigrammatic jadedness--the life measured out with coffee spoons, the women talking of Michelangelo. A later stage of response is to recognize the real depth of feeling that finally emerges from under the layers of wryness. It would be a distortion to turn Prufrock into an adolescent, but it isn't hard to recognize in him psychological patterns common in adolescence: a thirst for living disguised by introverted Weltschmerz, personal insecurity fortified by an elaborate, half-clowning cynicism directed half at oneself and half at other people, a world-weariness felt, or feigned, exactly because one has not yet really encountered the world.

1. "Prufrock" is a dramatic monologue. To what extent does it conform to the model perfected by Browning? Compare it especially with Browning's "Andrea del Sarto." What modernist changes has Eliot made in the genre?

2. Eliot often uses "expressionist" imagery, in which objects are projections of psychological states. The image of the evening as etherized patient in lines 1-3 of "Prufrock" is an example. Find others.

The immediately following lines include several.

3. Prufrock uses two seemingly opposite strategies in his monologue: the trivializing of what is important ("I have measured out my life with coffee spoons"--line 51) and absurd overstatement ("Do I dare / Disturb the universe?"--lines 45-46). How does this fact help define his personality?

4. Is Prufrock an emotional freak or does he embody problems many of us have?

5. Consider the last line of the poem: "Till human voices wake us, and we drown." Does this mean that (according to Prufrock) we unfortunately have to settle for real women instead of sex-fantasy mermaids, or can the line be read more positively?

6. Consider the poem's diction. What is it like? Is it appropriate to Prufrock?

This is not an easy question. For all his mannerism, Prufrock's vocabulary is generally clean and unpretentious, and at least once distinctly earthy: "To spit out all the butt-ends of my days and ways" (line 60).

William Faulkner

The choice of a Faulkner short story for the anthology was difficult because he wrote so many magnificent ones. "An Odor of Verbena" was finally chosen over the great stories of the modern South because of the way it presents a cluster of central Faulknerian themes with a combination of vivid, High-Noon melodrama and a moral and stylistic complexity.

1. Analyze the first two paragraphs of "An Odor of Verbena" carefully for what they tell us about Bayard and the dramatic situation. What is the effect of having Bayard remember the story from far in the future? What impression do we get of the mature Bayard? Look carefully at the last sentence of the second paragraph--one of Faulkner's famous long sentences. Is it merely self-conscious and mannered, or does it capture an important aspect of how Bayard's mind worked at the time of the action and works now, remembering?

2. How do Professor Wilkins and his wife regard the code Bayard is expected to follow?

3. What is Ringo like and what is Bayard's relationship with him?

4. Notice that Bayard, from the beginning of the story, knows what he is going to do, that he is going to stick to "principle" against "blood and raising and background." But we cannot understand what he means, since we do not know what has happened. What is the purpose and effect of this gap between Bayard's knowledge (at the time and in retrospect) and ours?

5. "There was plenty of time still for verbena although I would have to reach home before I would realise there was a need for it." What does Bayard mean by this? Trace the image of verbena; what does it come to mean? Why does Drusilla leave the verbena on her pillow?

6. Trace references to the killing of Grumby through the story. How has the episode affected Bayard's present attitudes?

7. "I realised then the immitigable chasm between all life and all print--that those who can, do, those who cannot and suffer enough because they can't, write about it." What light does this statement throw on Bayard's actions? On his relationship with Drusilla? On his writing the story? Should the statement be taken at face value?

8. Bayard's relationship with Drusilla amounts almost to a subplot to the main action of his avenging his father's death. How are the two plot lines related? What coloring does the semi-incestuous relationship with Drusilla give to Bayard's renunciation of his father's code?

9. What imagery does Faulkner use in connection with Drusilla? What kind of language does he have her use when she gives Bayard the pistols? What do the imagery and the language suggest about Faulkner's view of Drusilla?

10. What does Aunt Jenny mean by her story about the Englishman in Charleston who said "No bloody moon"? Why does Bayard repeat the line?

11. Bayard is a law student, and his confrontation with Redmond takes place in a law office. Trace the theme of law through the story. What "laws" do Colonel Sartoris, Drusilla, Bayard, and Aunt Jenny each live by?

Bertolt Brecht

Brecht should probably be taken on his own terms or not at all. Textbook editors (and presumably teachers as well) sometimes try to argue that Brecht's art "transcends" his politics and that, despite his theorizing, his plays draw upon traditional dramatic values. Both propositions, though well intended, are highly dubious. The Good Woman of Setzuan develops a single, clear theme: it is impossible to be good in a capitalistic society. And despite the emotional quality of his material, which includes young love, motherhood, and a whore with a heart of gold, he develops that material with a cool irony which makes us, if we are good readers (or playgoers), abandon stock responses and see some of the contradictions in a society that institutionalizes the survival of the fittest while at the same time admonishing us to love our neighbor as ourselves.

1. Brecht's descriptions of settings are rather sparse; the first reads merely: "At the gates of the half-westernized city of Setzuan." Sketch out settings on the basis of what is required for each scene. What should the visual style of the play be?

2. The Good Woman of Setzuan is like the Book of Job in that its action is triggered by a wager in Heaven and it develops a contrast between human and (presumably) divine power and morality. What do the gods mean by "goodness"? Consider such statements of theirs as the following: "We never meddle with economics," "Suffering ennobles," "The heavier the burden, the greater the strength," and "The world should not be changed." They say their views will be validated if a single person can be found who can be good and still survive, and they place their hopes on Shen Te. Does her story validate their position? Why do they not acknowledge defeat at the end?

3. Brecht does not idealize the poor, as some left-wing writers do; the people of Setzuan are grasping and exploitative of Shen Te. What point is Brecht making?

4. Examine the songs in the play. How are they related to the action of the scenes in which they appear?

5. The characters in the play frequently break the dramatic illusion by addressing the audience directly. What is the effect of this device?

6. How is the play structured? Notice how many major incidents take place between the scenes (Shen Te's engagement to the old widower, for example) and how each scene is like a little one-act play. Why does Brecht structure the play in this way? Can you outline a structure a more traditional playwright might have used to dramatize this story?

7. Brecht represents capitalistic society as deeply divided. The central division, of course, is that between the "good" Shen Te and the "self-protective" Shui Ta. What other divisions do you see in the play? (You might consider Yang Sun's line in scene V: "Shen Te is a woman: she is devoid of common sense.")

8. What are we to think of Yang Sun? Why does Shen Te fall in love with him? His mother thinks that going to work makes a "man" of him. Does it? Is he any better at the end than he was at the beginning?

9. How does love fare in Setzuan? Consider not only Shen Te's relationship with Yang Sun but also the relationships with the elderly widower and with Shu Fu.

10. Wong is a water seller, and Shen Te's first meeting with Yang Sun takes place in a heavy rain. What does water come to symbolize in the play?

11. In the epilogue, Shen Te tells us that we must write the happy ending to the play. What happy ending would you write?

Jean-Paul Sartre

Sartre's "The Wall" has many antecedents in literature as an account of a person confronting his own imminent death: Everyman and Tolstoy's The Death of Ivan Ilyitch, to name only two works from this anthology. But none is more harrowing in its psychological detail than "The Wall." The world changes for Pablo Ibbieta when he realizes that he is going to die shortly, as it does for Everyman and Ivan Ilyitch. But each of the earlier protagonists finds something positive to accompany him to the grave; Pablo Ibbieta finds only a frightening void. "The Wall" leads the existential protagonist only to the end of the first stage of his journey; the road through the absurd to commitment remains to be traveled.

1. "The Wall" opens abruptly with the prisoners' drum-head trial, and we never learn the details of their past lives. What is the effect of this omission of ordinary exposition?

2. What kind of person is Pablo Ibbieta? What do we learn about his background, his attitudes, and his temperament?

3. Ibbieta describes almost clinically the stages he goes through as he approaches his death. Identify these stages. Do you find them psychologically convincing? What sorts of defenses does he use to protect himself against his dreadful knowledge?

4. Almost as much attention is paid to Tom Steinbock and Juan Mirbal as to Ibbieta. How does each of them react to the prospect of death, and how do their reactions compare with that of Ibbieta?

5. What does each of the men find most fearful about death? Pain? The loss of future pleasure? Note Tom Steinbock's line: "I see my own corpse. That's not hard, but it's I who see it; with my eyes. I'll have to get to the point where I think--where I think I won't see anything more."

6. Trace the behavior of the Belgian doctor through the story. When Juan bites his hand, he "must have suddenly understood that we were not men like himself." How does his behavior illuminate Ibbieta's inner development?

7. By the time Ibbieta is taken to the interrogation room, he feels that his perspective has entirely changed. How does this change affect his behavior?

8. Why does Ibbieta refuse to betray Ramon Gris? Reread the paragraph in which he considers this question. He dismisses several possible reasons and concludes that it was merely because he was "stubborn." Is this an adequate or a convincing reason? Can you explain it differently?

9. When Ibbieta hears that Juan Gris was in the cemetery and then was killed, "everything went around in circles" and he burst into uncontrollable laughter. Why? What ordinary assumptions about the world have been called into doubt by the episode?

Albert Camus

One might do worse in teaching "The Adulterous Woman" than to put two columns on the blackboard, labeled "exile" and "the kingdom," and have the class fill them in. Some of the binary oppositions around which the story turns are obvious, but others are far from being so. Almost as in a lyric poem, even the smallest details in the story are organized around the central opposition. Of course, what such an analysis would not suggest is the way Camus integrates all these abstract splittings into a rich, believable portrait of Janine.

1. The housefly circling "on tired wings" in a closed bus opens the story with an image of imprisonment and futility. What kinds of imprisonment appear later in the story, and what other images are used to suggest them?

2. Marcel and Janine are both overweight. Marcel has a "heavy torso," and Janine rather optimistically thinks of herself as not fat, but "tall and well rounded rather, plump and still desirable." Who are the thin people in the story? What do fatness and thinness suggest?

3. What is the meaning of the opposition between French and Arab in the story? The thin French soldier on the bus is balanced by the proud, thin Arab who almost runs into Marcel and Janine later in the town square. Is Camus hinting at the political background, the inevitable clash of French and Arab in Algeria, that underlies Janine's personal division? Do the French represent "exile" and the Arabs the "kingdom"? Or is the contrast more complicated than that? (Notice that the French soldier and the Arab in the square are linked by their thinness.)

4. What are we to think of Janine's marriage? Notice that when Janine thinks about it, she emphasizes being loved and showered with attention. "By so often making her aware that she existed for him he made her exist in reality." Is this a good basis for a marriage? Has Janine been living in bad faith and self-deception in her marriage?

5. Janine fears "growing old alone" and values her marriage because "No, she was not alone." Trace the theme of being alone and being together through the story. Is it always bad to be alone?

6. What do dryness and water come to mean in the story? The landscape is very dry and seemingly sterile, and the references to water are frequently metaphoric. There is a "rain of sand" on the windows, the wind in the palm trees creates the "sound of a river," and then "the waters of the wind" dried up. Notice that at the climax of the story, as Janine looks out over the night desert, the "water of night" fills her. Notice, too, that in the last paragraph Marcel, who has earlier warned Janine not to drink the local water, drinks from a bottle of mineral water.

7. Janine visits the fort and views the desert twice in the story, once in the daytime with her husband and once at night by herself. Compare the two scenes. What happens in each? What draws her back to the fort at night?

8. Explore the title metaphor of adultery. On one level, the story denies our expectations that Janine will commit adultery, probably with the French soldier. But on another level, she does betray her husband. Trace sexual imagery through the story. Notice that Janine at one

point wonders if there is "another love than that of darkness, a love that would cry aloud in daylight." And the spiritual epiphany on the fort at night is presented in terms of orgasm: "the water of night began to fill Janine . . . rising up even to her mouth full of moans," and she falls on her back, moaning. How is sexuality related to the other themes of the story?

Jorge Luis Borges

The puzzle workers and detective story readers in your class will like Borges. The first challenge in reading him is teasing out the answers to his riddles. But students should not stop there. They should come to see the implications of Borges' view of life as infinitely mysterious and only imperfectly reducible to the order man's restless, pattern-making mind seeks. Borges, for all his love of ingenuity, is finally on the side of the divine labyrinth of life rather than the simplified one of Tlön.

1. Describe the structure of "Tlön, Uqbar, Orbis Tertius." There are two numbered parts and a lengthy Postscript; what does each contain? Can you retell the story, in chronological order, of the invention of Uqbar and Tlön? Which is the primary story--the creation of these imaginary worlds or the narrator's progressive discovery of their creation?

2. What is the narrator of the story like? Note that at the beginning of the Postscript he calls the earlier part of the story an "article," and note that the names and facts in the story are a complex mingling of fact and fiction. What is the purpose of this blurring of the boundary between life and art?

3. Note that at the beginning of the story the narrator and Bioy Casares have been discussing a "novel in the first person" whose narrator would engage in various sorts of trickery. Does this sound like a description of the story we are reading? What other self-referential elements do you find in the story? At one point, the narrator says that the possibility of a "lone inventor" of Tlön has been "unanimously discounted." Is this a bit of comic irony? What has Borges himself done? Does the story suggest that inventing an imaginary planet has something in common with writing a story about the invention of an imaginary planet?

4. Summarize the lengthy description of Tlön in section 2. What does Borges mean when he says that "the nations of this planet are congenitally idealist"? Why is psychology the central discipline in Tlön culture? Notice that "truth" and "reality" do not exist on Tlön; philosophers do not seek for truth but rather for "the astounding." What does this suggest about Tlön? Is Tlön the world of art? Is "Tlön, Uqbar, Orbis Tertius" about the truth or the astounding?

5. "Tlön, Uqbar, Orbis Tertius" was published in 1942, yet the Postscript is dated 1947 and refers to events that took place in 1944. What effect does this have on our reading of the story? Note that on Tlön "the present is indefinite, the future has no reality other than as a present hope, and the past has no reality other than as a present memory."

6. In the Postscript, the invention of Tlön is credited to a lunatic Tennessee millionaire who wanted to discredit God by proving that "mortal man was capable of conceiving a world." Tlön is said to be taking over the world because it is a labyrinth which obeys human laws, unlike the labyrinth of the real world, which obeys inscrutable, divine ones. What does this suggest about what Tlön symbolizes?

7. What is the tone of the ending of the story? Is it a good thing or a bad thing that Tlön is taking over the world?

8. In the last paragraph, the narrator says that he is revising "an uncertain Quevedian translation of Sir Thomas Browne's Urn Burial." Urn Burial was published in 1658; the Spanish poet Francisco Gomez de Quevedo y Villegas died in 1645. Is this an unexpected intrusion of Tlön and its hröns into the frame of the story? How?

9. The narrative structure, narrative voice, and tone of "The Circular Ruins" are very different from those of "Tlön, Uqbar, Orbis Tertius." Compare the two stories.

10. "The Circular Ruins" can be read, among other ways, as a parable of artistic creation. Explore the implications of the story when so read.

11. What does Fire seem to represent in the story?

12. "The Circular Ruins" recalls Pirandello in its suggestion of the relationship between human beings and works of art. Can you compare the theme in this story and in Six Characters in Search of an Author?

Samuel Beckett

The challenge of choosing one play for the anthology to represent the richness of dramatic literature since 1950 was an impossible one. But Krapp's Last Tape, despite its brevity, can stand for many of the qualities of the modern theater--its loosening of the bonds of realism, its prevailingly private, existentialist emphasis, and its achievement of an intensely poetic quality while rejecting verse.

1. In this fundamentally serious play, why does Beckett give his character an absurd, scatological name, a clown's appearance, and comic, music-hall routines to do? Do these comic elements, paradoxically, allow Beckett to deal more directly with serious and painful issues than he could otherwise?

2. Why does the play take place "in the future"?

3. Three points in Krapp's life are touched upon. Explain their ironic juxtapostions.

This may not be as easy a question as it appears; one prominent drama critic has interpreted the play as having to do with the self-deceptions of old age, by misreading the last lines of the play as spoken by Krapp in his present voice. Krapp is sixty-nine, he plays a tape recorded thirty years ago when he was thirty-nine, and on that tape he refers to himself as he was "ten or twelve years before," when he was, perhaps, about twenty-nine.

4. Krapp is a writer; why is this important in the play? Is there a suggestion of an analogy between writing and the sort of taped autobiography Krapp maintains? What is it?

5. The stage is dark except for the "strong white light" over the table and the tape recorder, and in the revelation recorded by Krapp at thirty-nine he realizes that "the dark I have always struggled to keep under is in reality my most--." What do dark and light stand for?

6. The thirty-nine-year-old Krapp resolves to stop eating bananas and reports resolutions when he was twenty-nine to drink less and lead a "less engrossing sexual life." Yet in the present he is eating bananas, drinking heavily, and pursuing a relationship with a "bony old ghost of a whore" named Fanny. Identify other such ironic links among the twenty-nine, thirty-nine, and sixty-nine-year-old Krapp. What do they suggest about the power of reason and good intentions?

7. Beckett has described his work as pursuing a via negativa, a negative way, or an attempt to strip away inessentials in pursuit of the fundamental elements in human life. Krapp's Last Tape follows this pattern in showing values and concerns important to Krapp as receding in importance as he gets older. What are these? What is the only thing that remains at the end?

8. How would you characterize the language of the play? What is the effect of the contrast between the abrupt colloquialism of such lines as "Couldn't do much, but I suppose better than a kick in the crutch" and the delicate lyricism of the description of the girl in the boat?

9. Beckett's plays are not built upon the traditional dramatic pattern of conflict/climax/resolution but rather develop single, poetic metaphors for human life. What does the central metaphor of a man tape-recording his life suggest?

Richard Wright

Both anthologists and teachers are frequently reminded of how difficult it is to represent a writer accurately with a single work. This is especially the case with writers whose work is quite heterogeneous, as Richard Wright's is. Early Wright and late Wright are quite different. The editors chose early Wright--the first story in his first book--not because it is "typical" but because it portrays, with a forcefulness all the greater because it is so unmediated by commentary or interpretation, the racism that was Wright's central subject.

1. The first three sections are almost like a play; they are almost all dialogue, with the third-person, past-tense narrator providing only minimal information about time, place, and action. What is the effect of this mode of narration, with the narrator withholding, for the most part, any explicit interpretation of the action?

2. Are Buck, Bobo, Lester, and Big Boy characterized individually as very distinct? Specifically, does Big Boy manifest any qualities that would allow us to anticipate that he would be the sole survivor of the day's horrifying events?

3. The idea of swimming in the forbidden swimming hole first comes from Buck, Bobo, and Lester, while Big Boy opposes the idea. "N git lynched?" he asks. But when they reach the swimming hole, Big Boy is the one who talks the others into going in. What leads Big Boy to make this fatal error? (Notice that just before they reach the swimming hole, Big Boy boasts, "Ahma smart nigger.")

4. The encounter with the white man and woman and the killing of Lester, Buck, and the white man are worth considering in some detail. The whites obviously have fixed expectations about blacks that lead them to badly misinterpret the innocent scene before them. What are they?

5. Once Big Boy is alone, in Section 3, the narration changes, alternating between the narrator's description of the action, in standard English, and Big Boy's interior monologue, in black English. Analyze the relation between these two voices. What is the narrator's tone?

6. The lynching is presented with great skill. Without softening the horror of the scene, Wright focuses it by weaving together three kinds of material: the shouts of the mob, the third-person narration, and Big Boy's interior monologue. Analyze this combination in sample passages.

7. The five parts of "Big Boy Leaves Home" are structured much like a five-act play, moving from exposition, to conflict, rising action, climax, and resolution. Trace this pattern through the story.

8. "Big Boy Leaves Home" seems to be set around the time of World War I; the man in uniform is perhaps on furlough from that war. The teens and twenties were a period of many lynchings in the South; they are now almost unknown. Does the story therefore have only historical interest?

Italo Calvino

Part of the fun of reading "Under the Jaguar Sun" is noticing how pervasively the story is presented in terms of eating. At one point, for example, a bus is said to be "disgorging and ingesting" its passengers. Trivial examples like this can lead the reader into larger uses of the image, which amount to what might be called a gustatory vision of the world, in which everything is in the process of either devouring or being devoured. And it is probably in the spirit of Calvino and of postmodernism not to worry too much about whether that vision is "true" or not but rather to trace closely the way the narrator's perceptions, including his perceptions of his girlfriend, are shaped by the template of eating.

1. The story begins with a description of the painting of the young nun and the old priest. How does this opening function to establish certain emphases in the story? Notice that (like the pronunciation of Oaxaca) it requires interpretation, a major element in the story. Notice, too, that the narrator and Olivia eventually interpret the painting as having to do with food.

2. The narrator is not altogether pleased with the way his relationship with Olivia is going. He comments that, "from the beginning of our Mexican journey, the physical bond between Olivia and me was going through a phase of rarefaction, if not eclipse." Trace as precisely as possible the course of their relationship in the story and relate it to the food references.

3. Alonso is, along with Salustiano Velazco, one of only two secondary characters in the story. What is he like? How do his characteristics bear on the themes of the story?

4. Comment on the same question in regard to Salustiano Velazco. What is his attitude toward human sacrifice? Notice that he has a "chivalrous certitude of male supremacy." How is this certitude related to the story's theme of cannibalism?

5. One of the most extraordinary passages in the story is that in which the narrator imagines being chewed up by Olivia. Comment and link with the passage shortly afterward in which the narrator eats instead of being eaten.

6. Analyze Olivia's attack on the narrator that begins, "How boring you are! How monotonous!" How does this fit in with the developing theme of the story?

7. Notice that the narrator and Olivia ask for fruit to be brought with their breakfast and that they like "fruits that conceal in the sweetness of their pulp subtle messages of asperity and sourness." Comment.

8. Why is the story called "Under the Jaguar Sun"? Where is the title explained? Notice that the jaguar sun is literally a relief carving on the Temple of the Sun and that the narrator has his giddy epiphany in "the light of the jaguar sun." What does it mean?

9. Read the last paragraph carefully. What is "the serpent that digests us all"? And in what sense is there "a universal cannibalism that leaves its imprint on every amorous relationship"? Has the story prepared us for this conclusion?

James Baldwin

The first word that might occur to someone thinking about "Sonny's Blues" is elegance. The subject matter is painful and sometimes brutal, but the pain and the brutality are given meaningful focus through great artistry. Only after reading the last great scene in the jazz club and then going back and re-reading the beginning can one see how carefully Baldwin has prepared us for that scene through building up rich, subtle images and unobtrusively repeating certain key words such as dark and there.

1. Who is the main character in "Sonny's Blues," Sonny or the narrator? Or are they equally important? Each one faces a challenge and achieves a victory at the end. What is the challenge for each? How do the challenges complement one another?

2. The news that Sonny has been arrested for possession of heroin shocks the narrator into beginning the transformation in his attitude toward his brother and toward himself that is completed at the end of the story. He describes his shock and fear as a "a great block of ice" that settled in his belly and "kept melting there slowly all day long." Trace imagery of water through the story. Is the narrator's transformation a kind of melting?

3. As the narrator leaves his classroom, he hears a boy whistling a tune "at once very complicated and very simple," and a little later he sees a barmaid dancing to something "black and bouncy." Trace these and other references to music through the story. What does music mean? How do these references prepare us for the final scene?

4. How does his meeting with Sonny's old school friend affect the narrator? What issues does it raise that are developed later in the story?

5. Examine the paragraph beginning, "This was the last time I ever saw my mother alive." What does "darkness" come to mean here? Trace the image through the rest of the story.

6. How is the mother's relationship with her husband like the narrator's with Sonny? Notice that the narrator tells her, "I won't let nothing happen to Sonny," but the mother says, "You may not be able to stop nothing from happening. But you got to let him know you's there." How does the story trace the narrator's growing understanding of what his mother meant?

7. "Well, Sonny," I said gently, "you know people can't always do exactly what they want to do--"
    "No, I don't know that," said Sonny, surprising me. "I think people ought to do what they want to do, what else are they alive for?

How does this exchange illuminate the contrast between the brothers? Does the story suggest that one is more right than the other?

8. Much of "Sonny's Blues" deals with ways that people cope with pain. Sonny uses heroin; what other ways of coping are illustrated?

9. In his letter to the narrator early in the story, Sonny mentions the death of the narrator's daughter Gracie, but we do not learn the details until much later. Why is this episode in the story?

10. Notice that Isobel's family tolerates Sonny only because he is the narrator's brother, but in the jazz club, the narrator is welcome only because he is Sonny's brother. How do the narrator and Sonny react to these situations? Does the narrator come to "belong" in the club?

11. The bass player Creole has an important role in the final scene, as almost a spiritual teacher. How is he a foil to the narrator?

12. What conception of the nature and function of art does the last scene develop?

13. Trace imagery of fire and water through the last scene.

14. What is the significance of the biblical allusion to the "cup of trembling" in the last line? What is the effect of having it refer to a glass of Scotch and milk?

Cynthia Ozick

If, as Ozick has repeatedly emphasized, it is hard to write about the Holocaust, it is hard to read about it, too. Not only are the details of Jewish suffering hard to read, it is also hard to find a comfortable moral stance toward the material. The sufferings of those who experienced the camps are such that it is hard not to grant them a sort of immunity from ordinary moral judgments. In The Shawl, can we afford to be too hard on a woman who has seen a Nazi soldier fling her baby against an electrified fence? And yet Ozick demands that we evaluate Rosa's beliefs and actions. It is not that she is a rigid, bluenosed moralist; she obviously has great compassion for Rosa. And yet she holds to her famous reversal of the modernist dictum that a poem should not mean but be. A story, Ozick wrote in the preface to Bloodshed, "must not merely be, but mean." The Shawl "means" in the sense that it is liturgical fiction, that it raises a moral issue and explores it in terms of Jewish belief. Rosa has broken the Second Commandment by turning the shawl and the memory of Magda into "idols" and by letting her pride in her status as an educated Pole stand in the way of her solidarity with other Jews, as represented by Mr. Persky.

1. The two-part narrative structure of The Shawl is quite unusual in its combination of the brief, horrifying first part and the much longer, much more relaxed and even comic second part. What relations can the class identify between the two parts? Notice, for instance, that Rosa has sworn never to wear stripes again and takes it as a sign of Stella's insensitivity that she has given her a dress with blue stripes. Where else do reminiscences of the camps appear in Part 2? Is Rosa living her concentration-camp trauma over and over?

2. How do the styles of Part 1 and Part 2 differ? Notice that many of the sentences in Part 1 are fragments and that the focus is so tight that sometimes it does not become clear what is happening until much later. The narrative style of Part 2 is much more conventionally realistic.

3. Magda is the product of Rosa's having been raped by a Nazi soldier, a fact that Rosa has repressed and denied. How does the reader gradually realize the truth?

4. The concentration camp and Miami Beach are both described with infernal imagery. What sorts of hells are they, respectively?

5. Language is thematized interestingly in The Shawl. Notice that there are three principal languages: Yiddish, Polish, and English. What are the associations of each? Notice that Rosa prides herself on her impeccable Polish but feels contempt for Yiddish and has never bothered to learn English well. (We are presumably to understand that her letters to Magda are in Polish, though we read them in English.) Could it be said that three value systems, as well as languages, are in play here?

6. In her letter about mailing the shawl, Stella writes, "Your idol is on its way, separate cover." The class should be alert to recurrences of the idea of idols. How might the shawl be considered an idol?

7. What is the place of the Professor Tree subplot in the story? It seems a fairly broad

piece of satire on pedantry; how does it fit into the story thematically?

8. Rosa tells Persky that "we" (presumably Holocaust survivors) have three lives: "The life before, the life during, the life after." She says that the life after is the present, the life before is childhood ("our real life"), and the life during was Hitler. What are we to make of this? Does Rosa have a distorted experience of time? Can it be "corrected"?

9. The spine of this story is clearly Rosa's prolonged attempt to deal with her concentration camp experiences, especially the murder of Magda. What do we learn of Rosa's life between the time of the murder and the time of the story? What happens during the course of the story? What happens at the end? Notice that "Magda" flees when Persky arrives. What does this mean? Does Persky, for all his vulgarity, represent life and an escape from obsession with the past for Rosa? The last sentence is, "Magda was away." Is this good or bad?

Athol Fugard

Athol Fugard has frequently expressed his admiration for and indebtedness to the drama of Samuel Beckett, rather surprisingly perhaps, since his own drama is so consistently realistic and so far removed from Beckett's Absurdism. And yet the more we think about it, the harder it is to imagine Fugard writing "Master Harold" . . . and the Boys if Beckett had not written his plays. Despite the surface differences between Beckett's and Fugard's plays, they have several deep similarities: the fondness for paired, complementary characters, the great economy of plot and character, the pared-down dialogue, the poetic theatrical imagery, the tension between an innate vitality and an existential pessimism. It is almost as if Beckett's example had been thoroughly internalized and emerged transformed in Fugard's personal style.

1. Ballroom dancing is obviously an important symbol in the play. Sam and Hally develop its most obvious meaning as they comically plan Hally's essay on "A World Without Collisions." But the symbolism is much richer than this. Trace dancing through the play, giving particular attention to the beginning and to the ending, and define what it comes to mean.

2. Fugard explores the relationships among his three characters very exhaustively. The initial relationship is between Sam and Willie, who become a contrasting, complementary pair. How are they contrasted, and what is the significance of the contrast?

3. Willie loses some of our sympathy when we learn that he beats his wife and dance partner, Hilda. Why does Fugard introduce this fact? How is Sam further characterized by his advice to Willie on this subject?

4. Corporal punishment is a recurring subject in the play. Not only does Willie beat his wife, but Hally has been beaten at school, Sam describes prison canings of blacks, and Hally strikes Willie with a ruler. How are these related? What does the play suggest about the psychology of corporal punishment?

5. In a fine essay on "Master Harold" . . . and the Boys, Rob Amato has suggested that Fugard's central subject in this play and in his entire work is "the hegemonic control of [the] psyche by an entrenched, distorting power structure." Even before Hally insults and spits at Sam, he has betrayed a profound condescension toward him, mingled with contradictory feelings of love. Trace these attitudes through the first part of the play.

6. An important structural feature of the play is the two tellings of the kite story, the first by Hally near the beginning and the second by Sam near the end. What has Hally "forgotten" about the incident? How does Sam's corrected account illuminate Hally's motivations?

7. Fugard is very conscious of the imagery of stage pictures and controls them carefully. Notice, for example, that through much of Sam's and Hally's discussion of education, Willie is scrubbing the floor on his hands and knees, a silent comment on their discussion. Analyze the effect of other stage pictures in the play, especially the final one.

8. The circle of light in the cafe and the dark, rainy weather outside are also important

visual symbols. ("You can't fly kites on rainy days.") Notice that at the end Hally slips out alone into the rain, unreconciled with Sam, separating himself from the human community Sam and Willie represent. Is this a final separation? Are we meant to believe that the breach between Sam and Hally will never be healed? Or that they will gradually regain their trust and affection?

Jamaica Kincaid

The most striking thing about <u>Annie John</u>, on first reading, is likely to be Annie's implacable hatred for her mother, a hatred that, contrary to narrative expectation, is not removed or softened at the end of the book. This aspect of the book is worth some careful attention. Most published criticism of the book does give it this attention, often citing Nancy Chodorow--either her book <u>The Reproduction of Mothering</u> (1978) or a key article, "Family Structure and Feminine Personality," in <u>Women, Culture, and Society</u>, ed. Michelle Z. Rosaldo and Louise Lamphere (1974). Chodorow is indeed illuminating (as are other psychoanalytic accounts of female maturation). But the class should not lose track of the fact that the mother-daughter hostility in <u>Annie John</u> is not a clinical fact but an artistic choice. In case the class is worried about the outcome of the relationship, Kincaid has stated in her interview with Selwyn R. Cudjoe, regarding her dislike for her mother: "Well, I hope it's an adolescent dislike, because now we get along very well." Having talked about the developmental logic of the dislike, the class might well go on to its narrative and thematic logic.

1. The eight chapters in <u>Annie John</u> read like separate short stories (and were originally published that way in <u>The New Yorker</u>). How do these chapters fit together? The class might pay special attention to the titles; some merely name the topic of the chapter ("Gwen," "The Red Girl"), while others highlight a key symbol ("The Circling Hand," "Columbus in Chains"). Close attention to these chapter titles can give a good overview of the book's structure.

2. The "figures in the distance" referred to in the title of the first chapter are mourners Annie John has seen going to the cemetery, especially those mourning dead children. Trace the theme of death through this first chapter. What does it suggest about Annie John? Must death be taken only literally here? Why is Annie's mother associated especially with death?

3. In Chapter 2, "The Circling Hand," Annie's fall from paradise occurs, her mother's rejection, in association with what psychoanalysts call a "primal scene," the sight of one's parents copulating. Examine the psychology of this incident. How do hands figure in the scene and its aftermath?

4. At the end of Chapter 2, Annie says, "At the end of the day, Gwen and I were in love," and Chapter 3 is primarily devoted to Annie's relationship with Gwen, the first of a series of such attachments. What is the psychology of the schoolgirl crush, as presented in <u>Annie John</u>? Why does Annie's preoccupation with Gwen follow so quickly her rejection by her mother? What does Annie seek in each of her crushes?

5. Annie's crush on "The Red Girl," as recounted in Chapter 4, seems quite different from her crush on Gwen, in that this relationship seems to express rebellion and lawlessness. Trace these themes through the chapter, and identify symbolic elements, such as the marbles, the library books, and the snake in the basket of figs.

6. In Chapter 5, "Columbus in Chains," the emphasis shifts from the psychology of individual development to the politics of colonialism, or perhaps we should say that the two dimensions of the narrative are blended. Trace postcolonial themes in the chapter,

especially the game of "band," which Annie and her friends play in the schoolyard, and the gatherings in the churchyard after school.

7. Chapters 6 and 7 tell the story of Annie's episode of clinical depression when she was fifteen years old. The progress of this illness should be traced very carefully, from the initial perception of an immensely heavy black ball within her body to the fullblown illness of Chapter 7. Elements that should be considered are dreams (especially the road dream of Chapter 6), the soured relationship with Gwen, Annie's negative view of her own body, the mother's attack on Annie as a "slut," the correspondence of the extended period of rain with Annie's illness, the incident of scrubbing the photographs, the visit from Ma Chess, and Annie's behavior in the aftermath of the illness.

8. The title of the last chapter, "A Walk to the Jetty," identifies the basic structural device, the walk that reviews Annie's life up to the point of leaving Antigua. The stages in this progress are worth careful review. Notice that the recurring line "My name is Annie John" throws the emphasis on identity and the role that previous experience has played in making her "Annie John."

9. What is the significance of the image in the last lines of the book, when Annie describes the waves lapping against the ship: "They made an unexpected sound, as if a vessel filled with liquid had been placed on its side and now was slowly emptying out"?

10. All maturation stories have a certain similarity, because we all have to learn certain things to become adults. But they differ, too, in ways that have to do with gender, culture, and historical period. What challenges has Annie John had to meet? How do they differ from those that other Bildungsroman protagonists that you know (Stephen Dedalus? Holden Caulfield? Huck Finn?) have had to meet?

SELECTIVE MEDIA GUIDE

No part of the Instructor's Manual is more difficult to keep current than the Media Guide. In the years since the first edition of <u>Literature of the Western World</u> appeared, the world of media has been constantly metamorphosing. The mimeograph machine and the 16-millimeter film have gone the way of the dodo, and we live in an educational-media world that is exciting but often bewildering: video tapes and players, large-screen projector TVs, laser disks, CD-ROMs, educational cable channels, electronic blackboards and voice hookups that allow us to teach students far away. The most revolutionary development has probably been the Internet, which offers instant access to a wide range of information to anyone skilled and patient enough to sort out the useful from the trivial and unreliable.

The Internet is evolving too rapidly for any guide like this one to offer much help; any tips we might offer would be obsolete by publication date. Instructors on the Net who want to locate sites useful in their teaching might get one of the directories with lists of Web sites classified by subject matter.

Even the more limited listing of available films, videotapes, sound recordings, and CD-ROMs in this guide is vulnerable to sudden obsolescence. New material is being produced all the time to feed the giant maw of the information industry, some of it of very high quality. Interested instructors might want to get on the mailing lists of some of the distributors; if they do, they need not worry about getting regular announcements of newly available material.

Distributors

American Audio Prose Library
P.O. Box 824
Columbia, MO 65205

Audio Learning, Inc.
44 Parkway West
Mt. Vernon, NY 10552

BFA Educational Media
2211 Michigan Avenue
Santa Monica, CA 90404

Benchmark Films
145 Scarborough Road
Briarcliff Manor, CA 90404

Brandon Films
8400 Brookfield Avenue
Brookfield, IL 60513

Caedmon Records
1995 Broadway
New York, NY 10023

Carousel Films
1501 Broadway
New York, NY 10036

Corinth Films
410 East 62nd Street
New York, NY 10021

Coronet Films
65 East South Water St.
Chicago, IL 60601

Counterpoint Films
14622 Lanark Street
Panorama City, CA 90402

Encyclopedia Brittanica Films
425 Michigan Avenue
Chicago, IL 60611

Filmic Archives
The Cinema Center
Botsford, CT 06404-0386

Films for the Humanities
and Sciences
PO Box 2053
Princeton, NJ 08540

GRJ Productions
c/o Kathryn P. Ruben
16330 Royal Hills Drive
Encino, CA 91396

Indiana University Radio &
Television Services
Bloomington, IN 47401

Insight Media
121 West 85th Street
New York, NY 10024

International Film Bureau
332 South Michigan Avenue
Chicago, IL 60604

Journal Films
930 Pitner Avenue
Evanston, IL 60602

Learning Corporation of America
1350 Avenue of the Americas
New York, NY 10019

McGraw-Hill Films
110 15th Street
Del Mar, CA 92014

National Public Radio
Publishing Department
2025 M Street, N.W.
Washington, DC 20036

PCI Aims Media
626 Justin Avenue
Glendale, CA 90202

Perspecctive Films
65 East South Water St.
Chicago, IL 60601

Phoenix Films
470 Park Avenue South
New York, NY 10016

Pyramid Films
PO Box 1048
Santa Monica, CA 90406

Sound Seminars
Jeffrey Norton Publishers
Department B
145 E. 49th Street
New York, NY 10017

Spoken Arts
310 North Avenue
New Rochelle, NY 10801

Time-Life Films
100 Eisenhower
Paramus, NJ 07652

University of Southern California
Division of Cinema
University Park
Los Angeles, CA 90007

Visual Resources Inc.
152 W. 42nd Street
Suite 1219
New York, NY 10036

The Old Testament

> The Bible: A Literary Heritage
>
> > A 27-minute color film made in Israel and starring Donald Pleasance. Surveys the Bible as a whole and includes excerpts from Genesis, Job, Psalms, the Song of Songs, Ecclesiastes, and Matthew (Learning Corporation of America).
>
> The Bible as Literature
>
> > A 30-minute videotape on how writers have drawn on the Bible (Insight Media).
>
> The Enjoyment of Scripture
>
> > 64-minute sound cassette by Samuel Sandmel (Sound Seminars).
>
> Readings from the Old Testament
>
> > Three half-hour sound cassettes recorded by G. B. Harrison (Sound Seminars).
>
> Genesis: The Creation and Noah
>
> > Sound cassette recorded by Judith Anderson (Caedmon).

Greek Civilization

> The Greeks
>
> > A BBC series of four one-hour videotapes based on the writings of Kenneth Dover and featuring British actors in performances of Greek literature and drama (Films for the Humanities and Sciences).
>
> Classical Civilization
>
> > Two 15-minute sound filmstrips (Films for the Humanities and Sciences).
>
> The Greeks: In Search of Meaning
>
> > 26-minute videotape; includes excerpts from Antigone, Lysistrata, and Plato's Apology, 1971 (Learning Corporation of America).
>
> The Ancient Mediterranean View of Man
>
> > 24-minute sound cassette by Arnold Toynbee (Sound Seminars).

A Recital of Ancient Greek Poetry

>Four cassettes of selections from Homer and the Greek dramatists read in Greek by Stephen G. Daitz. An accompanying booklet allows the non-Greek-speaking student to follow the text (Sound Seminars).

The Voyages of Ulysses and Aeneas

>A 34-minute videotape of the geographical settings of the <u>Odyssey</u> and the <u>Aeneid</u> (Insight Media). (CD-ROM version, Filmic Archives.)

<u>Homer</u>

The Perilous Journey: Homer's Odyssey

>Six videotapes, each 15 minutes, present six major episodes. The text is spoken by Michael Hordern, as Homer. (Films for the Humanities and Sciences).

The Odyssey

>Three half-hour videotapes on "The Structure of the Epic," "The Return of Odysseus," and "The Central Themes," presented by Gilbert Highet, 1965 (Encyclopedia Brittanica; Filmic Archives).

The Odyssey

>A half-hour videotape introducing the epic (Insight Media).

The Search for Ulysses

>A CBS special on a 51-minute color film about the real-life route of Odysseus. Narrated by Ernie Bradford, author of <u>Ulysses Found</u>. Excerpts from the <u>Odyssey</u> are read by James Mason (Carousel).

Homer's Mythology

>A 45-minute videotape (Insight Media).

Homer and the Birth of Tragedy

>85-minute sound cassette by Walter Kaufman (Sound Seminars).

Odysseus: The Eternal Optimist and Searcher for Truth

>84-minute sound cassette by Ralph Bates (Sound Seminars).

The Epic in Literature

    56-minute sound cassette by Ralph Bates on Homer and his influence (Sound Seminars).

The Odyssey

    Sound cassette of selections read by Anthony Quayle (Caedmon).

The Iliad

    Sound cassette of selections read by Anthony Quayle (Caedmon).

Sappho

    Songs of Sappho

        Five of Sappho's poems sung and danced by the New York Greek Drama Company. A 74-minute videotape (Insight Media).

Greek Drama

    The Ancient Greek Theater

        CD-ROM uses text, sound, and pictures to explore the theaters of Aeschylus, Sophocles, Euripides, and Aristophanes (1996) (Insight Media).

    The Origin of the Drama and the Theater

        1992 videotape (24 minutes) describing the origins of the Greek theater (Insight Media).

    Greek Tragedy

        Two 15-minute sound filmstrips (Films for the Humanities and Sciences).

    Greek Tragedy

        Excerpts from Greek tragedies performed by Katina Paxinou and Alexis Minotis (Caedmon).

    Greece 478-335 B.C.: The Theatre

        A 25-minute lecture-documentary with Prof. Eric Handley. Includes excerpts from a performance of Euripides' The Bacchae (Open University).

Aeschylus

> Aeschylus: The Oresteia
>
> > A great production by the National Theatre of Great Britain of all three plays, directed by Peter Hall. Three videotapes; Agamemnon is 90 minutes, and The Libation Bearers and The Furies are each 70 minutes. (Films for the Humanities and Sciences).
>
> Agamemnon
>
> > Videotape of a 1991 production of the play in English (120 minutes) (Insight Media).
>
> Aeschylus and the Death of Tragedy
>
> > 72-minute sound cassette by Walter Kaufman (Sound Seminars).
>
> The House of Atreus and the Great Chain of Evil
>
> > 95-minute sound cassette by Ralph Bates (Sound Seminars).
>
> Faster Pussycat, Kill, Kill!
>
> > An 83-minute black-and-white film directed by Russ Meyer. An amusing updating of the Eumenides, in which the Furies become killer go-go dancers, 1966 (Corinth).

Sophocles

> Sophocles: The Theban Plays
>
> > A magnificent production of Oedipus Rex, Oedipus at Colonus, and Antigone, with Michael Pennington, Anthony Quayle, and Juliet Stevenson. Produced by the BBC, in an effectively eclectic production style. Three videotapes, each 2 hours (Films for the Humanities and Sciences).
>
> Oedipus Rex
>
> > A 90-minute color film of the play by the Stratford, Canada, company directed by Tyrone Guthrie, 1956 (Corinth; Insight Media).
>
> Oedipus the King: The Rise of Greek Tragedy
>
> > 45-minute color film with a lecture on Greek tragedy and excerpts from the play, 1975 (Films for the Humanities and Sciences).

Oedipus the King: An Analysis

> A 1994 videotape (58 minutes) analyzing the themes of the play in their Greek context (Insight Media).

Oedipus Rex

> Four half-hour films featuring lectures by Bernard Knox on "The Age of Sophocles," "The Character of Oedipus," "Man and God," and "The Recovery of Oedipus," 1965 (Encyclopedia Brittanica; Insight Media).

Oedipus Rex

> Recorded performance of the play with Douglas Campbell as Oedipus (Caedmon).

Oedipus Rex

> 70-minute lecture on sound cassette by Walter Kaufman (Sound Seminars).

Antigone

> Videotape of 1962 film with Irene Pappas. In Greek with English subtitles (Insight Media; Filmic Archive).

Antigone

> 1991 production of the play in English, directed by Arlena Nys. Videotape (Insight Media).

Antigone: An Analysis

> 1994 videotape (58 minutes) analyzing the moral and legal dilemmas of the play (Insight Media).

Antigone

> Recorded performance of the play, starring Dorothy Tutin (Caedmon).

Euripides

Medea

> A 1986 production in the Classical Greek manner, with three masked actors. In Greek with English subtitles. Videotape (Insight Media).

Medea

>Videotape of 1959 black-and-white film, with Judith Anderson (Insight Media; Filmic Archive).

Medea

>The Kennedy Center production, again with Judith Anderson, but this time as the Nurse--Zoe Caldwell plays Medea. Videotape, 90 minutes. (Films for the Humanities and Sciences).

Medea

>Recorded performance of the play, starring Judith Anderson and Anthony Quayle (Caedmon).

Aristophanes

The Gods Are Laughing: Aristophanes, His Life and Theatre

>52-minute videotape, introducing Aristophanic comedy (Films for the Humanities and Sciences).

Lysistrata

>Production of the play filmed at the Acropolis (1987). In Greek with English subtitles (Insight Media).

Lysistrata

>Recorded performance of the play, starring Hermione Gingold and Stanley Holloway (Caedmon).

Plato

Plato's Apology: The Life and Teachings of Socrates

>32-minute color film, narrated by Mortimer Adler, 1962 (Encyclopedia Brittanica).

Plato, The Apology

>Performed on sound cassette by Ralph Richardson (Caedmon).

The Cave: A Parable

>A 10-minute color animated film, narrated by Orson Welles, 1973 (Counterpoint).

Plato's Cave

>A 20-minute color film (Pyramid).

Roman Civilization

The Romans: Laughter and Laws

>A 22-minute color film about Roman culture, 1971 (Learning Corporation of America).

Catullus

Selected Poetry of Catullus

>Sound casette of selections read by James Mason (Caedmon).

Virgil

Aeneas and the Aeneid

>13-minute videotape emphasizes the historical underpinning of the Aeneid (1990). (Insight Media).

The Aeneid: An Analysis

>Videotape (174 minutes) surveys the major critical issues in the epic (1994) (Insight Media).

The Golden Age of Rome

>Two 15-minute sound filmstrips on "The World of Virgil" and "The Aeneid as a National Epic" (Films for the Humanities and Sciences).

Virgil's Aeneid

>25-minute lecture on sound cassette by Gilbert Highet (Sound Seminars).

Ovid

The Book of Miracles (Ovid's Metamorphoses)

>15-minute lecture on sound cassette by Gilbert Highet (Sound Seminars).

Medieval Civilization

    Medieval Realms: Britain from 1066-1500

        A CD-ROM based on materials in the British Library. Comes with a 44-page instructor's manual to facilitate use in the classroom (Films for the Humanities and Sciences).

    The Middle Ages: A Wanderer's Guide to Life and Letters

        A 29-minute color film; includes excerpts from <u>Everyman</u>, the <u>Canterbury Tales</u>, and Dante's poetry, 1970 (Learning Corporation of America).

    The Medieval Mind

        26-minute videotape featuring a 1969 lecture by William C. Burke, author of <u>Origins of the Medieval World</u> (Insight Media).

    The Middle Ages

        46-minute videotape (1993) surveying medieval history and society (Insight Media).

Beowulf

    Beowulf

        A 38-minute videotape introduction to the poem (Films for the Humanities and Sciences).

    Beowulf and Other Poetry in Old English

        Sound cassette, read by Jess B. Bessinger, Jr. (Caedmon).

Dante

    Dante: The Journey of Our Life

        30-minute videotape written and narrated by John Hollander (1991) (Insight Media).

    Dante: Divine Poet and Wandering Exile

        A 38-minute videotape introduction to the poet's life and work (Insight Media).

    Dante's Inferno: An Analysis

        1994 videotape (116 minutes) (Insight Media).

Dante's Inferno

> Award-winning videotape by Peter Greenaway and Tom Phillips, creating an impression of the poem through juxtaposed images (88 minutes) (Films for the Humanities and Sciences).

Dante: Medieval Images of Order

> 52-minute lecture on sound cassette by Joseph Mazzeo (Sound Seminars).

The Divine Comedy

> Sound cassette of excerpts performed by Ian Richardson (Caedmon).

Sir Gawain and the Green Knight

Gawain and the Green Knight

> A 1973 British film directed by Stephen Weeks, which follows the story fairly closely (93 minutes) (Films for the Humanities and Sciences).

Chaucer

The Time, Life, and Works of Chaucer

> 25-minute videotape of visual material from the period (Filmic Archives). (CD-ROM version, Filmic Archives.)

Chaucer

> 1993 videotape (33 minutes) featuring an introduction to Chaucer's works by John Fleming (Insight Media)

Chaucer: The General Prologue to The Canterbury Tales

> 20-minute videotape (Films for the Humanities and Sciences).

Story-Tellers of the Canterbury Tales

> 18-minute color film based on the Ellesmere manuscript and using excerpts in Middle English (University of Southern California).

Chaucer's Canterbury Pilgrims

> 46-minute videotape on the pilgrims, with images from the Ellesmere manuscript and readings of excerpts from the poem (Filmic Archives).

Chaucer's England

>   30-minute black-and-white film, 1958 (Encyclopedia Brittanica).

Geoffrey Chaucer and Middle English Literature

>   A 35-minute videotape introduction (Films for the Humanities and Sciences).

A Prologue to Chaucer

>   A 29-minute videotape on Chaucer's world (Films for the Humanities and Sciences).

Chaucer: The Nun's Priest Tale and The Pardoner's Tale

>   Talks on sound cassette by Derek Brewer and A. C. Spearing (Audio Learning).

Chaucer's Canterbury Tales (in Middle English): The Pardoner's Tale and The Nun's Priest's Tale

>   A sound cassette recorded by Robert Ross (Caedmon).

The Canterbury Tales: The Miller's Tale and The Pardoner's Tale

>   A sound cassette performed in Modern English by Micheal Mac Leammoir and Stanley Holloway (Caedmon).

The Canterbury Tales: The Wife of Bath

>   A sound cassette performed in Modern English by Peggy Ashcroft (Caedmon).

From Every Shires Ende: The World of Chaucer's Pilgrims

>   A 38-minute color film featuring medieval art, architecture, and music recreating the culture of Chaucer's England, 1969 (Pilgrim Film Production).

Everyman

Everyman

>   Hour-long videotape of a production of the play on a medieval stage and in period costumes (1991) (Insight Media).

Everyman

>   Sound cassette of a performance featuring Burgess Meredith (Caedmon).

Renaissance Civilization

    Spirit of the Renaissance

        11-minute color film, 1970 (Encyclopedia Brittanica).

    The Renaissance

        A 48-minute documentary videotape (Insight Media).

    The Literature of the Renaissance

        12 videotape lectures, 45 minutes each (1993). Includes consideration of Dante, Shakespeare, Cervantes, and Milton (Insight Media).

Boccaccio

    Boccaccio: Tales from The Decameron

        Dramatization of six tales with shadow puppets (videotape, 71 minutes) (Films for the Humanities and Sciences).

Machiavelli

    Man and the State: Machiavelli and Political Power

        29-minute color film, 1972 (BFA Educational Media).

Cervantes

    Don Quijote

        Great epic film of the novel (video, 5 hours and 10 minutes). In Spanish with English subtitles (Films for the Humanities and Sciences).

    Don Quixote

        This rare early film starring Fedor Chaliapin is now available on videotape (Insight Media).

    Don Quixote

        The 1957 Russian film directed by Grigori Kozintsev, on videotape (Insight Media).

    Introduction to Don Quixote

        15-minute sound cassette by Gilbert Highet (Sound Seminars).

Introducing Don Quixote

>A half-hour videotape of background material (Insight Media).

<u>Shakespeare</u>

Henry IV, Part 1

>Videotape of the BBC Shakespeare Series production, with Peter Finch, Anthony Quayle, and David Gwillim (147 minutes) (Insight Media; Filmic Archives).

Henry IV, Part 1

>A production by the English Shakespeare Company (videotape, 2 hours, 52 minutes) (Films for the Humanities and Sciences).

Henry IV, Parts 1 and 2; Workshops 1 and 2

>Two 24-minute videotapes showing scenes from the plays being rehearsed under the direction of John Russell Brown (Films for the Humanities and Sciences).

The Time, Life, and Works of Shakespeare; Shakespeare's London; Shakespeare's Theater

>Three CD-ROMs (Filmic Archives).

Shakespeare: His Life, Times, Works, and Sources

>A competing CD-ROM (Films for the Humanities and Sciences).

Shakespeare: The Man and His Times

>1991 video documentary on Shakespeare's cultural, literary, and political contexts. 47 minutes (Insight Media).

William Shakespeare: Background for His Works

>1988 videotape, 22 minutes (Insight Media).

A Day at the Globe

>30-minute videotape about Shakespeare's theater (1977) (Insight Media).

The Staging of Shakespeare's Plays

> 45-minute videotape (1990), featuring an illustrated lecture by George Walton Williams (Insight Media).

The Theater in Shakespeare's Time

> 14-minute color film, 1973 (BFA Educational Media).

Behind the Scenes: Three Views of Shakespeare

> Three one-hour sound cassettes by Maynard Mack, Samuel Schoenbaum, and Daniel Seltzer. Topics are "Shakespeare in Our Time," "Shakespeare the Man," and "Shakespeare and His Theater" (National Public Radio).

Donne

John Donne

> A 40-minute videotape introduction to the poet and his works (Insight Media).

Milton

Milton and 17th-Century Poetry

> A 35-minute video documentary introducing Milton's life and works (Films for the Humanities and Sciences).

Paradise Lost, Books 1-4

> Performed on a sound cassette by Anthony Quayle (Caedmon).

Molière

Tartuffe

> 1984 film of a stage production, starring Gerard Depardieu. In French with English subtitles. Videotape, 140 minutes (Insight Media).

Tartuffe

> Production of the play by the Société des Comédiens Français. In French with English subtitles. Videotape, 119 minutes (Films for the Humanities and Sciences).

Tartuffe

> A production by the Shakespeare Drama Society on videocassette (Educational Record Sales).

Tartuffe

> Sound cassette; with a cast headed by William Hutt (Caedmon).

Tartuffe: An Analysis

> 58-minute videotape (1994) (Insight Media).

Molière

> A biographical videocassette. Produced by the Shakespeare Drama Society (Educational Record Sales).

Molière

> A 35-minute videotape (1985) discussing Molière's comedies, especially Tartuffe (Insight Media).

Racine

Phèdre

> A production of the play with Marie Bell. In French with English subtitles. Videotape (Insight Media).

Racine

> A 35-minute videotape (1985) which analyzes Racine's dramatic practice (Insight Media).

Racine: An Introduction

> Two talks on sound cassette by Martin Turnell (Audio Learning).

Swift

Gulliver in Lilliput

> A 1986 BBC production (107 minutes) (Filmic Archives).

Gulliver's Travels: The Houyhnhnms

> A reading on sound cassette by Michael Redgrave (Caedmon).

Gulliver's Travels

> Talks on sound cassette by Ian Thomson and J. C. Hilson (Audio Learning).

A Modest Proposal

> Performed on sound cassette by Patrick Magee (Caedmon).

Voltaire

Candide

> Excerpts in French; a sound cassette (Caedmon).

Voltaire's Candide: An Analysis

> 58-minute videotape (1994) surveys the major critical issues in the work (Insight Media).

Voltaire Presents Candide: An Introduction to the Age of Enlightenment

> A 33-minute color film, dramatizing scenes from Candide, with commentary in the character of Voltaire, 1976 (Encyclopedia Brittanica).

The Romantic Movement

The Spirit of Romanticism

> A 26-minute documentary color film, produced in Europe, 1977 (Encyclopedia Brittanica).

Romanticism: Revolt of the Spirit

> A 25-minute color film, 1973 (Learning Corporation of America).

Goethe

Goethe: His Personality and His Work

> An 83-minute sound cassette of a lecture by Albert Schweitzer with a sentence-by-sentence English translation by Thornton Wilder (Sound Seminars).

Goethe's Faust: An Analysis

> 58-minute videotape (1994) (Insight Media).

Romantic Poetry

Romantic Poetry

> Two 15-minute sound filmstrips, dealing with Blake, Coleridge, Wordsworth, Byron, Keats, and Shelley (Films for the Humanities and Sciences).

Blake

Blake

A 52-minute video documentary, narrated by Blake biographer Peter Ackroyd (Films for the Humanities and Sciences).

A Third Testament: Blake

A 53-minute color documentary film narrated by Malcolm Muggeridge, 1974 (Time-Life Films).

William Blake

A half-hour introduction to Blake and his poetry (Insight Media).

The Poetry of William Blake

Selections read by Ralph Richardson; sound cassette (Caedmon).

Blake and Manchild

A 36-minute talk on sound cassette by Benjamin DeMott (Sound Seminars).

Wordsworth

The Time, Life, and Works of Wordsworth

CD-ROM (Filmic Archives).

The Poetry of Wordsworth

A selection read by Cedric Hardwicke on sound cassette. Includes excerpts from The Prelude (Caedmon).

Wordsworth: The Lyrical Ballads

Talks on sound cassette by Angus Easson and Terence Wright (Audio Learning).

Beyond Dailiness: Wordsworth

45-minute talk on sound cassette by Benjamin DeMotte (Sound Seminars).

Coleridge

The Poetry of Coleridge

A selection on sound cassette, read by Ralph Richardson. Includes "Dejection: An Ode" (Caedmon).

Coleridge: The Fountain and the Cave

33-minute color film, 1974 (Pyramid).

Keats

John Keats: His Life and Death

A 55-minute videotape written by Archibald MacLeish, 1973 (Encyclopedia Brittanica; Filmic Archive).

John Keats

A 40-minute videotape introduction to Keats and his poetry (Insight Media).

Mary Shelley

Mary Shelley's Frankenstein

Kenneth Branagh's 1994 film with Robert De Niro is the most recent major filming of this much-filmed novel. David Wickes' Frankenstein (1993) gets higher marks for fidelity to the novel, if not for excitement (various distributors).

Frankenstein: The Making of the Monster

A 1993 video documentary on the history of Mary Shelley's monster in pop culture (50 minutes) (Filmic Archives).

Tennyson

The Poetry of Tennyson

Selections recorded on sound tape by Sybil Thorndyke and Lewis Casson (Caedmon).

Browning

> The Poetry of Browning and My Last Duchess and Other Poems
>
>> Two sound cassettes of selections read by James Mason. Includes "The Bishop Orders His Tomb," "My Last Duchess," and "Andrea Del Sarto" (Caedmon).
>
> Browning's Men and Women
>
>> Talks by Isobel Armstrong and Michael Slater (Audio Learning).

Melville

> Herman Melville: "November in My Soul"
>
>> A 29-minute color film, 1977 (BFA Educational Media).
>
> The Authors: Herman Melville
>
>> A 22-minute color film, 1978 (Journal Films).
>
> Bartleby
>
>> A 28-minute color film of the story, 1969. Also "A Discussion of Bartleby," a 10-minute color film with Charles Van Doren discussing the story and the film, 1969 (Encyclopedia Brittanica; Filmic Archives).
>
> Bartleby the Scrivener
>
>> Another dramatization of the story (1978; 30 minutes) (Insight Media).
>
> Bartleby the Scrivener
>
>> Yet another filming, this one with Paul Scofield and John McEnery (73 minutes) (Filmic Archives).

Dickinson

> The Belle of Amherst
>
>> Julie Harris in her one-woman performance as Emily Dickinson. Videotape, 118 minutes (Insight Media).
>
> Emily Dickinson: A Certain Slant of Light
>
>> A 30-minute videotape, narrated by Julie Harris, 1977 (Pyramid).

Emily Dickinson

>1988 documentary videotape surveying Dickinson's life and work (60 minutes) (Filmic Archives).

The Authors: Emily Dickinson

>A 22-minute color film, 1978 (Journal Films).

Emily Dickinson: A Self-Portrait

>Sound tape recorded by Julie Harris (Caedmon).

Poems and Letters by Emily Dickinson

>Sound tape recorded by Julie Harris (Caedmon).

The Life of Emily Dickinson

>A 56-minute sound cassette of an interview by Heywood Hale Broun of Richard Sewell about his biography of Dickinson (Sound Seminars).

Whitman

The Time, Life, and Work of Whitman

>CD-ROM (Filmic Archives).

Walt Whitman

>1988 documentary videotape surveying his life and works (60 minutes) (Filmic Archives).

Walt Whitman: Poet of Humanity

>1992 videotape (27 minutes) emphasizing Whitman's glorification of the individual and his sorrow over the Civil War (Filmic Archives).

Walt Whitman's Civil War

>A 23-minute color film, 1969 (GRJ Productions).

Crossing Brooklyn Ferry and Other Poems; Leaves of Grass: I Hear America Singing; Leaves of Grass: Song of the Open Road; Walt Whitman: Eyewitness to the Civil War

>Ed Begley reads Whitman's poems on these four sound recordings (Caedmon).

Walt Whitman

>Taped talks by Gay Wilson Allen and Arthur Golden (Audio Learning).

Walt Whitman

>Taped talks by Quentin Anderson and Robert Spiller (Audio Learning).

The American Parade: Song of Myself

>Rip Torn plays Walt Whitman in this 31-minute film, 1975 (CBS).

Dostoevsky

>Fyodor Dostoevsky
>
>>1988 videotape introducing Dostoevsky and his novels (58 minutes). From the series The Modern World: Ten Great Writers (Insight Media; Filmic Archives).
>
>Dostoevsky: 1821-1881
>
>>A 55-minute color documentary film, narrated by Malcolm Muggeridge, 1975 (Learning Corporation of America).
>
>The Grand Inquisitor
>
>>A 28-minute film starring John Gielgud (BBC).
>
>Dostoevsky: Realism Transfigured
>
>>A 49-minute sound cassette by Ernest J. Simmons (Sound Seminars).
>
>The Brothers Karamazov
>
>>A 154-minute color film in Russian with English subtitles, 1972 (Corinth).

Tolstoy

>The Death of Ivan Ilyich: An Analysis
>
>>58-minute videotape (1993) surveys the major critical issues in the story (Insight Media).
>
>A Third Testament: Tolstoy (1825-1910)
>
>>A 53-minute color film documentary narrated by Malcolm Muggeridge, 1974 (Time-Life Films).

Tolstoy: Totality of Life

> A 55-minute lecture on sound cassette by Ernest J. Simmons (Sound Seminars).

Ibsen

Henrik Ibsen

> A 1988 videotape documentary (58 minutes). Part of the series The Modern World: Ten Great Writers (Filmic Archives).

A Doll's House

> 110-minute color feature film with Jane Fonda, David Warner, and Trevor Howard, 1973 (Learning Corporation of America).

A Doll's House

> A performance of the play with Claire Bloom and Anthony Hopkins. Videotape (Insight Media).

A Doll's House

> A production, somewhat compressed, with Julie Harris, Christopher Plummer, and Jason Robards. On videocassette (Educational Record Sales).

A Doll's House

> Two half-hour color films--"The Destruction of Illusion" and "Ibsen's Themes"--narrated by Norris Houghton and incorporating scenes from a modern-dress production of the play, 1967 (Encyclopedia Brittanica).

A Doll's House

> A performance of the play on sound cassettes, featuring Claire Bloom and Donald Madden (Caedmon).

Chekhov

Chekhov

> A biographical and critical documentary. Video, in Russian with English subtitles, 53 minutes. (Films for the Humanities and Sciences).

Anton Chekhov: A Writer's Life

> A 37-minute videotape, narrated by Eli Wallach (Films for the Humanities and Sciences).

The Cherry Orchard

> A performance of the play on sound cassettes, with Hume Cronyn and Jessica Tandy (Caedmon)

The Cherry Orchard

> Two videotapes, 22 minutes each, with lectures by Norris Houghton on "Chekhov: Innovator of Modern Drama" and "Comedy or Tragedy?" (Insight Media).

Chekhov and the Moscow Art Theater

> 13-minute videotape shows archival footage of a production of The Cherry Orchard at the Moscow Art Theatre (Insight Media).

Chekhov: Humanity's Advocate

> A 46-minute lecture on sound cassette by Ernest J. Simmons (Sound Seminars).

French Symbolist and Modernist Poetry

Charles Baudelaire, Les Fleurs du Mal

> A sound cassette with poems read in French by Eva LeGallienne and Louis Jourdan (Caedmon).

Freud

Young Dr. Freud

> A 99-minute German documentary with English subtitles (Films for the Humanities and Sciences).

Sigmund Freud

> A one-hour radio documentary, on sound cassette, narrated by Fritz Weaver (National Public Radio).

Conrad

> Joseph Conrad
>
>> A 1988 documentary (58 minutes). Part of the series The Modern World: Ten Great Writers (Filmic Archives).
>
> Heart of Darkness
>
>> The fine 1994 film of the novella, directed by Nicholas Roeg with Tim Roth and John Malkovich (Filmic Archives and various other distributors).
>
> Apocalypse Now
>
>> Francis Ford Coppola's 1979 version of Heart of Darkness, reset in the Vietnam War (various distributors).
>
> Conrad's Heart of Darkness
>
>> A 20-minute videotape that emphasizes the historical background of the story in Africa and the ivory trade (Insight Media).
>
> Heart of Darkness
>
>> Sound cassette, performed by Anthony Quayle (Caedmon).
>
> Joseph Conrad: The Three Lives
>
>> Interview on sound cassette by Heywood Hale Broun of Frederick R. Karl about his biography of Conrad (Sound Seminars).

Yeats

> Yeats Country
>
>> A 19-minute color film made in Ireland, 1965 (International Film Bureau).
>
> W. B. Yeats--A Tribute
>
>> A 22-minute black-and-white documentary film, made in Ireland and featuring Micheal Mac Liammoir and Siobhan McKenna, 1950 (Brandon Films).
>
> Yeats Remembered
>
>> A 30-minute videotape featuring archival footage of Yeats and of the poet reading his own poems (Insight Media).

W. B. Yeats

> A 65-minute videotape (1991) analyzing six of Yeats's best known poems: "No Second Troy," "September 1913," "The Fisherman," "Sailing to Byzantium," "Among School Children," and "The Circus Animals' Desertion" (Insight Media).

Dylan Thomas Reads the Poetry of W. B. Yeats and Others

> Sound cassette includes "Leda and the Swan" and "The Circus Animals' Desertion" (Caedmon).

The Poetry of William Butler Yeats

> Sound cassette; read by Siobhan McKenna and Cyril Cusack (Caedmon).

Yeats

> Talks by C. J. Rawson, Marjorie Perloff, J. A. Berthoud, and A. J. Smith (Audio Learning).

On William Butler Yeats

> A 60-minute lecture on sound cassette by Robert Pack (Sound Seminars).

On William Butler Yeats

> A 60-minute lecture on sound cassette by Theodore Weiss (Sound Seminars).

W. B. Yeats

> A 45-minute lecture on sound cassette by Stephen Spender (Sound Seminars).

Pirandello

Luigi Pirandello

> A 1988 documentary (58 minutes). Part of the series The Modern World: Ten Great Writers (Filmic Archives).

Six Characters in Search of an Author

> A 55-minute color film of a compressed version of the play, 1976 (Films for the Humanities and Sciences).

Six Characters in Search of an Author

> One-hour condensed version of the play on videotape (Insight Media).

Mann

> Thomas Mann
>
>> A 1988 documentary (58 minutes). Part of the series The Modern World: Ten Great Writers (Filmic Archives).

Joyce

> James Joyce
>
>> An 80-minute videotape documentary produced by Irish National Television (Films for the Humanities and Sciences).
>
> The World of James Joyce
>
>> Video documentary (116 minutes) produced with the assistance of Richard Ellmann. Shot in Dublin, Trieste, Rome, London, and Paris (Films for the Humanities and Sciences)
>
> James Joyce
>
>> A 1988 documentary (58 minutes). Part of the series The Modern World: Ten Great Writers (Filmic Archives).
>
> James Joyce (1882-1941): Silence, Exile, and Cunning
>
>> A 42-minute black-and-white film, narrated by Anthony Burgess, 1969 (Time-Life Films).
>
> Walking into Eternity
>
>> Half-hour documentary videotape filmed in Dublin (Insight Media).
>
> The Dead
>
>> John Huston's 1988 film with Donal McCann and Anjelica Huston. Videotape (Insight Media and other distributors).
>
> The Joyce of Music
>
>> A recording by James Hurt and The New Hutchinson Family Singers of 25 songs from Joyce's fiction, with commentary. Includes songs from The Dead (University of Illinois Press, 1983).
>
> James Joyce, Dubliners
>
>> Talks on sound cassette by Angus Easson and Terence Wright (Audio Learning).

James Joyce

    A 36-minute talk on sound cassette by Brendan Behan (Sound Seminars).

Woolf

Virginia Woolf

    A 1988 documentary (58 minutes). Part of the series The Modern World: Ten Great Writers (Filmic Archives).

A Room of One's Own

    1990 videotape of Eileen Atkins' one-woman show based on Woolf's life and works (55 minutes) (Insight Media).

Virginia Woolf: The Moment Whole

    A 10-minute color film featuring actress Marian Seldes, 1972 (PCI Aims Media).

Virginia Woolf

    A set of audiocassettes featuring discussion by Leonard Woolf and Vanessa and Quinton Bell, and the only surviving recording of Virginia Woolf herself (American Audio Prose Library).

Kafka

Franz Kafka

    A 1988 documentary (58 minutes). Part of the series The Modern World: Ten Great Writers (Filmic Archive).

The Trials of Franz Kafka

    A 15-minute black-and-white videotape, narrated by Kurt Vonnegut, Jr. (Films for the Humanities and Sciences).

Franz Kafka: His Life and Works

    A 25-minute sound cassette by Max Brod and Alex Aronson (Sound Seminars).

Metamorphosis: Nabokov on Kafka

    Christopher Plummer delivers Nabokov's witty lecture on "The Metamorphosis" (videotape, 1989; 30 minutes) (Filmic Archives).

The Metamorphosis: An Analysis

    58-minute videotape (1994) (Insight Media).

The Metamorphosis

    Read on sound cassette by James Mason (Caedmon).

Lawrence

Anthony Burgess on D. H. Lawrence

    Videotape, 30 minutes (Filmic Archives).

The Horse Dealer's Daughter

    1984 dramatization of the story (videotape, 30 minutes) (Filmic Archives).

D. H. Lawrence

    A 58-minute lecture on sound cassette by Stephen Spender (Sound Seminars).

Dinesen

Babette's Feast

    Gabriel Axel's fine 1987 film of the story, featuring Stephane Audran (various distributors).

Eliot

T. S. Eliot

    1988 videotape documentary (58 minutes) Part of the series The Modern World: Ten Great Writers (Filmic Archive).

The Mysterious Mr. Eliot

    A 63-minute videotape, featuring a number of interviews with Eliot's friends, 1973 (McGraw-Hill).

An Introduction to T. S. Eliot's Poetry

    39-minute videotape surveying Eliot's career (Filmic Archives)

T. S. Eliot Reading The Love Song of J. Alfred Prufrock

    Sound cassette (Caedmon).

Pound and Eliot

    Talks by M. L. Rosenthal (Audio Learning).

T. S. Eliot

    Talks by John Chalker and Edward Hall (Audio Learning).

On Eliot

    A 58-minute talk on sound cassette by Theodore Weiss (Sound Seminars).

Faulkner

  Faulkner

    23-minute videotape presenting Yoknapatawpha County, drawing illustrations mainly from The Sound and the Fury (1985) (Insight Media).

  William Faulkner's Mississippi

    A 50-minute black-and-white film, made in Mississippi and with excerpts from Faulkner's works, including "The Unvanquished," read by Montgomery Clift, 1965 (Benchmark Films).

  William Faulkner

    A one-hour radio documentary on sound cassette, narrated by Colleen Dewhurst (National Public Radio).

  An Introduction to William Faulkner's Fiction

    45-minute videotape, emphasizing the social organization of Faulkner's Mississippi (Filmic Archives).

  William Faulkner

    Talks on sound cassette by Irving Howe and Alan Trachtenberg (Audio Learning).

Brecht

  Bertolt Brecht

    55-minute video documentary, emphasizing his background and his theatrical innovations (Films for the Humanities and Sciences).

Bertolt Brecht

    90-minute documentary on sound cassette (National Public Radio).

Camus

Albert Camus: A Self-Portrait

    A 19-minute color film, 1971 (Learning Corporation of America).

Albert Camus Reading from His Novels and Essays

    Sound cassette in French (Caedmon).

Borges

The Inner World of Jorge Luis Borges

    A 28-minute videotape, narrated by Borges himself (Films for the Humanities and Sciences).

Borges: Profile of a Writer

    A 79-minute documentary on videotape, featuring an interview with the writer (Insight Media).

Beckett

Waiting for Beckett: A Portrait of Samuel Beckett

    An outstanding videotape documentary (86 minutes), made in 1993. It includes excerpts from performances, archival photographs, and interviews with Beckett and his associates (Insight Media).

Samuel Beckett: Silence to Silence

    An 80-minute videotape featuring Billie Whitelaw, Jack MacGowran, and Patrick Magee in excerpts from Beckett's plays (Films for the Humanities and Sciences).

Krapp's Last Tape

    A production of the play with Jack MacGowran. Videotape (Insight Media).

Krapp's Last Tape

    A production with Richard Cluchey, using Beckett's staging (Insight Media).

Krapp's Last Tape

>A sound recording of the play, performed by Donald Davis (Spoken Arts).

Wright

An Introduction to Richard Wright's Fiction

>45-minute videotape narrated by Valerie Smith (Filmic Archives).

Baldwin

James Baldwin

>A 1994 documentary videotape introduction to Baldwin's life and works. Part of the Black Americans of Achievement series. 30 minutes (Filmic Archives).

James Baldwin

>An audiocassette featuring Baldwin reading from his work and being interviewed (American Audio Prose Library).

Fugard

Master Harold. . . and the "boys"

>Michael Lindsay-Hogg's good 1986 film of the play, with Matthew Broderick and John Kani. Videotape (Insight Media; Filmic Archive).